VOICES
from
THE FRONT

VOICES
from
THE FRONT

Durham Light Infantry in World War Two

Peter Hart

Pen & Sword
MILITARY

First published in Great Britain in 1999 by
LEO COOPER

Reprinted in this format in 2010 by
Pen & Sword Military
an imprint of
Pen & Sword Books Ltd
47 Church Street
Barnsley
South Yorkshire
S70 2AS

ISBN 978 1 84884 401 8

A CIP catalogue record for this book is
available from the British Library

Printed and bound in England
by CPI

Pen & Sword Books Ltd incorporates the imprints of
Pen & Sword Aviation, Pen & Sword Maritime, Pen & Sword Military,
Wharncliffe Local History, Pen & Sword Select,
Pen & Sword Military Classics and Leo Cooper,
Remember When, Seaforth Publishing and Frontline Publishing

For a complete list of Pen & Sword titles please contact
PEN & SWORD BOOKS LIMITED
47 Church Street, Barnsley, South Yorkshire, S70 2AS, England
E-mail: enquiries@pen-and-sword.co.uk
Website: www.pen-and-sword.co.uk

Contents

Victory Parade 1945

Preface

I am greatly indebted to the old comrades of the 16th Battalion, Durham Light Infantry without whom this book would not exist. The DLI Sound Recording Project to which they contributed was initiated by The Imperial War Museum Sound Archive in conjunction with Steve Shannon of the DLI Regimental Museum in 1986. It now consists of over 200 interviews with an average length of eight hours each. By patiently tape recording their memories these veterans have opened up their lives to allow us to better understand the reality of the Second World War.

All I have done is to choose some of the most evocative extracts from those 30 interviews that concerned the 16th Battalion DLI in the Italian Campaign of 1943-1945 and linked them together within a broad historical context. I therefore must particularly thank – in alphabetical

Carrier Platoon, Support Company, 16th Battalion Durham Light Infantry, during field firing training near Athens, 1945. Lieutenant Russell Collins extreme left (binoculars around neck), Captain Harry Myhneer on the far right. Sergeant Chilvers seated at front wearing beret; Private Philips at front with beret and radio equipment.

order – Gerry Barnett, George Bland, Tony Cameron, Sam Cawdron, Tommy Chadwick, Russell Collins, James Corr, William Cowans, Lionel Dodd, Ronald Elliott, Robert Ellison, Gordon Gent, Edward Grey, Henry Harris, Alan Hay, Dick Hewlett, Tom Lister, Kenneth Lovell, Jackie Milburn, Ernest Murray, Ian Neal, Charley Palmer, Tony Sacco, Ronnie Sherlaw; Laurence Stringer, Leslie Thornton, Douglas Tiffin, Tom Turnbull, William Virr and Viz Vizard.

It is true that not all are widely quoted in this particular book, but they all played a vital part in building this archive which I am sure others will use to far greater effect in the future.

As ever I am up to my eyes in debt to my fabulous comrades in arms at the Imperial War Museum Sound Archive:- Margaret Brooks, Jo Lancaster, Rosemary Tudge, Richard McDonough and Conrad Wood. They are the custodians of an archive which grows exponentially in value as the years drift by. Of course I am particularly grateful to the other interviewers who assisted in our recording programme, of which the most important in this case is the indefatigable Harry Moses. Harry has worked on the DLI Project right from the start and brings an unbelievable diligence, skill and knowledge to his work. I cannot recommend too highly his book 'History of the Sixth Battalion DLI'

published by County Durham Books. Nigel de Lee has also carried out several interviews from which I have quoted. In charge of proof checking and occasionally making caustic comments about my shaky grammatical skills were Bryn Hammond of the IWM Information Systems, Nigel Steel from the IWM Department of Documents and my very good friend Polly Napper. The staff of the IWM Photographic Archive were extremely helpful in providing copies and giving me permission to reproduce many of the photographs in the text. Terry Charman was invaluable in resolving historical problems with his usual urbane charm. I must especially thank Tom Tunney whose exhaustive research into his father's war service has been an example to us all of hard work. Tom not only checked the manuscript but also supplied the Roll of Honour.

Thanks are due again to Polly Napper who prepared the maps without a murmur of complaint. Many of the photographs were supplied by the veterans themselves, particularly Colonel Russell Collins, Dick Hewlett, Kenneth Lovell and Major Viz Vizard. Particular thanks are also due to Major Laurence Stringer, author of 'The History of the Sixteenth Battalion Durham Light Infantry' published in 1946.

I am indebted to Colonel Russell Collins, Major Ronnie Sherlaw and Major Viz Vizard who were kind enough to read advance copies of the manuscript.

Roni Wilkinson of Pen & Sword Books is as ever my hero for producing the silk purse you now hold. As usual I remain responsible for those few howlers I have cunningly concealed in the text to entertain and amuse the superior reader!

The interview extracts have been lightly edited and re-ordered only where necessary to improve readability or clarity. The general accuracy of the information within the quotations has been checked against the regimental history and the relevant war diaries kept in the Public Record Office. The original tapes are available for consultation by appointment at The Sound Archive, IWM, Lambeth Road, London SE1 6HZ. Open Mon-Fri: 10am-5pm. Please telephone for an appointment: 0171-416-5363.

Peter Hart,
Oral Historian, IWM
February, 1999

Introduction

Morale is a precious resource at every level in war. From the mass of humanity that is a modern army, to the individual alone in his slit trench, morale is a key element in determining military efficiency. It must be treasured and hoarded to avoid national or personal humiliation and defeat. It can be spent all too easily – thrown away in a single moment of ill judged stupidity in action; or ground down into dust by repeated exposure to danger over a long period of time. Good morale, the cheerful acceptance of whatever befalls them, can allow men to endure hardships and take risks that would be beyond them if they were demoralised. It truly marks the difference between a leaderless rabble and a disciplined body of men working purposefully together in pursuit of a common cause despite the fears that wrack each individual.

If this book has a theme it is the sheer unadulterated courage with which the men of the 16th Durham Light Infantry struggled to maintain their morale in the face of imminent death for what seemed a lifetime in the prolonged Italian Campaign of 1943-1945. Far too many were in fact only released by death from that unending strain. Others, damaged in body or mind, are still suffering today. Casualties were such that the battalion was in a constant state of flux from the moment it went into action. New drafts arrived and they too were promptly killed, wounded or rejected as unsuitable soldiers for active service. Very few men were lucky enough to pass through this maelstrom unscathed. For this reason is difficult to follow specific characters throughout the campaign as most had their time with the battalion cut brutally short.

It is invidious to comment on an individual's response to extreme stress from the comfort of one's armchair but it is my belief that *however* they responded – whether bravely, falteringly or in fear and trembling – these men were all heroes who fought, however unwillingly in some cases, to save their collective future. These men were not regular soldiers who had trained for years, fully realising that, at least in theory, they had sold their lives for the 'King's Shilling'. Most of them were ordinary civilians called from their peaceful vocations to fight for their country in a war unsurpassed for sheer evil brutality. They shared no homogenous geographical or cultural Durham background and in fact came from the length and breadth of the country. For the most part they did not even train together, but were drafted in dribs and drabs from their parent regiments as the exigencies of war demanded. It was only after serving together in the 16th Durhams that they gained a unified identity and became proud to be 'Durhams'.

The Durham Light Infantry have their origin in the Eighteenth Century wars against France. The Government decided to increase the size of the Army by simply asking the existing regiments to form a second line unit. As a result on 25 August 1756 the 23rd Regiment of Foot began to form a second battalion. At this point regiments had not yet been given 'County' names and thus, when the two battalions were separated in 1758, the 2nd Battalion became known as the 68th Foot. In 1760 the 68th Foot were based at Tynemouth Barracks and naturally most of the new recruits originated in County Durham. The regiment served in North America and the Caribbean where they first earned their honorific title 'Faithful'. On their return to Tynemouth the regiment's links with Durham were formalised when it was linked to the county for recruiting purposes.

Founder of the Regiment, General John Lambton, 1710–1794

In 1808 the 68th Foot were designated as the 68th Light Infantry receiving a new uniform, new weapons, the bugle insignia and began to march at the light infantry pace. They served in the Napoleonic Wars, playing a distinguished part in the Peninsula War Campaign in Portugal and Spain. After a long period of garrison duty, often in Canada, the 68th Light Infantry were called into action again in 1854 when they entered the Crimean War. Here their most conspicuous success at the Battle of Inkerman became a regimental

The 68th Foot in action during the Nineteenth Century.

Officers of the 68th Light Infantry during the Crimean War. The Battle of Inkerman became a regimental battle honour celebrated annually on 5 November as 'Inkerman Day'.

battle honour celebrated annually on 5 November as 'Inkerman Day'.

Meanwhile the East India Company had raised a new unit in the 2nd Bombay European Light Infantry in Poona on 18th December 1839. Following the dissolution of the East India Company after the Indian Mutiny of 1857, this unit was taken into the British Army proper and renamed the 106th Bombay Light Infantry. Despite its name the unit largely recruited in County Durham.

In the 1881 re-organisation of the army the two units which recruited in the Durham area were formally unified and became the 1st and 2nd Battalions, The Durham Light Infantry. The regiment served in the Sudan, India and South Africa before it faced its greatest challenge in the First World War. In all no less than 37 battalions took part in the Great War where the slaughter of the Western Front left an indelible mark on the consciousness of pit villages and towns across the county.

Between the wars the Durham regular battalions served in the Army of Occupation, Afghanistan, India, Egypt, Sudan and China before once more the world was at war in 1939. The regulars went off to war with the British Expeditionary Force under the command of Lord Gort. The first and second line territorial battalions quickly mobilised and they too joined the fray in France and Belgium in time to see the end of the Phoney War and the awe inspiring German blitzkrieg which burst through to force the British evacuation of France in May 1940.

The 16th Battalion Durham Light Infantry owed its existence to the disaster that had befallen the British Army at Dunkirk. As the country faced an uncertain future across the English Channel the need for more trained troops was both obvious and pressing and some of the normal refinements of training were put aside in the rush. New battalions for existing regiments like the Durham Light Infantry were therefore created from fresh drafts of recruits from wherever they were available. Many were base southerners who had never even been to County Durham! Most were unsullied by even the most basic of training.

During the next two years, experienced officers and NCOs supplied the backbone around which the battalion was made flesh, as the recruits learnt the training manual from scratch. Originally brigaded with the 14th and 17th Durham Light Infantry who were also 'Dunkirk' Battalions, they were soon selected to join 139 Brigade of 46th Division, with whom they trained until active service beckoned in December 1942. The 2/5th Sherwood Foresters and 2/5th Leicestershire Regiment were to be their comrades in arms for the rest of the war.

The Durhams left Liverpool on 25 December 1942. The date exaggerated the poignancy of the moment as they left on active service for the first time.

> It was Christmas Day, I was one of hundreds of 16th Bn. The DLI soldiers aboard a Troopship. We were all excited – not at the thought of the festive celebrations but because, that day, we were setting sail and our ultimate destination was the Battle Field. At last the ship's anchor was drawn up and we moved down towards the open sea. Nearly all the troops on board were lining the ship's rails and no doubt, like me, wanted to see as much of dear old England as they could before She faded from view, perhaps for ever. I was leaning over the rail of the port side and was feeling pretty miserable – my thoughts were of the folk at home. Suddenly I was startled by the sound of loud cheers. The noise came from the starboard side and I made my way across to find out what it was all about. After a struggle I managed to get to the rail and saw a little British destroyer steaming close alongside us. She was displaying a big white sheet and printed on it in block letters was a message of good will: "A Happy Christmas to all on Board." I shall remember that greeting as long as I live. *Company Sergeant Major G Gates*[1]

The 46th Division joined the First Army which had landed under 'Operation Torch' in North Africa in November 1942 and was slowly pushing its way towards Tunis mirroring the progress of the indomitable Eighth Army which had been edging east ever since the victory of El Alamein in October 1942. The 16th Durhams landed at Algiers on 3

Eisenhower and Alexandra in a conference break, 18 September 1943. IWM NA 6877

January 1943 and initially occupied a quiet part of the line in the Green Hill sector near the village of Sedjenane.

In late February the real war burst upon them as the Germans thrust forward and the Battle of Sedjenane began. It was a cruel introduction to warfare, for although the German offensive was eventually held off, the inexperienced troops of 139 Brigade suffered heavy casualties. Further battles followed as the Allies slogged their way forward through Tunisia but the Germans had shot their bolt. Ever increasing numbers of Allied troops poured into North Africa and Tunis fell in May 1943. On the completion of the campaign the Durhams spent a considerable time on mountain training in the Atlas Mountains whilst based at Blida before moving up to Bizerta ready for whatever their masters might command.

The next stage in the Allied master plan was the conquest of Sicily with the intention of clearing the Mediterranean and thereby securing a safe sea route direct to the Middle East and via the Suez Canal to India. It would also allow Allied air bases to move a step closer to their objectives. Direct invasion of the Italian mainland was originally ruled out as it would inevitably develop into a major land campaign which would suck in troops and resources needed for the intended 'Second Front' invasion of Europe planned for 1944. The Allied forces available were the 15th Army Group commanded by Field Marshal Harold Alexander It consisted of the British Eighth Army under General Bernard Montgomery and the United States Fifth Army commanded by General Mark Clark.

The invasion of Sicily was launched on 10 July with Operation Husky. Although there were problems and hold-ups, overall the campaign was a success, assisted as it was by the Allies' complete naval and aerial domination of the area. The Italian Army had also been less than enthusiastic, offering only token resistance. This severely handicapped the Germans who found the Italian formations to be a liability in the line of battle.

This went so well that it was decided to push on by launching a limited offensive into Southern Italy. The strategic objectives were to finally complete Allied control of the Mediterranean and secure air fields in the Foggia area from which heavy bombers could strike into the industrial centres of Germany and the Balkan oil fields. It would also act as a diversion by sucking in German divisions from the main battlefields of the Eastern and Western Fronts.

It was decided that the Eighth Army would leap across the Straits of Messina which separated Sicily and Italy to land on the 'toe' and 'heel' of Italy and then fight their way up to link up with the Fifth Army which was to land at Salerno.

The Eighth Army successfully landed at San Giovanni and Reggio on 3 September 1943. Subsidiary landings succeeded in capturing the crucial Italian naval centre of Taranto on 9 September. The two German divisions withdrew in good order before them on the orders of the senior German commander Field Marshal Albert Kesselring who had rightly guessed that the main Allied landing would be higher up the 'leg' of Italy, probably at Salerno, in the Gulf of Gaeta.

The scene was set for the Allied landings at Salerno.

CHAPTER ONE

Happy Landings

The Salerno landings, code named 'Operation Avalanche', were to be carried out by the Fifth Army under General Mark Clark. Salerno had been selected because it was relatively near the vital port of Naples and had beaches suitable for landings within the area for which air cover could be provided from the newly captured airfields in Sicily. The Salerno landings had been conceived against a backdrop of ongoing negotiations between Eisenhower and Marshal Pietro Badoglio's Italian government who had taken over from Mussolini on 25 July 1943. The Italians were maintaining a fiction of remaining in the Axis Alliance to avoid further German troops pouring into Italy, but were secretly intent on signing an Armistice with the Allies. After intensive negotiations it was agreed that all Italian forces would surrender on the eve of the planned Salerno landings.

The US Fifth Army consisted of the British X Corps (46th and 56th Divisions) and the US VI Corps with additional attached Commando and Ranger units. The X Corps commanded by Major General Sir Richard McCreery was to land on the northern section of the Salerno beach whilst the VI Corps landed south of the River Selle. The Commandos and Rangers were to land and hold the two passes through the hills leading to Naples. Once the immediate beachheads were secure the two main corps were to move inland to form an advanced perimeter in the hills which surrounded the beaches like an amphitheatre. The plan was predicated on establishing total naval and aerial superiority in the Salerno area.

The 46th Division under the command of Major General JLI Hawkesworth were ordered to secure their section of the beachhead between the River Pienttino and River Asa. Meanwhile 56th Division would land on a wider front to their right. The 16th Durham Light Infantry

General Hawkesworth – 'the little man with the big stick'. IWM NA 6847

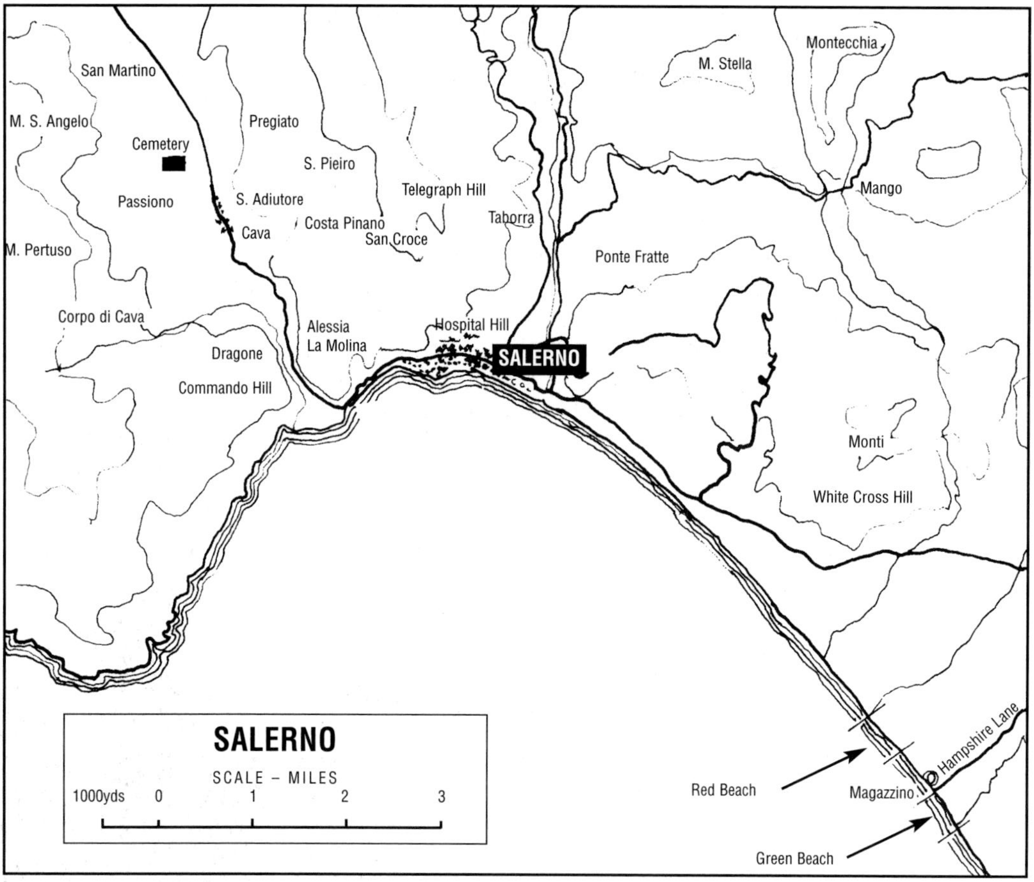

(Durhams) were unaware of the strategic implications or plans that lay behind their role with 139 Brigade in the landings. They only knew they were preparing for a landing but they were not even officially aware of their target. Test embarkations, practise landings, route marches and weapons testing filled the frenetic last two weeks at Bizerta in August 1943.

> We began some fairly hard training. The Officers and Warrant Officers were given an idea of their future target by being taken to a geographical formation the silhouette of which resembled what we ultimately found when we got ashore. We were told that this was such and such a place a) b) c) d) e) and so on. We were told the outline of what we were expected to do. Nobody told us where it was, but everybody had guessed that it would be Italy. Two weeks of fairly intensive preparation for the tasks that were to be

set us. In the meantime the rifle companies carried on some pretty hard work. We'd never been as well equipped since we'd come abroad. We were really given everything that we could possible have asked for in the way of clothing, boots with a warning from the Colonel that if we got the boots wet we should not get any further boots for three weeks after arrival! The weapons and armaments that had become depleted during the African fighting were all replaced. *Major Viz Vizard, A Coy, 16th DLI*

The chance to replace his uniform would have been a blessing to one recently-arrived soldier who had not yet had the chance to wear his uniform in action. Nevertheless he had made a bit of a mess of it!

Company Sergeant Major Baker had given me the job of trying to keep down the germs in our rather primitive latrines. To give some sort of privacy some big 80 gallon petrol drums had been laid longwise around their sides. He said, "Get some cans of petrol, pour the petrol in and chuck a match on top. It won't do much but it might keep the germs down!" I did this with a couple of other chaps and we got to the last one. There wasn't much petrol left so I chucked it in, set light to it and sent one of the other chaps to get another can of petrol. When he returned I threw some earth into the pit to smother any remaining flames. Then, satisfied it was safe, I threw the contents of the can in. There was a hell of a 'WHHOOSSHHH!' and a bloody great sheet of flame shot up towards me – I thought the most sensible thing would be to jump through it because the wind was blowing the flames towards me. I jumped but instead of landing right on the top of one of the drums I landed on the reverse slope. With my steel-shod boots I didn't have much chance, and despite all my efforts, I fell back and with a splash landed into the shit! They say the more you stir it the more it stinks – I can assure you that's very true! Fortunately I went in with such a thump that it sort of spread the burning petrol away from me and one of my lads grabbed my hand and pulled me out. I wasn't burnt but my hair was singed a bit. I walked the few hundred yards to the sea and I just laid down in it for about two hours till I was thoroughly cleansed! *Private Kenneth Lovell, D Coy, 16th DLI*

Kenneth Lovell, 1944

Almost every night the Luftwaffe launched bombing raids on the tempting concentration of Allied landing craft and troops which filled Bizerta harbour to the brim.

These planes used to come over and the sky was lit with the

searchlights from all the ships. When they got on to him there was beams going on from every which way and they never got out of it, down they would come in flames. Poor devils. The first night we were parked with our three trucks. We'd seen the view of the bay from the top of the hill not far up from the trucks, a beautiful view. When the planes came over we went up to the top to watch the fireworks. The bombs were dropping and the anti-aircraft fire from the ships. Then we heard a whacking great thud somewhere – very near! We thought, "To hell with this – we'd better get shelter!" We went and got under our trucks because they had a sheet metal base. Our lads were camped in little two man tents and next morning they found a piece of old shell bottom, a great big lump of horrible metal, bigger than your hand with great raw gashes, had gone right through the bottom of their washing tin and it was a foot into the ground when they dug it out. That had just missed a tent. So we were very cautious after that! *Driver Gordon Gent, MT Section, HQ Coy, 16th DLI*

As the climactic moment approached they were let into the big secret. The 128 Brigade, formed entirely of battalions from the Hampshire Regiment, were to be first to storm ashore on Red and Green Beaches on 9 September. The 139 and 138 Brigades were to form the second wave consolidating and enlarging the putative bridgehead the same day.

Men of D Coy at Blida, July 1943.

46th Division vehicles waiting to be embarked at Bizerta docks, 3 September 1943.
IWM NA 6354

The Durhams rifle companies were to embark on three Landing Ship Infantry (LSI).

> We had a talk from the American Admiral Moran, he gathered all us chaps together from the 46th Division. The Officers, Warrant Officers and senior NCOs of the leading companies went to the cinema. Big cinema it was and there must have been 800 fellows in there. He gave an address and he had some maps. They weren't very detailed maps but we were destined for what was known as Green Beach. He went through what they intended to do and he was an amusing fellow – he wound up the speech by saying, "Well gentlemen, that's about all, there are too many of you to take questions. I'm not going to guarantee that my buddies will actually land you on Green Beach, but sure as hell I can guarantee that we will land you in the right country!" *Major Viz Vizard, A Coy, 16th DLI*

The battalion transport and Headquarters Company were to follow on the Landing Ship Tanks (LST). The loading of the vehicles was a major task, posing logistical problems which would have baffled any scientist unwise enough to believe that a given space is not infinitely expandable.

> There were certain things laid down by the quartermaster, by battalion headquarters and by the company headquarters as to

what had to be taken and what was not allowed to be taken. The drivers were very ingenious about how much they seemed to squeeze into their trucks. There was a fifteen hundredweight truck which had about thirty hundredweight of stores stacked into it! It was a question of getting on everything you possibly could but only in such a way that the vehicle would still actually drive on to the landing craft and drive off again at the other end. *Lieutenant Russell Collins, Support Coy, 16th DLI*

Russell Collins on commissioning into the Duke of Cornwall's Light Infantry and shortly before embarkation to North Africa where he was posted to the 16th Durhams, 1943.

Collins himself, a very young and newly commissioned officer who had only just joined the battalion, began his active service career in an inauspicious manner.

I made a bit of a fool of myself just at this crucial moment. Of course one of the biggest hazards, not only in North Africa, but also in South Italy, was malaria and everybody had to take a certain quantity of mepacrine tablets. They were given out at meal times and one stood in the meal queue and made sure every soldier had his mepacrine tablet – and took it. So they were supervised and they didn't slip up. But after all that, by the time I got into the Officer's tent to have my own meal, I occasionally slipped up and didn't take my own tablet. So shortly before the invasion, unfortunately, I went down with a mild attack of malaria – I didn't get many brownie points for that! George Ballance, gave me a pretty sound, severe ticking off. Very well deserved really because that's the sort of thing officers shouldn't do. But it was only a very mild attack, I've never had a recurrence and it didn't keep me out of action for very long. But it did mean I missed the first phase of the battalion landing, I came in on the second phase. *Lieutenant Russell Collins, Support Coy, 16th DLI*

Other anti-mosquito precautions were considered ludicrous by many of the Durhams.

We had bee-keepers' nets to put over our helmets to keep the mosquitoes off our faces. And cotton gauntlet gloves. They expected us to go into action in the evening and put on bee-keepers' mosquito nets and gauntlet gloves – it's unbelievable. Nobody ever did of course. I never put mine on and I didn't see anybody else put his on. I kept the net for straining juice out of grapes! *Lieutenant Gerry Barnett, C Coy, 16th DLI*

A and C Companies were designated to land first on Green Beach and

46th Division vehicles embarking aboard LSTs at Bizerta docks, 3 September 1943.
IWM NA 6351

A Company embarked aboard LCI 345 crewed by American sailors.

> We embarked, there was good deal of grumbling but nobody was any better off than anybody else. It was very democratic – the troops were cramped, the Warrant Officers were cramped, the NCOs were cramped, the officers were cramped... There was a tiny wardroom topsides in the conning tower section which accommodated the skipper and his Number 1, myself and Tom Reynolds. That's all you could get in. Tiny! *Major Viz Vizard, A Coy, 16th DLI*

Many of the troops were heavily laden but the signallers had a ridiculous amount to carry. One decided to take unilateral action to ease his burden.

> I had six batteries this time plus my other gear. As we were going up there was about a two foot gap between the ship and I said, To hell with this, I'll never need these batteries!" And I just plonked three of them into the sea. Corporal Reynolds spotted it

and he said, "Right, you'll be reported!" I said, "Please yourself, I'm like a flaming pack mule here, I cannot carry more than this!" *Signaller Anthony Sacco, D Coy, 16th DLI*

Embarkation was completed by the afternoon of 5 September and they set off for Sicily. At first they encountered some rough seas which had the virtue of distracting the men, at least for the moment, from a prolonged contemplation of what lay before them.

Cairo, March 1944. Back row left to right: *A Sacco, L Smith, Ronald Elliott.* Front row: *C Grey, D Jordan.*

With the LCIs being pretty shallow draft and flat bottomed, it felt twice as bad as on a normal sort of boat. I was fortunate, I'm a good sailor, I wasn't seasick, there were very, very few others who weren't seasick. Every officer on board was seasick, half the crew were seasick and the mess decks were absolutely awash with vomit. If we had been going straight in to Salerno from there and had landed the men just wouldn't have been able to break through the skin of a rice pudding, let alone the German defences. I think they'd have just gone ashore and put their hands up they were in such a terrible state. Next morning I went up on deck about 5 o'clock and it had calmed considerably and the sun was coming up. Then we anchored in, I believe, the Straits of Pozzo, waiting for the rest of the invasion fleet to gather. All troops were ordered topside, the crew of the ship hosed the mess-decks out and men were given permission to go swimming in the sea. Those who had soiled their clothes just emptied their pockets, took off their boots and went in fully clothed. After swimming around for a little while they came back took off their clothes, laid starkers, hung their clothes out to dry and got themselves respectable again. *Private Kenneth Lovell, D Coy, 16th DLI*

As they recovered from their ordeal by water, news came of a breathtaking announcement as the Italians finally showed their hand.

The night before the invasion we were having an inspection when over the Tannoy in the American style came, "Hear me, hear me," and the voice of the Captain told us that he had been commanded to inform all that, "The Italian government had surrendered and all Italian troops had been ordered to lay down their arms." A cheer rang through the ship. *Private Kenneth Lovell, D Coy, 16th DLI*

To the sweating troops packed below decks it seemed for fleeting moment that their prayers had been answered.

We thought, "Brilliant, landing at Naples, at a harbour and it'll be all over – just a matter of occupying Italy!" We were wrong! Sergeant Threadgold said, "Don't you believe it, make sure your weapons are clean!" He was right! *Lance Corporal William Virr, B Coy, 16th DLI*

The optimistic vied with the pessimistic as the reverberations of the message sank in across the invasion fleet.

I thought it was bloody stupid, we were all sort of pretty young chaps, we'd been trained up, we were tensed up, we didn't know what we were going into, but we expected the worst. And then you had this announcement which seemed to take the edge off things. Lieutenant Woodlands called us to order and told us to get any idea out of our mind that we were going to stroll ashore on a Roman holiday, that intelligence reports indicated that the area was being held by veteran German troops and he certainly did his best to nullify the effects of that stupid message. We had no certainties as to what we were going to face when we landed and I think this possibly helped to dissipate the feeling of euphoria that went through the ship on the announcement – it went pretty soon. Whether the men ever got completely back up to their battle tenseness I don't know. *Private Kenneth Lovell, D Coy, 16th DLI*

Lieutenant Woodlands was not the only officer left seething at the impact of the news on his men.

Nothing would satisfy the Padre but that he had a drumhead service of thanksgiving on board. I took him aside and I said, "Now look, if you do this you're going to put the wrong sort of emphasis into troops' minds. They think there's going to be the local mayor and a brass band ready to receive them the Italians having surrendered. The chances are the Germans will have foreseen that the Italians were getting ready to jack it in and will have plenty of their own forces in reserve to take over." "No, No!" He said, "It was a gift of God!" And so forth. So we had to have a service – a short service! *Major Viz Vizard, A Coy, 16th DLI*

Herded like cattle below decks, the atmosphere amongst the men became for the most part subdued as they approached their destiny on the beaches.

A lot of us were going into action for the first time, I certainly became a little more pensive than I was normally – a lot of men became rather quieter. Some of the men became much more chatty. I wondered what it was going to be like. I wondered what my reaction would be, whether I'd be able to stand up to it, worried lest I might turn coward. I prayed that if anything happened to me I'd rather be killed rather than losing my limbs or sight; death was preferable to being maimed for life. I wondered what it would be like to have people shooting real bullets at me. It's funny how looking back now, that faced with the prospect of death in a few hours, I was extremely calm. I think most of the lads were too. The married men in the platoon were a little bit more concerned obviously, they had responsibilities, thought about their children and there were a lot of family photographs brought out, passed round and commented on. On the whole I think more men were subdued than chatty. And I think we were kinder to each other than perhaps we would normally have been. Just before the landing we paraded and Woodlands, our platoon commander had a weapons inspection. Then he suggested it would be a good idea if we commended ourselves to God and asked his protection. We said the Lord's Prayer together. I don't think I've ever in my life heard it said so fervently as it was on that occasion! *Private Kenneth Lovell, D Coy, 16th DLI*

As they sailed into the Bay of Naples they were called up on deck. All around them was evidence that although they were just anonymous cogs in the war machine, it was a truly vast and powerful engine of destruction that was directed at the hapless German defenders of Salerno.

We came up on deck and saw this vast invasion fleet. Just to our

The invasion fleet at sea entering the Bay of Naples, 9 September 1943. IWM NA 6575

left was the Warspite blasting away with its 15" guns, the shells going through the air making the sound of railway porter running with his devil along the platform. *Private Kenneth Lovell, D Coy, 16th DLI*

Ahead of them they could see their destination slowly getting closer and closer.

We had this profile of the hills and I could see it quite clearly, – the training had been good, the profile was there – except all the angles were much steeper and they'd warned us about that. So I knew where we were going to and I could see the town of Salerno on my left and we were pretty much on Green Beach. As we got closer I could make out Positano not far down the coast. *Major Viz Vizard, A Coy, 16th DLI*

Ahead of them the Hampshires prepared to make their landing. As the first wave approached in the dim moonlight the rocket ships opened up in a final blistering bombardment. On Red Beach everything went well as the 1/4th Hampshires moved inland and occupied the low lying hills in front of them. Unfortunately the 2nd Hampshires intended for Green Beach were landed on the wrong side of the River Asa and hence against German positions relatively untroubled by the preparatory naval bombardment. As they rushed ashore they came under heavy fire but with the help of the 5th Hampshires they managed to cross the Asa and begin to move inland as originally intended. Elements of 138 Brigade also landed, but Green Beach remained under shellfire and soon a threatening German counter-attack developed and the situation was in flux.

Now it was the Durhams' turn. A and C Companies were the first ashore.

They had 88mm Tiger tanks hull down on the sand dunes and they were banging away. 128 Brigade were about a 1,000 yards inland, they'd had a lot of trouble and a good deal of the trouble was still there, because they'd over-run some of it. These Tiger tanks were still banging away at us. Bits were flying off the LCI, we started to get off and I said to the skipper, "Well don't hang around, you'd better get yourself off!" "Oh," he said, "I'm stopping here till you're all ashore." And he did. *Major Viz Vizard, A Coy, 16th DLI*

Led by their officers the Durhams charged ashore.

I was the lead man off, there were two ramps. Tom Logan took one and I took the other. Then we had two subalterns, they were standing behind and we organised ourselves into three platoons. Number One Platoon moved off to its right, rushed up the beach, Number Two rushed off moving to the centre and Number Three

Salerno beach, 9 September 1943. IWM NA 6630

to the left. So as they came off they went in their different directions. The Sergeant Major had organised the disembarkation so that, fairly roughly you got a fellow moving that way, a fellow moving that way and a fellow moving this way. Which dispersed them, there were no solid targets on the beach at all. We all got ashore and ran like hell up the sand. *Major Viz Vizard, A Coy, 16th DLI*

Across the sands they ran in the footsteps of the ill fated Hampshires. The other companies landed behind them.

Behind us was the big ships firing into the mountain range round the beachhead and the noise was terrific. There seemed to be hundreds of small boats hovering, waiting of the Beach

Commander calling them forward. The Hampshires had already landed, early morning, and word got back to us that they were in a terrible state. They decided that certain groups out of different battalions would go in to make a second landing. We were among this lot. We didn't quite hit the beach, we were waist high in water going in, having to keep all our equipment up above. As we were coming off the boat there was people trying to get back on. They'd got off and ran up the beach and they'd hit land mines. Maybe four or five were killed at that point and six or seven wounded were coming back on the boat with blood pouring off them. So it was a bit of a shambles. They were trying to get up the planks as we were going down, which was totally wrong – but what could you do. We were told to go to the left as we got off the beach and not to go forward because of the mines. Obviously we'd landed somewhere that hadn't been cleared. Lying on the beach there was a lot of flak coming over but it was landing in the sea. Our ships were firing back in – it was horrendous the noise. *Private Robert Ellison, D Coy, 16th DLI*

When B Company came ashore they had rather more luck to start with.

I always say we went off the landing craft and I never even got my feet wet, because we were lucky! The others further along at either side, they were having to wade in. When we got in he must have hit a nice shelf of beach and when he put the ramps down we went straight onto the sand. Straight away we were under fire from machine guns and small arms. When we got so far up the beach there was a wall. There was a gap in the wall and he had a fixed gun on the wall. One or two tried to get across this gap and got hit by machine guns. *Corporal Tom Turnbull, B Coy, 16th DLI*

Salerno beach 9 September 1943. IWM NA 6631

Although the beach had been taken by the Hampshire Brigade the amount of German fire directed at the beach was still quite considerable.

> There was a lot of small arms fire, some mortar fire, and a good deal of shelling. The sand was constantly being thrown up by quite large calibre shells. I think they were the 88s firing from the sand dunes. It was general fire but I think they were principally aiming at the vessels because there were quite a few LCIs coming in. There were seven casualties on the move up the beach. *Major Viz Vizard, A Coy, 16th DLI*

One junior NCO froze in front of his men.

> We came down the ramp and spread out, got down on the sands. Mr Coutts was our platoon commander. The Corporal just lost it, went to pieces, he couldn't move, he said, "No, I can't..." Mr Coutts ordered him back on the boat. I had to take over the section. *Lance Corporal William Virr, B Coy, 16th DLI*

Their instructions had stressed the importance of clearing the immediate beach area as soon as possible.

> We were pleased to get across the beach and into the field on the far side. Once we got in there the fire finished for the time being because it seemed to be concentrated on the beach. We knew that some of the people either side of us were in difficulties. Unfortunately the company couldn't find the rest of the battalion and we joined up with Brigadier Harding of 138 Brigade on our left. *Lieutenant Ronnie Sherlaw, C Coy, 16th DLI*

The Durhams moved forward and took up defensive positions about quarter of a mile inland. All seemed to be well.

Overall the landing had been successful and the 46th Division was safely ashore. By the evening of 9 September the Allies had established a bridgehead which was some 30 miles long, although it was shallow in depth and the Germans still overlooked them from the hills. Kesselring and his subordinates reacted swiftly. The divisions facing Montgomery's Eighth Army were ordered to harry and delay his advance while the rest of Kesselring's forces concentrated in the hills above Salerno. So the Germans gathered their sinews for a counter-attack to drive the Allies back into the sea with unimaginable losses.

> We followed the platoon commander and after a little while we came into a little wood with a lovely clear stream running down into the sea. We were told to rest, we were staying there until further orders! *Private Kenneth Lovell, D Coy, 16th DLI*

The German Army had however no intention of leaving them in peace.

CHAPTER TWO

Hospital Hill

The Durhams spent the night at the assembly area and next day the remainder of the battalion landed. Although German harassing fire on the beach continued the situation appeared under control. Nevertheless a couple of bright sparks in the Motor Transport (MT) Section aboard an LST got a shock as they ran in to land on the beach.

We were shifted off the decks, everybody had to be piled down in the hold with the exception of the people that were concerned with the vehicles on the deck. You always get one or two smart Alecs and they'd found this large cupboard in the bulkhead. They had a light in there and they were playing cards and smoking. We were approaching this landing. The ship hove to and they dropped the anchor – now what we didn't know was that we were immediately next to the chain locker! These anchor chains were rattling away – it sounded just like all the bombs that ever were were being dropped! It was absolutely deafening, we had to put our fingers in our ears. We crouched on the floor in sheer panic, thinking, "We're going down, this is great, we've got here and we're going to drown before we get ashore." It was a terrible noise! This American Chief Petty Officer was laughing his head off, he'd known all about what would happen and hadn't warned us. *Driver Tom Lister, MT Section, HQ Coy, 16th DLI*

Walking along Salerno beach Generals Alexander, Clark and McCreery, 15 September 1943. IWM NA 6822

Despite such alarums the Durhams' concentration was completed by lunch on 10 September. They moved forward to occupy defensive positions above the River Grancano valley north of the San Sevino road. As they moved forward there were grim reminders of the permanent nature of the 'game' they were playing.

We moved up and it was on my way I came across my first dead German. I climbed over a wall and just in front there was a bush. Suddenly a huge cloud of flies came up and there was a terrible stink. A sweet sickly smell, something I had never smelt before. As I went past the bush there was a German half track that had received a direct hit from a shell. The whole lot, nine or ten men had been killed, all sprawled in grotesque attitudes, many of them black from burns. I spewed my heart up, it really made me sick, the smell, the stench and the sight of seeing men so violently killed. *Private Kenneth Lovell, D Coy, 16th DLI*

Despite the absence of hard fighting many of the men were already beginning to understand the enervating effects of lack of sleep and stress which distinguish active service from any battle exercises, no matter how realistic, in England.

One or two aeroplanes came over strafing and you were praying for darkness to come. It got dark – then you were praying for it to be light – you didn't know who was creeping up onto you! No sleep. It was black dark – all you could see was the flashes of the guns but most of the battle was down in the valley to our left. *Private Robert Ellison, D Coy, 16th DLI*

Officers, NCOs and men alike had to cope with the tension

We reached the road we had been given as our immediate target on the second day. We spent a very fretful night, I don't think anybody slept at all. In fact I don't believe anybody slept for three days. It can be done when you're that age. It dulls your senses a bit but when your senses are being stretched like violin strings – it's the aftermath rather than at the time. *Major Viz Vizard, A Coy, 16th DLI*

Their position was certainly not without personal danger, for the Germans were maintaining a considerable amount of fire into the bridgehead from the surrounding hills. As the Allied units poured ashore there was soon such a profusion of targets that it was difficult for the German gunners to miss.

Jerry was up on the heights and he sees everything that's happening. Another battalion was being brought in and all these troops were disgorging off buses down the main street. We were going back for ammunition, he was shelling away and I saw one or two shells hit the top corner of a five storey building, bricks and mortar coming down into the street. I thought, "Hell, I'm not going to drive through this lot – I'll wait till it quietens down." I could see why he was shelling it because these troops were being brought in. Then there were screams as some people were hit. My mate he was a young lad, he didn't have his wits about him! He didn't think about taking precautions and hanging back a bit. He drove through where the shelling was and he was wounded. *Driver Gordon Gent, MT Section, HQ Coy, 16th DLI*

On the 11 September, the 16th DLI were ordered to relieve the 6th York and Lancs on the hills below the mental sanatorium which gave the whole area the designation of Hospital Hill. They were the final buffer to protect the port of Salerno. The relief was completed by 20.00. D Company took up positions just left of the Hospital, whilst C Company occupied a slight promontory known as 'The Pimple' in time honoured manner. In reserve were A and B Companies positioned in the vineyards on either side of the Hospital road leading back into Salerno. The 2/5th Sherwood Foresters were to their right on the main road. To the left lay rough country with the nearest British troops the Commandos on Castle Hill. The Durhams were holding a crucial front line bulwark of the slender Allied bridgehead as the German pressure and counter-attacks escalated. It was now that the German mortars began to really

Bren carrier passing through Salerno, 10 September 1943. IWM NA 6790

make their presence felt. The most distinctive of them was the Nebelwerfer.

> It was awful, really terrifying. We could hear them start off, because they used to be fired electrically from six barrelled mortars, we used to call them 'Wurlitzers'. They had a note as the barrels fired in rotation. Then you knew you had about 20 seconds before the bombs arrived. Terrifying it was. You used to lie at the bottom of this hole, looking at a beetle or something, wishing you were somewhere else. *Lieutenant Gerry Barnett, C Coy, 16th DLI*

The German mortar fire was accurate and unremitting, inexorably searching out the Durhams cowering in their hastily dug slit trenches.

> Bill Crummack and I had a most miraculous escape – a mortar shell landed in our trench and didn't explode. It landed between our feet. It did shake us! We scrambled out of the bloody trench faster than you've ever seen anyone scramble out of a trench. *Private Kenneth Lovell, D Coy, 16th DLI*

The shell may not have gone off, but this was the real thing, not an exercise.

> It is a situation you can't reproduce. You can have machine guns firing on fixed lines but you know, however hard it is, that nobody is actually trying to kill you. And that's the difference between an exercise and the real thing where you've got some rotten bugger

Nebelwerfers – German six-barrelled mortars with the projectiles caught by the camera.
IWM STT 5572

trying to kill you. It was a fact that you knew you stood a bloody good chance of being killed, that was the difference. *Private Kenneth Lovell, D Coy, 16th DLI*

The screaming mortar shells were a terrible introduction to battle as the scything shrapnel swept across the trenches.

There was a lot of shelling on the position and it was my first experience of being shelled in that way. I was surprised to find that quite a number of the younger soldiers, who had already been in action, took very badly with it. I remember one young fellow started screaming and I had to guess how to handle it. I just gave him a good clout in the face and he stopped. We eventually had to get him out of the line but he cooled down. Some of these chaps, more the chaps who'd been in the line than the chaps who hadn't, took badly with this shelling. I suppose they'd seen more of what happened when you were shelled than we who hadn't been in action before. I was and am a great fatalist and I have a very strong faith too – I'm not saying that I wasn't frightened – I had the same sort of fears and apprehensions as anybody does when this sort of thing happens, but I refused to let it worry me, put it that way, so I always got through things that way. I think it's just sort of ingrained in me – my mother always used to say, "You can't help being frightened but never show it!" And I didn't! *Lieutenant Ronnie Sherlaw, C Coy, 16th DLI*

Even under shellfire the men still had to eat and they were fed through the devoted efforts of the Regimental Quartermaster Bert Newman and his faithful team. Rations were generally the composition type which was to become familiar to them all through their time in Italy. Although packed for ease of transport and distribution they posed considerable problems for harassed junior officers and NCOs in the front line.

We had 'compo' rations. A wooden box with a day's rations for seven men in each box. They were lettered from A-G, each letter denoting a different menu. Some were favourites, some weren't. The food in them was of very good quality. It included not only the three meals; but tins of tea, sugar and powdered milk, all in one mix; tinned plum pudding which was so good that you could eat it cold with great relish; tinned bacon, sausages and ham; toilet paper to last the day; a tin of 50 cigarettes which meant that every day every man had a ration of seven cigarettes; hard boiled sweets and of course a tin of hard biscuits – which were the 'bread' you might call it of the ration. The biscuit tin made a very good tea boiler and the wood from the packing case made a fire. After the war I used to have nightmares as most people do – but it wasn't about the shelling it was about distributing the rations. It's a terrible mathematical conundrum when you work it out. For example you get a tin of butter and in the hot weather it goes soft.

Well, how do you get butter from a tin which supplies seven men to your men on the ground under fire. It doesn't come in a little tin you can just hand out, it's half molten in a big tin! The American rations came in little tins for one man – that was easy – you could throw them to them. It was all right if you could bring seven men, just sit round in a little tea party and have a picnic, but they weren't even packed for an infantry section. If they'd come in nine men to a box you could have given the box to the section leader. *Lieutenant Gerry Barnett, C Coy, DLI*

One sniper went too far when he interrupted a communal brewing up of a section of 18 Platoon.

We were stood down and brewing up. We had a fire going with an empty biscuit tin with the water in boiling away. The tea and sugar ration you got was in a powder mixture and you put a few spoonfuls into the water and let it boil up – that made your tea. We were just getting to that stage when this sniper up in the hospital put a bullet right through the tin. The water ran out and put the fire out! Somebody said, "Right, we've got to get this bugger!" *Private Robert Ellison, D Coy, 16th DLI*

On the morning of 13 September, A Company, under the command of Major Vizard, tried to infiltrate on to the hill feature known as 'The Fort' to the right of the Hospital. He was not aware that the Germans too were building up their counter-attacks all along the Allied front-line.

I had 1 Platoon on the left, 3 Platoon on the right and I was in the middle with the reserve platoon, moving up this heavily wooded hill, a sort of pine trees. We really began to come under quite strong sustained fire from the right flank particularly. A lot of mortar fire, in fact at one stage I rang on my 18 Set and spoke to the Colonel and said, "Are you quite sure that we aren't too far forward and that we're not running into our own mortar fire?" "No", he said, "what you're getting is from Jerry!" And we were getting a lot! We moved on further up through these wooded pines spreading out as far as possible. There were no mines, they hadn't laid any mines. I could see defended positions, they were sort of dugouts, but the troops had gone. The Germans were mostly up and around the hospital at the top of the hill. I think we may have moved slightly further forward than the Guards on the right, they were having a hard time and I could understand that. But we were moving forward and as a result we were getting not only opposition from the front but we were getting it strongly from the right flank. We were moving through part of this wadi and there was tremendous burst of Schmeisser machine pistol fire from it, it couldn't have been more than 300 yards away on the right hand side. Simultaneously Sergeant Major 'Nutty' Wilson, I and Tom Logan jumped. Unfortunately, poor Tom, he jumped a bit too late.

Major Viz Vizard

I landed on top of the Sergeant Major and Tom landed on top of me. But he'd been wounded badly through the stomach. We got him dressed as best we could, got him on a stretcher and evacuated him but he died. *Major Viz Vizard, A Coy, 16th DLI*

Rightly or wrongly, Vizard felt personally responsible for Logan's death.

I always felt very badly about this because I thought it was my job to jump last, I should have pushed Tom in and got in after him – but it's instinctive. A Schmeisser will fire at 800 rounds a minute – you jump! I went to see his mother after the war and explained it all to her, told her it really ought to have been me, not Tom. She said, "Well in the circumstances as they were I can't find it in my heart to blame you...." So I felt a bit better then, but it should have been me.... *Major Viz Vizard, A Coy, 16th DLI*

After calling for mortar support, Vizard re-arranged his platoons and sought to establish a clear superiority of firepower so that their advance could continue.

I swung Number 1 off its axis, up the hill slightly to face the right hand side, I moved Number 3 forward and we half veered to the right, so we were facing where the trouble was coming from. We gave them everything we'd got, I heard later that Support Company had been laying into them – they'd got some Vickers medium machine guns and they'd mounted those and they were raking the whole of that area. But it was quite clear that this was where Jerry was putting in one of his principal retaliatory attacks to try and force us back to the beach. I don't think we were more than 1,500 yards inland. We had everything we had got going at them steadily, we had a nice reasonably protected situation in these great gullies with the gnarled roots of these pine trees. We were able to lie in there and give them all we'd got. We'd only got 12 Bren guns but you can do quite a lot of harm with 12 Bren guns. *Major Viz Vizard, A Coy, 16th DLI*

Having at least quietened down, if not silenced this flank attack, they were able to resume their move forward.

I sent Miller and Number 1 Platoon over to the left and 3 and 2 moved forward – we all moved forward, we no longer had reserve platoon – we were moving on a company front. The mortar fire became much more intense and we began to sustain quite a lot of casualties. The stretcher bearers were at work, it was mostly shrapnel splinters, I don't remember anyone getting a direct hit but it still did a lot of harm. It was quite clear that they had switched from the flank – they were now coming over the hospital. The poor old nuns inside must have had a rotten time of it. *Major Viz Vizard, A Coy, 16th DLI*

They struggled on another 200 yards further up Hospital Hill under a hail of mortar shells. But, at about noon, Vizard's own luck ran out.

I was crouched and one of these mortar bombs landed to the right of me and a splinter zipped through and got me at the bottom of the back. It wasn't particularly painful at first, it was very largely a flesh wound, but it had damaged the spine a bit. It was difficult to walk. I got patched up and continued moving forward. But the Medical Sergeant who was with me said, "You ought to jack it in, you're losing blood!" I said, "Well, no, it's all right!" Tom Logan had gone you see, if Tom had been there it would have been a different matter. So we pressed on and in the end the Sergeant was right because I passed out from loss of

British troops pass a road block in Salerno, 10 September 1943. IWM NA 6785

blood. Nothing I could do about it. *Major Viz Vizard, A Coy, 16th DLI*

Vizard was evacuated by stretcher for the urgent treatment his wounds required.

They'd started the job with me at the main dressing station, I got 96 stitches in the back and I got clips put in which halted most of the bleeding. The trouble was the spine was chipped. All regimental aid posts and dressing stations were very gory places. Like a butcher's abattoir. It was shocking! Fellows covered in blood from head to foot. All over their hair and faces and everything else. Because they were really at the sharp end. Blokes coming in and they only had a matter of minutes to save a life. Amputations were carried out with incredible speed. I saw one fellow have his leg taken off and it didn't take more than a minute and a half. Away it went. They did a hard, a very good job. *Major Viz Vizard, A Coy, 16th DLI*

Despite his personal problems, Vizard still found time to think of his men.

The officers had an ammunition box for their private possessions. Vizard and his second in command were wounded and he sent word down with the Quartermaster to open these and get out all the cigarettes. The officers always had a good supply of cigarettes – they acquired them! But they'd thought about the cigarettes in those boxes and Major Vizard ordered us to pass on all these cigarettes to the QM to dish out amongst the lads – which was a thoughtful gesture. Driver Gordon Gent, MT Section, HQ Coy, 16th DLI

The MT Section lorries were often stacked full of ammunition and were extremely vulnerable as the German shells probed the Durhams' rear areas behind Hospital Hill and in the outskirts of Salerno.

I'd lost contact with the lads altogether and there was no point in staying up there – I was doing nothing. Battalion HQ was just 200 yards down below where we'd been parked up the hill. I popped down to see if I could find out from HQ where A Company had got to. I got down there and there was a triangular little orchard with fruit trees. They'd got trenches and the Commanding Officer was in a trench with his retinue. The shells started coming over, good and fast, six barrelled mortars and God knows what. It was hectic. "Get your heads down!" That was the thing. I dived in with the CO's driver. You got squatted down just below the level of the surface. These shells were coming over and exploding. I suddenly felt a shoot of pain through my leg. I grabbed it and said, "Oh hell, I think I've been hit!" When I looked down there was a little tiny bit of shrapnel, red hot! It had burnt a hole in my trousers and it burnt my leg! Then a voice went up, "There's a truck on fire at the gate, Sir!" The CO pops his head up in the next trench. He said, "Anybody know who's it is?" I popped my head up and I said, "Yes, it's mine, Sir!" He said, "What have you got on board?" I started reading the ammunition list! "Oh my God!" He says. I got out of the trench but there was nothing I could do. The flames were belting out, the back was on fire and there was only one answer – she would blow up when it got to the ammunition! And it did! Whooh! What an explosion! These Piat mortar bombs – they were fierce things, blast, purely and simply blast, very powerful. Things were flying, bullets were going off – poor old truck! There was trucks with camouflage netting on in this spinney and all the netting was on fire, all from the blast of my ammunition tuck going up. We were frantic, dashing around dragging these burning nets off the other trucks. *Driver Gordon Gent, MT Section, HQ Coy, 16th DLI*

The Germans' counter-attacks were raging all along the line but in the Hospital Hill sector they culminated as dusk fell on the night of 15 September. German infiltrators swept over the positions of D Company on 'The Pimple'.

Whoever were in the forward observation post were either knocked out or they hadn't been watching and Jerry got right up on top of the hill. The first thing we knew he was starting to fire down. I put my hand out along the slit trench to get a hold of my rifle and the bullets smashed it – the butt was blown to bits! There was no question of getting the rifle it was just a matter of trying to keep down. We had a couple of grenades and we lobbed them back. What saved the day was somebody wired down and the mortar platoon started firing up there. *Private Robert Ellison, D Coy*

Further back down the hill, Lovell had just stripped down his Bren gun when the warning reached his platoon.

German troops at Salerno move up for a counter-attack against the invaders.
IWM MH 235

Suddenly Lieutenant Woodlands came galloping up and said, "Right, fix bayonets, we're going to go into a bayonet charge!" He led us, at the front, up the hill, over the slope and into the Germans. We really ran as fast as we could, Lieutenant Woodland called out, "CHARGE!" and we charged! Now the Germans were virtually amongst the positions of 16 and 18 Platoons. We went in using the battle cry we pinched from the 'Paras'. Evidently the battalion had been attached to 1st Paras in North Africa. We got stuck into the Germans. I hadn't got my Bren gun because it was still in pieces but I'd got a Tommy gun, I think Mr Woodlands gave it to me. As we were going I was firing from the hip. I suddenly saw a German lying down behind a machine gun. He looked at me and I looked at him – I pulled the trigger and nothing happened so I just swung the Tommy gun round, grabbed it by the barrel and smashed him over the head. I didn't know whether I'd killed him or whether he was unconscious or what. I went on. I think they were taken by surprise. There's a lot of stories that the Germans don't like cold steel but I don't think anybody does come to that! I think if some bugger had come at me with a bloody bayonet I might have done a side-step or something. The Germans fled into a box barrage that our mortars had put down behind them. We took quite a number of prisoners, killed quite a few. I went back and saw this German that I'd slammed. I don't think it was the fact that his head was stove in, but rather the idea of having killed another human being. All right, he'd have killed me if he'd got the chance, but nevertheless I was physically sick, I vomited. *Private Kenneth Lovell, D Coy, 16th DLI*

A stunning surprise awaited Lovell as he watched the German prisoners observing the decorations that indicated they were veterans. One man in particular caught his eye. Surely he was familiar?

Most of them were wearing the Russian front decoration. They were all experienced soldiers, some of them were wearing the close combat clasp which they didn't exactly chuck away in the German Army. A number of them had the Iron Cross 2nd Class, a couple had the 1st Class. The prisoners were taken up to company headquarters; one of them was ranting and raving in English about the fact that the Germans were going to win the war and about the glorious Fuhrer. At school I used to sit next to a German named Mittelhauser and I turned round, looked at this German Lieutenant who was ranting and raving and said, "Why don't you shut your mouth, Mittelhauser, you were just the same when you were at school!" This was a boy I had sat next to at school! His father had worked for some German company in London but in 1938 the family had gone back to Germany. One of those amazing coincidences. He said, "What the hell are you doing here?" "Same

Salerno Bay: Kenneth Lovell came across an old school chum among one batch of PoWs. TAYLOR LIBRARY

as you!" From ranting and raving he then started talking. *Private Kenneth Lovell, D Coy, 16th DLI*

The German counter-attacks all along Hospital Hill undoubtedly caught the Durhams on the hop – but this was most especially so in the C Company area commanded by Major Jobey.

George Jobey had his company headquarters on the rear slope in a tiny gardener's hut used by the Italians no doubt in the vineyards. It was on one of the terraces where there were these few vines. At dusk he sent for us, the three platoon commanders for what we called an 'O' Group for orders. We all gathered in this tiny hut but we never got round to getting the orders, I don't know what they would have been, because there were sounds of firing from outside the hut. Someone flung open the door and said, "We're under attack!" Sure enough the Germans were coming down the terraces, throwing grenades and firing with Schmeissers. They'd come up the forward slope, presumably at dusk. It was a great mistake actually to call us away from our platoons at dusk because they are the critical times, dusk and dawn. They were right through our positions. We were at the rear of our company positions and the Germans were round the hut virtually. The Sergeants must have been with us. *Lieutenant Gerry Barnett, C Coy, 16th DLI*

The situation was desperate – there were no troops for the young officers to command – they were the troops themselves and all that remained between the Germans and a dangerous local breakthrough.

There was a box of grenades in George's hut so we all grabbed a handful of grenades. That brings me to a little criticism of army uniform in that there is nowhere on a British infantryman's uniform to carry grenades. So you stuff them down your shirt and hope your belt's tight enough to hold them up. We grabbed some grenades and ran out. Of course there was no sort of orders or directions, we just started attacking back up the hill. It's just an instinct really – when you see Germans in the flesh to attack – there's nothing else you can do, you can't run away, we didn't know how to, it never occurred to us. Sort of unwilling but duty bound. *Lieutenant Gerry Barnett, C Coy, 16th DLI*

The situation was horribly confused as the light rapidly faded on Hospital Hill.

I was going forward with a .38 pistol in my hand, which is a useless implement. As I crawled up a sort of slit trench I put my head over it and there was a German helmet came up! I immediately pulled the trigger and I shot him – not very straight! I had a horrible feeling, that was the first time I'd ever been face to face and it was fortunate I had shot him because if I hadn't he'd have shot me! *Lieutenant Ronnie Sherlaw, C Coy, 16th DLI*

Perhaps the sheer desperation of their attack caught the Germans by surprise.

The Germans retreated and we slowly collected odd bods from our trenches where they'd been over-run and not observed and increased our strength a bit. But really it was an officers' and Sergeants' attack that was going on! We used grenades and I had my Tommy gun. Darkness came as we moved back up the hill until we reached the little saddle below the final 'Pimple'. By that time it was dark but bright moonlight. *Lieutenant Gerry Barnett, C Coy, 16th DLI*

Barnett and Sherlaw paused to reconsider the situation. It was at this point that Sherlaw made an error of judgement that could quite easily have cost him his life.

The Germans were obviously on and around the final 'Pimple' because I could hear them talking in loud voices as they seemed to be digging in while they used a machine gun to fire at us. Ronnie for some reason thought they were some other company's troops, ours, and he stood up in bright moonlight in his fairly light coloured KD uniform – you could see him for miles, stood up and shouted, "Stop firing, you bloody fools, this is C Company!" I said, "It's the Boche, Ronnie!" On which he dropped down smartly under cover! *Lieutenant Gerry Barnett, C Coy, 16th DLI*

German panzer grenadier in action with a Schmeisser machine carbine (MP38/40) in Italy. IWM MH 196

It was obvious that the Germans were still on the Pimple.

Complete confusion – the whole battle had been confused but this was very confused. Anyway we made the final walk up the hill, a small summit sloping away on all sides and there must have been a group of Germans about 20 feet away. They were within grenade-throwing range anyway. We could see the flashes coming from their Schmeissers as they fired at us. There were about five of us at the most on our side on the top. There wasn't room for any more anyway! We were firing at them and throwing our grenades; they were firing back and throwing grenades. I was lying down between bursts of fire, then kneeling up so I could see just over the crown of the hill, see their flashes and then firing back with my Tommy gun – when it worked. The first time when I got up there I pressed the trigger and there was just a rough grating noise as the bolt slid forward because the dust was slowing the action. So I got back, lay down again, pulled the oil bottle out of the butt, oiled the bolt and like a good soldier put the oil bottle back in the butt. I got up and it worked, fortunately, it fired then. It's a very heavy weapon of course, a .5 round, a most dreadful thing really to use in action, a very slow rate of fire – a sort of 'Bop-Bop-Bop' whereas a Schmeisser is more like a raspberry. It has a safety catch with three places, safe, which means you can't fire, single shot, which means that every time you pull the trigger you fire one shot, but the bolt re-cocks itself, or rapid fire. You always kept it on rapid fire because it was such a slow action that you could actually fire single shots – you had time to let the trigger go in between shots. That's how we used it – every shot was re-aimed though it was quite fast firing. Then I heard a little noise as I was lying there to my left and glanced, just as a grenade went off about two feet away, just alongside my face. Nothing seemed to be wrong so I carried on firing and then I noticed that my Tommy gun was getting very slippy. Of course we were in moonlight and you can't see colours you know. When I relaxed again I could feel the warm blood coming onto the weapon, felt around and found that it was coming from my chin, I had a flap hanging down, an artery had gone and it was spurting out. All in the midst of this mess we were in. Ronnie said that the Corporal had been killed. So I bandaged myself up, put my chin back on and wrapped my field dressing round it because I'd heard it said that if you put the flesh back it seals. Wrapped my field dressing round my head and put my tin hat back on to hold it on. I carried on and the action finished very shortly after that. We captured two prisoners, one wounded, the rest had gone. I said to Ronnie, "Well I'll take these down because I'll have to go and get this chin sealed up – I can't stop it bleeding!" It was dripping you see. I walked down the hill with these two Germans. There was always a sort of friendship immediately prisoners were taken – I suppose we were all in the same boat because we were all relieved to be out of it, there's an instant strange friendship. *Lieutenant Gerry Barnett, C Coy, 16th DLI*

The German attack was beaten back all around the perimeter. The beachhead had survived and that survival allowed ever increasing quantities of artillery and armour to be safely ushered ashore ready to launch a breakout towards Naples.

The next day a rare target of opportunity arose which allowed the Durhams' twinned artillery unit to show its paces.

We saw a great convoy of German vehicles travelling up the road. I was with a chap from the gunners, Mike Frewer, Forward Observation officer of 449 Battery, 70th Field. They were always with us. We called on him to do what he could to do something about this. He brought the Navy in, he brought in AGRA, the army guns, 5 inchers, he brought in his own Field Regiment of course and after we'd got all that on, he had a bit of RAF. So we really did them an awful lot of damage. That was my first experience of using a Forward Observation Officer and first time I'd ever seen an attack of that nature – it was very spectacular and it gave me an insight into what could be done by the Royal

Artillery, by just having an FOO with you. *Lieutenant Ronnie Sherlaw, C Coy, 16th DLI*

Vital artillery support was also supplied in the early stages by the Royal Navy ships cruising in the Bay of Naples. Naval guns were powerful engines of destruction when they were accurately ranged onto their target.

There was a Royal Navy monitor arrived offshore to try and counter this 210mm gun. There was obviously only the one 210 and they had an idea where it was, but they weren't too sure. They sent this young Lieutenant, a Petty Officer and another bloke. He was a gunnery officer and he wanted to go up as far as he possibly could to get to look across the valley and observe. I took him up this place. We stayed there about three hours and there was no sign of any activity at all. He was quite a nice young fellow and he was advisedly supplied with rum so we got a nip of rum now and again, plenty of cigarettes. It emerged, I didn't see it, from a railway tunnel, just about the extreme range of his glasses – and they were good ones. "Now, "he says, "I've got the bastards!" He had the radio and he directed the fire from the monitor. They were 12″ guns I think, and they were firing and honestly you could see the shells sailing through the air. He overshot the first lot and he gave some fresh directions and they just blew the entrance to this tunnel to bits, it just disintegrated and you could see it all collapse – he let me see it. He said, "Well that'll do...." *Driver Tom Lister, MT Section, HQ Coy, 16th DLI*

Meanwhile Lieutenant Russell Collins had recovered from his mild attack of malaria and had been posted to A Company. On 18th September he was immediately thrust into an awful situation which caused him to doubt not only his training but his own abilities as an officer. His new company were a couple of hundred yards above and to the left of the corner of the hospital wall. To their left were D Company under the command of Captain Frank Duffy.

I was required to go to battalion headquarters, I was briefed by the commanding officer that the enemy were believed to be withdrawing from around Salerno to a range of hills further behind. It was just a question of me taking my platoon and going forward to find out how far they had gone and whether the ground in front of us was clear and so on. It was a fighting patrol, I was to take my whole platoon. We'd had these simulated situations, innumerable times on training and I was well able to cope with them with distinction, although I say it myself. But here I felt totally confused, totally unequal to the situation. The CO was going on about covering fire from the ships in the bay and so on and so forth. And there were American troops nearby, and so on and so forth and all would be well – and off I was supposed to go. In those days, the radio communications were not very good. I just had a small portable, an eighty-eight set or something like that, which my orderly carried. But the thing was totally unreliable and it didn't range more than a hundred yards. *Lieutenant Russell Collins, A Coy, 16th DLI*

What befell him was a vivid illustration of the effect of the sheer confusion and terror of war on a young immature officer with no active service experience. Collins set off keeping the Hospital on his right-hand side.

I hadn't gone I don't suppose more than 100 yards, at the very most 200 yards, before we were fired on from a position beside the hospital about a 150 yards down on the right. There was a light mortar detachment there and they were firing mortars off in our direction. We were on a slope leading down towards the hospital and machine guns were also being fired at us. I was on this bank completely exposed to fire, although a little bit concealed from view and I could see the bullets hitting the bank either side of me. I thought well this isn't on, I can't go on on this basis. So I tried to call up the Company Commander on the radio for fresh orders, because it seemed to me that the situation was entirely different from what I had been told. I was weighing up in my mind what do I do about these people, do I ignore them and go on? I hadn't really positively identified them. I decided that really they were too close on my line of attack and that I couldn't go on. So I sent an orderly to run back to the battalion, to the company headquarters, with a written message to say what the situation was, and say what I was proposing to do. Namely trying to sort out this irritation on the right flank and then continue to advance. About ten minutes later the orderly came back a gibbering wreck, telling me he'd run

German assault gun at Salerno firing on British positions. MH 6325

into some Germans between where we were and the company headquarters, which as I say wasn't more than a very few hundred yards back, so that seemed pretty drastic. Certainly there were Germans in very close proximity to us and as far as I was aware there were or could have been Americans as well. Their steel helmets are very similar in shape, particularly in poor light or when partly concealed and camouflaged. Well they could have been, or he could have just seen an apparition, but he was pretty frightened by something. I just had to assume or infer that they were Germans. I formed the conclusion that, far from the enemy having withdrawn, they were very much on the doorstep. So I determined to make some sort of attack on this post that was firing on us, going around the right flank which took me to the right back towards the hospital wall below our position you see. As we approached the hospital wall all hell was let loose and our own battalion mortar platoon brought down the defensive fire slap on top of my platoon. Well it was the first time for me, it wasn't the last time, but it was the first time. I mean one is just cringing, there is nothing you can do, it's no good running, because if you run you're bound to be caught in the blast or shrapnel of the next mortar bomb. The only thing you can do is to hug the ground as closely as possible and just hope and pray that the next one isn't going to land on top of you. I think we were about twenty nine people and only five survived it unscathed. *Lieutenant Russell Collins, A Coy, 16th DLI*

They were not out of the metaphorical, or figurative woods, for at that very moment Collins' own Company Commander Captain Pritchard led a full scale assault to finish off the enemy he imagined before him.

They followed up the concentration with an assault with bullets and bayonets. I was screaming mad with them really. I'd been slightly hit myself in the hand – a tiny bit of shrapnel through the knuckle. I just stood up in front of this onslaught of bullets and bayonets with these chaps charging and waved my arms and said "You bloody idiots, can't you see it's us!" *Lieutenant Russell Collins, A Coy, 16th DLI*

Collins was in a desperate position.

Somebody said, "Jerries". But it was Collins and them coming back. They started firing the bloody mortars at our own men. Russell Collins, he'd only be about 19, he came charging down, "Stop the bloody mortars, stop the bloody mortars!" They killed quite few of our own men. It was terrible. *Signaller Anthony Sacco, HQ Coy, 16th DLI*

Nothing could seem more poignant than the bleeding corpses and groaning of wounded men hit by their own side.

Of course then everybody was very crest-fallen. We tried to see to the wounded and pick up the pieces of those who had been blown to bits, it was that bad. So that was a rather nasty baptism of fire. But if I had the time over again, I don't see what else I could have done. I think if I was more experienced I might have played it differently, but I'm not quite sure how. To have gone on with, as I understood it, enemy troops around and behind me, would have been even more foolhardy. I would have just walked straight into the bag, so there was no point in doing that and I couldn't get through to the company commander. I'd only just arrived on the scene not more than 36 hours earlier. I was new in that company, I really hadn't got my bearings, and the communications were poor – the whole thing was what we also call an 'MFU'. If you don't know what that is it's a 'Military F...k Up'. *Lieutenant Russell Collins, A Coy, 16th DLI*

In war, lives can be lost wholesale without the officer in command having actually made any definable mistake. Collins had survived but his situation was embarrassing.

I was very shaken, but I felt with a few deep breaths that I would be all right again. But I was made to go back to the regimental aid post for a check up as they said. Then I had to go and tell the CO Johnny Preston what had happened and even then he was very sympathetic and understanding, he said, "Well, don't worry about it now." Then, to my astonishment, the Medical Officer decided I was to lie down with the casualties who were going to be evacuated further back. I said, "Well, wait a minute, there's some mistake here, I've only got this little bit of a nick through my knuckle." *Lieutenant Russell Collins, A Coy, 16th DLI*

General Mark Clark greets General Bernard Montgomery on Salerno Bridge 24 September 1943. IWM NA 7108

A quiet period followed and the battalion was relieved on the night of 19 September to spend a period in the brigade rest area.

I was absolutely shattered from lack of sleep. When they brought us off to go along to the far end of Salerno for a

rest we marched so far and stopped on the road and I just went dead in the ditch. The first thing I knew was my friend shaking me and saying, "Come on, we're moving again!" Absolutely fatigued.
Private Robert Ellison, D Coy, 16th DLI

The Germans were by now withdrawing in response to the increasing threat of being trapped between the Fifth Army and the Eighth Army. Pivoting on their right flank secured on the Sorrento Peninsula, they fell back to their next chosen line of defence along the River Volturno. Behind them they left their rearguard formations to defend the passes that led through the hills to Naples.

****

While the 16th Durhams had been holding the perimeter there was a mutiny of sorts amongst reinforcements intended to join the battalion. Amongst them was Signaller Ronald Elliott who had originally been drafted out to join the 9th Battalion, DLI in Sicily in July 1943. After a very short exposure to action he had been lightly wounded and evacuated for hospitalisation in North Africa. On recovery he was sent with a draft of other 50th and 51st Division men who had recently recovered from their wounds. Montgomery had promised both these formations that they would be coming with him to England for the long awaited opening of the 'Second Front'. The men felt deeply aggrieved that having done their bit and been wounded in the 'cause', they were now being separated from all their comrades and exposed to immediate, rather than deferred, danger in the company of strangers.

We were in this field with nothing else to do but just talk amongst ourselves about the situation. The Jocks said that they definitely weren't going to go and fight, they would definitely refuse to go. They had the sort of tribal feeling about it in terms of their argument that they were Scottish soldiers and should be in a Scottish division. So it was a nationalistic thing from their point of view as well as everything else. The Durhams didn't have that sort of aspect to it. Most of it was more like trade union solidarity than it was anything else, "We'll all stick together lads and they can't do anything to us!" It had little to do with war. I was in two minds, I thought that perhaps I ought to help them but on the other hand I really had only been in the 9th DLI about three weeks, so I really hadn't very much of a case if truth be told! There was this tall red-headed Geordie Sergeant and I went to him and said, "What shall I do?" He said, "Ahhr lad, you should support the Jocks and the Durhams – they've been treated badly and if we all stick together we'll be all right – you stick with me!" Fair enough then! Signaller Ronald Elliott

Such arguments were powerful incitements and Elliott remained with the 'mutineers'. The situation was not irreversible however.

So we were all then officially on a mutiny. They provided us with food, compo rations, and there was this large area of tomatoes growing quite close by so we had tomatoes with everything. We stripped this fellow's field of tomatoes for him! We lived quite well, we cleaned up our weapons and talked about the situation – it was quite a pleasant two days. It really didn't crystallise until they actually brought up all our kit. When you get your kitbags and big pack that means you're complete, then you can move, then you are mobile. That came up one morning and after that point in time we really didn't have any excuse for not going anywhere. Before that we couldn't have gone anywhere because we weren't fully accoutred as it were. At that point in time we were in a mutiny situation. A fellow came and chatted to us first and then we all were paraded and this Major or brigadier said in effect that there had been mistakes made, they were sorry that it had happened the way that it did and that every effort would be made to try and get people into their proper formations. But for the moment we really didn't have any option but to obey orders and report for duty and we would be posted to appropriate battalions within the Fifth Army. Then the Riot Act was read out. Having that read out to you, then you sort of appreciate the enormity of what you're into, that quite clearly you are disobeying lawful orders and could be shot. When the Riot Act is read out in those situations it brings a chill to anybody. *Signaller Ronald Elliott*

Ronald Elliott, 1946

Now the writing was really on the wall. The executions of the First World War had been mercilessly carried out only 25 years before and the situation was fast escalating out of control into an ugly confrontation. Elliott was becoming aware of the risks of his own personal 'stand'.

The order was then given that all of those who wished now to obey their lawful orders were to go with all their kit into the centre of this field. I thought to myself after all this, "I'm a bloody fool really, what have I got that I can say is any sort of excuse for doing what I'm doing?" So I wandered off to the centre with my kit and 'lo and behold' there was my friend, the red-headed Sergeant, organising the collecting together of the kit! I said, "I thought you said we all ought to stick together and we'd be all right!" He said, "Ahhr, lad, you have to obey

> orders at the end of the bloody day! You can't beat the army!" So I reckoned if he went then the least I could do was go as well! Quite a number of people, a good half, collected themselves together, were marched off and subsequently we at least ended up with the 16th DLI. *Signaller Ronald Elliott*

Hardier, or more foolish spirits, stuck it out. Colonel Johnny Preston decided to go down and talk to the Durhams in the group to see if he could persuade them to end their protest and join his battalion.

> I was in Salerno itself, in Headquarters Company and the Quartermaster came out and he said, "Get your bike, I want to go down to the beach, will you take me down straight away!" Johnny Preston was making a speech to them about how we needed them, how the Durhams were desperate for them, they were Durhams, they were in a battalion of Durhams – he didn't know what they were worried about – because they would just have been going to train for another landing and we had made a landing for them. This was his sort of style. He finished up, he says, "I give you my firm promise as an officer, and Johnny Preston always keeps his word, that as soon as the situation here resolves you will go back to your own battalions – you've got my firm word on that!" Well, all but a few then decided to come to us, just a handful stayed. *Private James Corr, Anti-Tank Platoon, HQ Coy, 16th DLI*

Surprisingly perhaps, there was not much sympathy in the 16th Durhams for the mutineers.

> I took Preston down in the Humber, with the adjutant. He addressed these blokes – some of them agreed to join the battalion but some stood fast. In the old days they would have been shot, but some of them were court martialled anyhow. I don't think many of us had much sympathy for them because we accepted that they'd had a pretty hard time, a lot of them had been wounded and they were cheesed off, but you're in the army and you do what you're told or suffer the consequences – that's the point. *Driver Tom Lister, MT Section, HQ Coy, 16th DLI*

Ultimately a hard core were left to face the music. They were court martialled and the ringleaders were given punitive prison terms.

To some extent the whole affair was unnecessary because the existing troops in the bridgehead had managed to repel the German attacks and the bridgehead was in no danger at all by the time the mutiny was in full flow. Thus the 'mutineers' never need have been diverted from returning to their own units. With less panic from the army authorities and a greater sense of realism from the 'mutineers' the situation need not have escalated in the way it did.

In the end the former 'mutineers' were used to provide replacements for the casualties lost in the Salerno campaign.

CHAPTER THREE

Breakout to Naples

The passes leading to Naples had to be forced. Their German defenders were determined to buy vital time to allow for defensive lines to be consolidated behind them and in front of Rome. The 46th Division was given the task of bursting through to allow the 7th Armoured Division to pour onto the plains around Naples. It was not an easy task and 138 Brigade, with the Durhams under special command, were given the responsibility of clearing the Northern exits of the Vietri defile. The heights to the right of the road were allotted to 2/4th King's Own Yorkshire Regiment and the 6th Lincolns. Simultaneously the Durhams and the 6th York and Lancs were to seize the village of Corpo di Cava and the nearby La Crocella Spur feature on the right hand side. Colonel Johnny Preston developed a bold plan which called for a 'silent' night march foregoing any preliminary artillery support. By approaching through a deep ravine it was hoped to avoid any contact with the Germans until they were actually on their objective.

At 01.00 on 23 September, D Company set off from the start point

The blown bridge at Cava. 24 September 1943. IWN NA 7102

at Dragone and successfully moved behind the German lines to take up positions on La Crocella Spur whilst B Company captured Point 600.

We set off, all in single file. It was that dark that we had to hold each others' bayonet scabbards, like elephants holding each others' tails. It was pitch black. There were frequent stops as though whoever was leading us wasn't quite sure if we were going in the right direction. Each time we stopped, everybody seemed to go straight to sleep, everybody was that worn out. We had to more or less kick them awake. Eventually we went through a farmyard, crossed a road and started up this hill. There'd been no reaction from the Germans at all. We went up this hill to the top and planted ourselves up there. *Lance Corporal William Virr, B Coy, 16th DLI*

The Germans were caught by surprise and at first could offer no serious opposition. This was perhaps as well for Private Ellison on La Crocella Spur.

My rifle was dirty with climbing round the hill and I had it all to bits cleaning it – and here's a Jerry officer coming down! What do you do – stick him up with a rifle with no bolt in? My colleague was doing his rifle as well! We learned a lesson there – never both to be doing it together! The Jerry officer gave up, said, "I've had enough!" He put his hands up in the air and he handed his Luger over. He'd seen the situation and he wasn't going to get killed! *Private Robert Ellison, D Coy, 16th DLI*

The two companies consolidated their positions by noon. However behind them there still remained an area of difficult wooded and hilly terrain from which pockets of German resistance were difficult to eradicate. Communications were thus by no means secure and Lieutenant Sherlaw was given the task of escorting a forward observation officer up to B Company on Point 600. The risk of ambush made it a difficult task.

I had to find a route through to Corpo di Cava which was a small village at the foot of the hill. I took 12 people with me and an FOO called Len Garland, who was a

German field guns in the midst of a vinyard firing towards the British positions after the landings at Salerno, September 1943. IWM MH 6297

> Captain with 449 Battery of the 70th Field. We kept three or four yards apart, we had a couple of 'points' who looked forward, generally a Corporal or Lance Corporal for that sort of job. I led behind the points. We went as fast as ever we could go. There was an urgency in getting the FOO to the top and to some extent the faster you went the less likely you were to be hit anyway. We had a few skirmishes. As we were walking up there were little attacks from our right where the Germans were. On the left was woodland, we were above the valley, we walked above it and looked down to it. There were Germans all the way along on the right in little patches. As we were going along they would have a go at us and we would stop and have a go at them. Then we would move on. When we got about half way along some of the chaps got so fed up that they left – they just disappeared. They would say that they got lost... To some extent you had to sympathise with the ones that couldn't stand being shot at all the time and as long as you could carry out your mission you wouldn't make too much of an issue – unless it was affecting everybody. In this particular instance these fellows said they got lost but they turned up eventually. So I had to accept in some ways that they had got lost, although my own view is that they went and hid themselves out of the road until it was safe to go on. Well half a dozen of us and the FOO struggled on until we got there. *Lieutenant Ronnie Sherlaw, C Coy, 16th DLI*

Corpo di Cava was in the hands of a detachment from the 6th York and Lancs.

> They were in trouble with tanks which couldn't actually get into Corpo di Cava because they couldn't get across the bridge – it was too narrow for tanks. But they could shoot at us quite easily! What we did until it was dark was just lobbed 2" mortars at them which didn't worry the tanks but it stopped the infantry or the tank crews getting out and coming across. *Lieutenant Ronnie Sherlaw, C Coy, 16th DLI*

Meanwhile up on the hill a patrol was sent toward Corpo di Cava to locate a supply route.

> Lieutenant Stoddart said, "You go in that direction, so far, to see if you can find the cross-roads and we'll go in this direction." We went down and we grabbed an Italian coming up the road and by using a stick in dust made a map to direct us back to where the cross-roads was. When we got towards it there was an abandoned German anti-tank gun in a sunken road where the fields were higher than the road. The anti-tank gun was facing down to Corpo di Cava. As we were walking past one of the lads comes flying down, "You've got to come back", he says, "Lieutenant Stoddart has seen some Jerries going into a house and they're going to get

as near as possible! He's gone forward with Corporal Smith and another one of the chaps. He says you've got to lie up here till he comes back." So we get on this bank side with our legs facing the road. I'll always remember the chap next to me saying, "Tom, there's a tank or something coming up the road behind us!" I said, "Get-a-way man, that'll be the carriers coming up with the rations!" I'd no sooner said that then, "BRRRRWWRRR!" He opened out at us. He killed the bloke alongside of me and scattered us with the machine gun from the tank. We didn't know till later on that the three tanks were coming up the road. They'd come past Captain Sherlaw's company and they'd come up to pull the anti-tank gun out. Captain Sherlaw had engaged them before they got to us. We had the artillery spotter on this hill with us and he brought artillery fire down. So you can quite imagine, us on the patrol, we were in the middle of it. We had to scatter back up the hill. You've never seen anybody go up a hill as fast as what we did! *Corporal Tom Turnbull, B Company, 16th DLI*

To their fury, D Company on La Crocello spur got the full benefit of the artillery fire.

We were dug in only about 100 yards from the tanks. We got a fearful stonking from our own 25 pounders. Frank Duffy had been out somewhere or other and during a lull of a couple of minutes in the bombardment he went to dash over to Company HQ. The bombardment opened again and he dived into my slit trench and I noticed that he'd only got a half of a revolver. A shell fragment had evidently cut his revolver right in two – he'd lost the barrel of it. He went a little bit white when I told him. There was another little lull and he got back to company, got back on the radio again and they dropped the guns. They never hit the tanks. *Private Kenneth Lovell, D Coy, 16th DLI*

Panzergrenadiers and armoured troop-carrying half tracks awaiting the order to counter-attack, September 1943. MH 6298

However the artillery were successful in driving off the tanks and the supplies were brought up that evening by the ubiquitous jeeps. Soon the whole position was made secure.

Over the next few days, first 128 Brigade and then the 7th Armoured Division, exploited the gains to push forward through the Vietri Defile, across the plains that lay beyond and finally Naples fell on 1 October. Meanwhile to the south Montgomery had succeeded in capturing Foggia. The primary objectives of the Italian campaign had now been secured and it could have been assumed that the desired strategic objectives could now be harvested without any further major offensives in Italy. However, as First World War Generals had learnt to their cost in Gallipoli, Mesopotamia and Salonika, once a campaign has begun it seems to generate its own momentum. The Americans undoubtedly fought shy of committing any more resources in Italy which they saw as an unwelcome distraction from the all important and appropriately named 'Overlord' landings which would launch the Second Front in 1944. The British, however, saw merit in extending the campaign to seek the capture of the Italian capital Rome. Churchill argued that the capture of such a potent symbol would have a significant political and psychological impact on the whole Allied war effort and in this he may well have been right. However in truth Churchill had another agenda. The architect of Gallipoli, was still an aficionado of the whole concept of attacking Germany through an imagined 'soft under-belly' – in this case moving from Italy through into the Balkans. After a vigorous tussle the Americans gave in on condition that on the capture of Rome there should be no more prevaricating and all significant resources would be devoted to 'Overlord'.

Meanwhile the Durhams had a well deserved rest away from the front-line. One unique feature of the Italian campaign had by now been observed by the men – excessive consumption of grapes could have devastating effects even before they were made into wine!

> If you were anywhere reasonably permanent you had to make provision for latrines. These were generally speaking dug out of the soil to a depth of about two yards and about a yard wide. They had a trestle on with a big telegraph pole and you squatted on the pole and did your business. These holes were filled with lime or whatever. The funniest thing was that we were there at the time that the grapes were just about ready. People were gulping grapes down as fast as they were growing – and were getting dysentery on that account. At one point in time we had one of these latrine pits in a vineyard. So people could sit on the pole and pick up handfuls of grapes from the vines just above their heads, while they were sitting on the pole. We reckoned that was the nearest one could get

to perpetual motion in this world! *Signaller Ronald Elliott, Headquarters Coy, 16th DLI*

The Durhams made their own triumphal entry into Naples on 6 October.

The battalion went through Naples in the lorries and all the inhabitants came out and cheered us. It was great fun, we went right through Naples in these lorries, with everybody cheering you. It wasn't the same as being on foot because they couldn't embrace you or whatever. What happened in the end was quite funny in a way – they pelted us with apples. It was the apple season, they were just collecting them and they pelted us with apples all the way along! Well apples are quite hard and people were getting hurt by them so we threw them back again! And before we got to the end of the run through Naples there was a battle going on between people firing out apples from the lorries back at the civilians – so it finished up quite a conflict truth be told. *Signaller Ronald Elliott, Signal Section, HQ Coy, 16th DLI*

The Italians had been their enemies only a month before and the situation was to remain strange for several months. Some of the Italians hadn't quite got over being enemies and their hostility was real.

There was crowds of people lining the pavements, watching us going past. The girls were, as usual, shrieking and offering you drinks of wine. One of the young lads stepped out, spat right in my face and told me, I had enough Italian to understand, "I hope you'll be killed!" That's a brilliant welcome that, you know! I was sorely tempted to dive out, but you couldn't. *Driver Tom Lister, MT Section, HQ Coy, 16th DLI*

Italians' joyful reception for the first troops of 7th Armoured Division to arrive in Naples. IWM AN 7436

Chapter Four

River Crossing

The decision to continue the campaign had been taken, but the Germans were falling back onto a powerful series of prepared defensive positions. They too recognised the crucial significance of Rome and they built a series of defensive lines right across Italy from the Mediterranean to the Adriatic. It was a complicated system but two main lines can be identified in front of Rome. The Winter Line ran from the mouth of the River Garigliano, passed through the fortified massifs of Mount Camino and Mount Lungo and stretched across to the River Sangro. Behind this lay the main defences of the Gustav Line which were solidly anchored on Mount Cassino. In addition the Germans were hard at work on completing further defence lines across the Liri Valley.

The infantryman's enemy – mud!
IWM NA 7672

The Allies had made their decision and Field Marshal Alexander ordered the Eighth Army to hammer its way up the Adriatic coast while the US Fifth Army attempted to batter its way through the Germans' mountain lines on the direct west coast route from Naples to Rome.

Following the fall of Naples the Germans retreated north and decided to make their next stand on the River Volturno. Both sides were aware that every day the Germans could delay the Fifth Army would give their slave labour Todt organisation vital time to complete the main defensive lines blocking the roads to Rome. Every day also brought deteriorating weather conditions as the Italian winter began to bite. Without hesitation General Mark Clark ordered the British X Corps and US VI Corps forward to launch a general attack all along the Volturno. The 46th Division was allotted the coastal sector which they approached across a flat flood plain overlooked by the Germans on the other side of the valley.

The Durhams moved up to Villa Literno on 7 October and immediately began a series of probing patrols forward to the Volturno to try and establish whether there were Germans on the south bank of the Volturno and to glean intelligence for use in the ultimate crossing. One of the first patrols was sent out under the command of Lieutenant Collins who had quickly recovered from the trivial hand wound he had suffered during the debacle at Hospital Hill. He had naturally assumed he would be returned to the Durhams but he was soon brought face to face with the realisation that his battalion may not have wanted him.

> I was sent for by the CO Johnny Preston. Then there was another psychological shock for me in a way. When he saw me he said, "Well, I'm glad to see you, I had asked for you back." That absolutely took the wind out of my sails - it hadn't dawned on me before then that of course he might have decided that under no circumstances did he want this officer back! It was nice of him to try to put me at my ease like that. *Lieutenant Russell Collins, A Coy, 16th DLI*

For his own peace of mind it was perhaps fortunate that he was immediately back in action with a chance to prove himself as an officer. Patrols were of two different kinds.

> A reconnaissance patrol was very lightly equipped and armed and you might wear rubber shoes and no helmets, no equipment - just a personal weapon each and perhaps a compass. Very little else, the idea being to see and not be seen and to take evasive action if encountering any enemy. Now the fighting patrol, that was quite different, a fighting patrol was stronger and it may have been up to platoon strength, but perhaps usually rather fewer than that. They took light machine guns, personal weapons and spare ammunition. They wore steel helmets and were prepared to fight for the information. *Lieutenant Russell Collins, A Coy, 16th DLI*

This was definitely a reconnaissance patrol and they set off on the night of 9 October.

> Ray Mitchell and I took our patrols on the same night to the river. We were provided with some very good aerial photographs of the approaches to the river and the crossing points. I spent hours poring over these things and committing them absolutely to memory. I was to concentrate on the approaches to the river on this side, Ray was not to bother about that, but to get to the river, get himself across in a boat and examine the landing areas on the other side. In my patrol there were only perhaps three or four of us, I think there were rather more in his. This was not exactly fenland, but it was the water basin of the river Volturno. In winter it may have flooded, but there were certainly a lot of dykes around

and the roads were very often raised with ditches on either side. The main route up there was such a road. We progressed up the road mainly in single file with me leading. The next chap keeps a sharp lookout to the right, the chap behind that keeps a short lookout to the left, and the chap behind that keeps a sharp lookout behind – so one makes progress. We did my reconnaissance on this side of the river and I ascertained what I wanted to ascertain. When I got to the objective and turned to come back, I remembered one very important lesson from training patrols and that was that you don't come back the same way you went out. So I struck another route across country. It turned out to be a very propitious one because we went right through a melon field, the place was stacked with beautiful melons and they were all ripe. We were sitting in the middle of that field, eating these melons while straight ahead of us lay Mount Vesuvius – a pillar of fire by night, a pillar of smoke by day. We were lying there enjoying these melons when all hell broke loose on the road that we'd gone up by. Poor old Ray Mitchell's patrol had come back down that same road and the Germans were lying in wait, they had put an ambush there to get him on the way back. Then they had to fight, but I just felt very gratified that I'd remembered that lesson, that you don't go back by the same route. *Lieutenant Russell Collins, A Coy, 16th DLI*

His rehabilitation was clearly under way for he had been successful, not only in avoiding casualties, but had also found a suitable approach route to the river.

Meanwhile D Company was ordered to proceed to Castel Volturno where a party of Royal Engineers were engaged in constructing a Bailey Bridge across the Regi Lagni Canal some four miles on the Southern side of the River Volturno. D Company began to cross the canal with the intention of providing an infantry screen around the fledgling bridge.

The bridge wasn't finished. The engineers said there'd been no German activity at all. They didn't have an infantry screen in front

Bailey Bridge erected by Royal Engineers across the canal in front of River Volturno, 9 October 1943. IWM AN 7642

of them – it hadn't turned up. So they were just on their own putting this Bailey Bridge across. We went across in our canvas and wood assault boats. They had a wooden bottom, canvas sides with a wooden frame at the top. You sort of lifted them up, pushed two or three struts in position to keep them rigid, just got in and paddled across. They took about six men. We got across the canal which was about ten feet deep. *Corporal Kenneth Lovell, D Coy, 16th DLI*

Once they were across they began to move forward to establish a reasonable defensive perimeter around the bridge.

We were straddled across the road. In the distance I observed a couple of Jerries running across the road carrying a machine gun. I told the Corporal, passed word back and he just ignored it – he didn't want to know, we were blind – "No, " he said, "there's nobody up there!" I said, "There is!" He wouldn't have it – he was back nearer the canal. Whether they'd had false information previously I don't know. I wish we'd taken it upon ourselves to fire our gun along the road. But we were so disciplined we daren't. *Private Robert Ellison, D Coy, 16th DLI*

Corporal Lovell of 17 Platoon also suspected that there were Germans in the area.

I told the 18 Platoon Sergeant, 'Soss' Martin that we'd seen Jerries over there. He just laughed at us and told us we were a load of bloody amateurs. They were told when they got to the other side they could have ten minutes rest. My platoon came across and I had words with Ray Sykes our Platoon Sergeant. Ray said, "Soon as you get over, get into those trenches and take up fire positions!" Which we did. Company HQ was coming across next. *Corporal Kenneth Lovell, D Coy, 16th DLI*

As a signaller Elliott was attached to D Company headquarters to handle their wireless communications.

The boats were somewhat difficult to manoeuvre and after the usual problems of going round in circles which one tended to do, we all got across. The platoons fanned out ahead of us, we were in the Company HQ which was close to the bank. We'd taken off the set, put it down and were establishing communications with the base. We'd taken our kit off. All of a sudden there was this hullabaloo, grenades were thrown, shots were fired at us. *Signaller Ronald Elliott, D Coy, 16th DLI*

Ellison and the rest of 18 Platoon had not yet taken up proper defensive positions and were terribly exposed as the Germans charged forward.

We had to scarper back to the canal. They were lobbing these little stun grenades, and I got quite a few shrapnel wounds on my wrist and arm. Only small bits in the muscle. You didn't know it had happened just a flash at the side of you. But the other lads were getting bullets in them unfortunately. We lost quite a lot of blokes there. It was completely flat, like a playing field. There wasn't enough cover just behind the embankment, the water was pretty high up so to get under cover we were stood in the canal up to the chest in water. Jerry came down and he was firing on them in the canal, as they were trying to get over the canal. *Private Robert Ellison, D Coy, 16th DLI*

A German fighting patrol, which had crossed the Volturno and pressed on to the Regi Lagni Canal was responsible for this startling ambush.

All hell broke loose. Machine guns opened up at us from every bloody quarter – from behind us, from our sides, from the front. The Germans had set up a beautiful ambush. 'Soss' Martin's platoon got cut up, he got badly wounded. We had taken up fire positions, we opened up, we could see flashes. 'Brothel Baby' was next to me, he was my Bren gunner and he got a bullet through the wrist. After a little while he said to me, "Here, Corporal, give us a drink will you?" I felt for my water bottle and found I'd had a burst of machine gun bullets go through it, I cut my hand quite badly where the metal had been ripped to pieces. The Germans were just a few yards away. The buggers! We opened up and it was very, very dicey. *Corporal Kenneth Lovell, D Coy, 16th DLI*

The shock of sudden death and the shattering noise of automatic weapons and grenades at close range meant that it was not surprising that panic spread like wildfire amongst some of the company.

There was a rush back to the canal. Either I got into or I was pushed into the canal, some people got into a boat, I found myself in the canal and not being a good swimmer was in some danger of drowning. I got a hold of the boat which was floundering around as was its wont. Someone either deliberately or unconsciously waved a paddle around and knocked my glasses off. Whether he was trying to knock me off the boat I don't know – but I had no intention of being knocked off – I hung on grimly. Eventually we all got to the other side, I was soaking wet, without my glasses on, didn't know where to go, didn't know where the Germans were. Meanwhile pandemonium was still going on on the far bank. Some of the platoons were fighting back and clearly it wasn't a total retreat, but some small number had retreated – including me! So there was I a pretty sight, wandering around, with the mosquitoes around, not able to see very far and waving my Beretta in the air prepared to defend myself, though quite how and in what way I don't know. *Signaller Ronald Elliott, D Coy, 16th DLI*

Those that remained fought back hard.

Coporal Lewindon and Sergeant Sykes were at the parapet of the bridge lobbing grenades back on to the top. They killed quite a lot of Germans and saved the day. This Sergeant Ferrell was there and he'd been mortally wounded. As things quietened down, we got out of the canal on the bank and I was told that he had about 22 bullets in him, he'd taken the full flak. He died next day. *Private Robert Ellison, D Coy, 16th DLI*

Sergeant Ray Sykes was awarded a well merited Military Medal for his actions. The German patrol was repelled, although D Company suffered some 40 casualties killed, drowned, missing and wounded. Lieutenant Whitehead was reported to have saved several men from drowning before he was himself was tragically lost in the canal.

****

While the Durhams occupied Villa Literno the nights went by filled with patrolling but during the day they could try and locate the German artillery and mortar positions.

When enemy guns fired, what one does is to take a quick bearing with a compass, the bearing from which the flash comes and the time of day. Then you count the interval between the flash and shell arriving and then report it on a little form that's handed in. You spent a long time doing that and of course the gunners where able to deduce from that where the enemy gun batteries were. *Lieutenant Russell Collins, A Coy, 16th DLI*

On 11 October, a 139 Brigade Conference was held and the plans for the assault crossing were finalised. A Company under Major John Morant was selected to lead the assault but Lieutenant Collins was given a big responsibility.

I was detailed to lead the battalion up to the river because I'd reconnoitred the route. The outline brigade plan was that the unfortunate Foresters were going to decoy for us. We were going to make the actual crossing a little bit further down the river. The Bofors light anti-aircraft gun fired tracer rounds and the scheme was that every five minutes they would fire a burst of five rounds along the axis of attack, so that everybody moving forward could keep their bearings and know that that was the direction they were to go. I was leading the entire battalion party and we were due to cross the river at H hour. Now I don't know whether I performed particularly well there, because I was very cautious in leading the battalion up because I had it very much in mind that our patrol had been ambushed only a night or two before and I didn't want the whole battalion to walk straight into an ambush – it was my responsibility to make sure we got safely through and there were undoubtedly Germans on our side of the river. So I proceeded rather cautiously – to the point that we lost a bit of time. The Adjutant, Captain Pritchard, came up to know why on earth I was being so slow. I said "Well, because there are Jerries around the place on this side of the river and I don't want to walk the battalion into them." Anyway we had to get a bit of a move on and so in due course we got to the river. *Lieutenant Russell Collins, A Coy, 16th DLI*

The cold, swirling currents of the river loomed before them. The Volturno was around 4 foot 6" deep and some 300 feet across. This was a real obstacle to the diminutive Collins.

Then with my platoon leading we had to make the first crossing. We hoisted our packs up as high as we could on our shoulders, put our rifles in our out-stretched arms above our heads and the first few of us waded into the river. Ray Mitchell must have established the depth of it, but it was certainly up to my armpits, if not up to my shoulders, being a rather shorter chap! We had to take a rope across and secure the rope at the far end. Then the boats were brought up; that rope was the guideline and people pulled themselves across in the boats. The whole company got across. While we were crossing the Germans weren't aware of our presence, at least there were no signs that they were aware. *Lieutenant Russell Collins, A Coy, 16th DLI*

Unfortunately behind Collins and the leading elements of A Company, one man lost his nerve as the other companies began their crossing.

We were crossing, not making a sound, I was up to my neck, holding on to the rope. The slopes to get up on the top – you've never seen mud like it. It was shiny black, just like coal tar. Some people had to get on the top and pull you up – we were covered in this black slime But we didn't make a sound. But further up they

Infantry crossing River Volturno in assault boats, 13 October 1943. IWM NA 7729

Above and right: *Troops practising for crossing the River Volturno, 11 October 1943.*
IWM NA 7630 & IWM NA 7633

> were crossing in dinghies. Suddenly this lad started screaming, – he was a Cockney lad – we got all sorts after Sedjenane! He was screaming, "I'm drowning, I'm drowning, I'm drowning!" He must have woke the whole German Army up. Somebody was saying, "Drown, you bugger, drown! *Signaller Anthony Sacco, A Coy, 16th DLI*

B Company decided not to wait for the boats to return.

> I had to get in the water and wade across. We got across and by God it was a cold night. You can quite imagine with the depth of water nearly up to your shoulders and you're going across with your weapon above your head. *Corporal Tom Turnbull, B Company, 16th DLI*

In front of them Collins and the rest of A Company were feeling their way forward.

> Then we fanned out to some extent, controlled by word of mouth and I remember then our first objective was a high dyke, 200-400 yards to the north of the river. It seemed like a mile because when we were about half way across somebody fell into the river and cried out – that alerted the Germans and suddenly we found all along this dyke were machine gun posts as we came

under fire. I had one of my more painful experiences there. One of my young soldiers, well probably no younger than I was, about the same, called Anderson[2], was hit, badly hit, and he felt he was dying, mortally wounded. I was kneeling beside him and he was giving me messages to give to his girlfriend right in the middle of this. It was mainly machine gun fire and fortunately for us it was plunging fire – they were sited above us shooting down. With plunging fire, the bullets just go into the ground wherever they happen to hit, whereas if the machine gun is on the same level as a standing man they can sweep the ground. One amusing incident there: Sergeant Major Wilson was as cool as a cucumber, whenever he got an order he always said, "Very good, sir!" Major John Morant was a bit laconic and eventually he said, "Sergeant Major!" "Sir!" "I've been hit!" "Very good, sir!" We got under the lee of the dyke and we were in such numbers that the enemy probably withdrew to a concentration area. *Lieutenant Russell Collins, A Coy, 16th DLI*

Once across, B Company swung to the right, heading for their objective which was a dried up canal. They came under heavy fire.

We were getting hit left, right and centre with machine guns. Jerry was on fixed lines, sweeping this field. We were crawling in this open field. The lad next to me was behind a Bren and he inched his way up to stretch his back with lying down all the time. He stretched up and as he stretched up a burst of tracer hit him. It seemed as if it was going in and dropping out at his back – the tracer – I'll never forget it. He went down. They started shouting the stretcher bearers and when they crawled towards us I said, "It's no use, he's dead!" I heard him die, the rattle.... A lad called Private Tuck[3]. The lads on the other flank, one of our sections, put the machine gun out of action. Our section gave covering fire when they went in. We went over these fields and we came to a dried up canal. We always seemed to be bloody unlucky, our section out of our platoon! We got sent on another patrol to find a road across the canal. Another patrol had been across and come back and said that there was nothing along there. So they sent us! We just got about 200 or 300 yards and a Jerry came over the bank side. He says, "Achtung!" He practically said, "Share that amongst you!" We watched the grenades come over our heads and it hit three of the last lads in the patrol. So naturally we had to get back. One was wounded about the face, one of the Corporals lost his heel and the other lad – it was his nineteenth birthday the day before and it had shattered his arm. We fixed them up and then we dug in. *Corporal Tom Turnbull, B Company, 16th DLI*

Sniping was a problem and there was a steady trickle of casualties.

We came under a lot of sniper fire, we lost a few men killed and wounded. One particular poor fellow, he went to answer the call of nature, had dropped his trousers, more or less finished his business and he got a bullet right through both cheeks of his arse and fell back in his own mess. *Corporal Kenneth Lovell, D Coy, 16th DLI*

The wounded were evacuated to the Regimental Aid Post which had been established on the north bank of the Volturno.

I was the only member of the Royal Army Medical Corps attached to the Battalion. No RAMC members were forward of myself. My own stretcher bearers were members of the Infantry. There was a convenient house near the river, on the lower side, convenient for the Aid Post and Advanced Dressing Station. However, the river crossing and getting the wounded across to the RAP was under the Infantry stretcher bearers, so I had to move out and establish a small Aid Post in some bushes on the far bank of the river. This meant that the problem of getting the wounded across the river to the Advanced Dressing Station was in the hands of the Field Ambulance and RAMC. I was unable to do much in the bushes for any of my patients except to evacuate the wounded as quickly as possible. *Medical Officer Captain Jones, HQ Coy, 16th DLI*[4]

The Durhams were in fact doing remarkably well. Colonel Preston crossed the river and established his headquarters in some farm buildings. He sent for Collins and gave him a dangerous task.

There was a pocket of enemy some few hundred yards to the east who were holding up progress and I was to go and try and sort

Mortar crew in action on the northern bank of the Volturno. IWM NA 760§

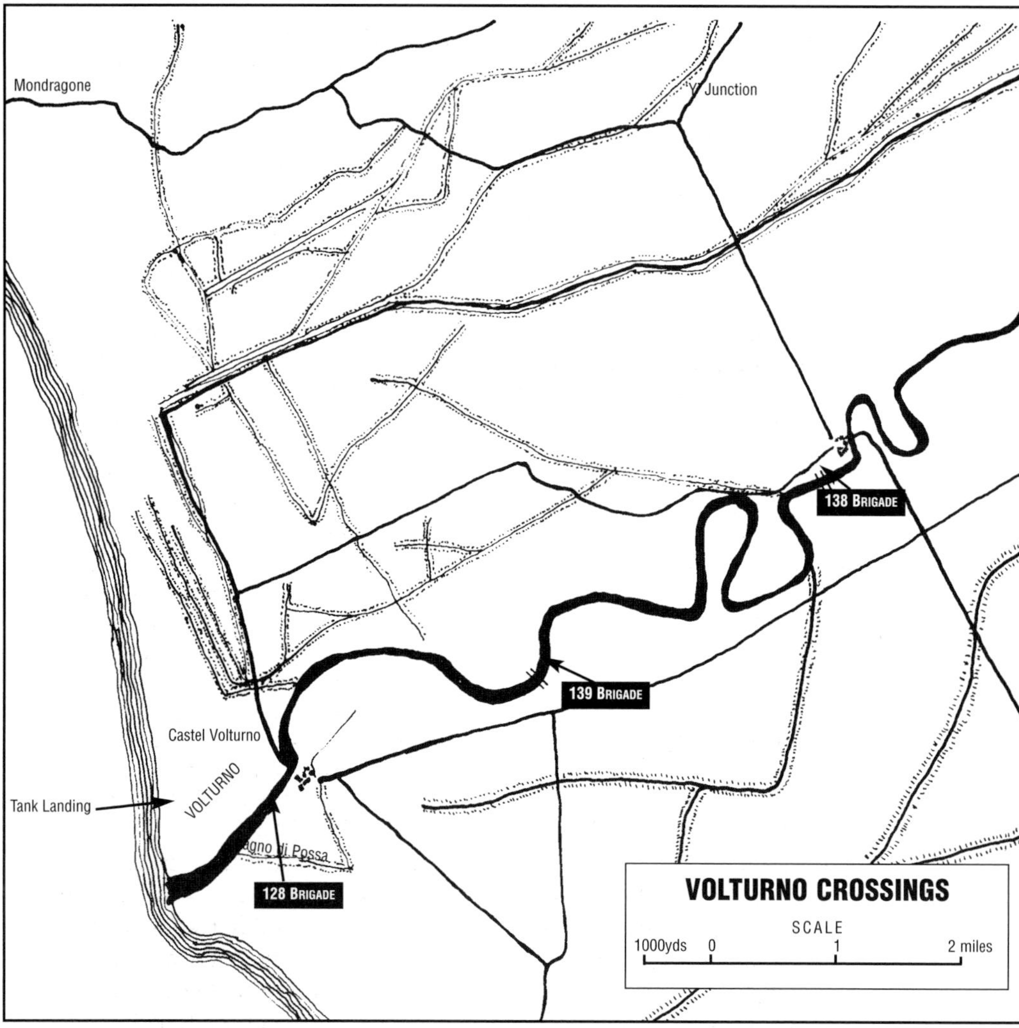

it out. I got up onto a high vantage point where I saw John Smith, who was the Mortar Officer. He had located this area and worked out the range. I quickly conferred with him, told him that I was going to have to attack and I really didn't know what to expect. This tall dyke had ditches on either side. I quickly made a little plan that I would take a number of men, perhaps half my platoon and go along the dry channel beside the dyke, which afforded cover from view. I said, "Right, I'm going to move along the dyke, you put down six rounds rapid, just six, no more, no less, and then we'll go in!" I hadn't pin-pointed the machine guns, but the

> Mortar Officer had seen them. So I mean it was by guess and by the grace of God really! I just said, "Right, Fix bayonets!" Everybody lined up behind me and I set off. We just crept forward first of all and then down came these six bombs, one, two, three, four, five, six – and then we up and ran full tilt. About 100 yards on, there was a junction in the gullies, one going off at right angles in a northerly direction. Just as I arrived at that point I saw the last German's backside disappearing into the bunker – they'd got bunkers dug into the walls of the end of the dyke. I'd got them absolutely like rats in a trap, they hadn't even time to turn around and look out of their foxholes. I was right upon them and in total command of where they were. I just called on them to come out and of course they had no choice, because I was standing there with my weapon in the entrance. So I winkled them out one at a time – they came trooping out, officers, NCOs – it turned out to be the company headquarters. I quickly gave orders for these chaps to be disarmed and we just shunted them out, one by one, with their hands above their heads. Then we took them all back. I think I must have shouted at some time because I remember when the CO interviewed me, not a quarter of an hour afterwards, my voice was a bit husky. He was very pleased and recommended me to higher authorities for an immediate award for distinguished service. I was as lucky in that as I was unlucky at Salerno. There's a big element of luck in these things. I mean the bombs could have fallen on us, or I could have got there and it might have been bomb proof, or they might have been just fifty yards further down waiting for us as we came round the corner. But it was a good plan, well executed and it just happened to work absolutely like a dream. *Lieutenant Russell Collins, A Coy, 16th DLI*

In all 16 Germans were taken prisoner in the company headquarters, including two officers and three NCOs. With them were all their communication equipment and two machine guns. After the triumph of the moment there was an inevitable physical and mental reaction.

> When we eventually got into one of the farm buildings, we were given very, very strict orders, that we were not allowed to light any fires. There was a fear that the smoke would give away our locality you see. We hadn't had any hot food and we'd been wet through – we were getting at a pretty low ebb by this time. I had some cigarettes I'd managed to keep dry and I got down on this bed smoking a cigarette. I woke up with the mattress burning and I was so tired that I went to sleep again without putting out the fire. I was absolutely knackered, as they say these days. *Lieutenant Russell Collins, A Coy, 16th DLI*

This action fully established Collins' reputation and he soon acquired the admiring nickname of 'Winkler' because of his repeated success in ‘winkling’ out the Germans from such strongpoints.

The Durhams managed to maintain their bridgehead and both assault brigades of 46th Division made progress. Meanwhile, although 56th Division failed on their right flank, the US 3rd and 34th Divisions both got across and began to purposefully move forward. Inevitably the Germans pulled back once they were certain that the integrity of their river line was breached. Their next major holding operation was along the line of the River Teano.

The Durhams moved forward to Francolise overlooking the River Teano. Once again the patrols crept forward and Lieutenant Sherlaw led his men across the river on 27 October.

> The Colonel was quite specific about how far he wanted you to go. What he couldn’t be sure about was what obstacles were in the way, so he had to give you a certain amount of leeway about the direction you took. But he would always want to know what was there between Point A and Point B. If he knew anything about the area he would tell you. So often you went out knowing a little bit about what might happen. We’d usually travel as lightly as we could because we were not going to take anybody on, or very rarely anyway. I wouldn’t bother with a small pack. I’d have a Tommy gun and plenty of ammunition. They’d all have one or two grenades in their pouches. You didn’t bother with your steel helmet because it made a noise and you were hoping you wouldn’t need it. Maps if you needed them. You blacked your face with dirt as long as it was something that didn’t reflect. Wherever you had to go out or come back, they were normally told and you usually had a password. We’d take a ‘V’ formation and point would be the patrol commander. You wouldn’t let the Germans know if you could help it, but the chances are that he knew you were there – that is how you found him! You found him because you came under fire! Your concern then was whether or not he was in strength or whether it was just an isolated post. If it was a long way short of your ultimate objective, you had to find some way of getting past him and finding out what was beyond. That wasn’t always easy. We actually crossed the Teano, just waded through it. It wasn’t very a very deep river at all and we got to the other side. We were travelling down a big built up hedge and it was from there that we eventually got machine gun fire. There was a set Spandau and a certain amount of Schmeisser. It was haphazard, they didn’t know where we were, they were just firing because they could hear somebody. I think if they’d have seen us they’d probably have hit us. Of course they would see us once we fired back. We guessed that it was a little pocket of probably half a dozen Germans – that meant of course that this was the outpost probably of a decent sized company. We messed about quite a bit – we fired back and

German soldier operating the 7.92mm dual purpose MG 34. IWM STT 3360

then moved, we had a couple of lads who were pretty good at this, they wriggled about to try to find out exactly where they were. We fired again and we got fire from further up. We returned fire because we were hoping to get further, but in fact it became so heavy that we eventually abandoned it and came back. We didn't see any point in launching in and getting half of us killed. We came back and reported. I went to see the battalion Intelligence Officer, who then asked you what you'd found, what you'd seen, what the terrain was like, if you could identify any particular hazards and obstacles. You told him as best you could and used the map or an aerial photograph to try and mark things on. If he felt you hadn't done the job he would tell you! *Lieutenant Ronnie Sherlaw, C Coy, 16th DLI*

The attack was set for the night of 29 October. The Durhams were to attack to the left of the 2/5th Leicestershire Regiment.

On getting to the other side the plan was that the tanks would go first and we would come up behind them. We discovered that being close to the tanks was the worst thing in the world, because in going for the tanks, the German shells found us. So we let the tanks go over one side and we went over the other side! This was the first time we had ever worked with them. We let the tanks soften the Germans up and then we moved in separately from them. *Lieutenant Ronnie Sherlaw, C Coy, 16th DLI*

From further back the situation was both chaotic and fraught. The

Private Charley Palmer

Divisional 'Tac HQ' had been established on high ground at Francolise to watch the battle as it developed on the morning of 30 October. With them was an artillery officer of 70th Field Regiment who normally acted as FOO with the forward companies of the Durhams. In this account he is known by the nom de plume of 'Jones' and the Divisional Commander was Major General J L I Hawkesworth.

The Divisional Commander surveyed the battleground. There were the Sherman tanks. Where were the Durhams? "Jones, can you see the Durham?" Answer: "No, Sir!" A pause of five minutes. "Jones, can you see the Durhams?" Answer: "No, Sir, they are probably making use of ground and cover." Jones knew the Durhams well and had read some infantry textbooks. A pause of ten minutes. "Jones, can't you see the Durhams yet?" Answer: "No, Sir. Those tanks are very slow, aren't they?" An effort to divert attention from the Durhams – Jones was a very loyal officer. A five minute pause. "Jones, have a good look and see if you can see the Durhams!" Answer: "No, Sir, they are probably on their objective. They generally get their objective." Full marks for loyalty and devotion. A final pause and then: "Jones, where are those WRETCHED Durhams?" No reply. The news soon reached the battalion and another historic battle had been won. It was not until March 1945 that I summoned up the courage to tell the Divisional Commander how proud the Battalion were to earn such a title from him! *Lieutenant Colonel Johnny Preston*[5] *HQ Coy, 16th DLI*

Preston himself was concerned to find out what was going on when he lost contact with B Company.

This is part of the bewilderment of action. It doesn't all go according to plan. Battalion Headquarters had moved into forward position. Colonel Preston was there and Brigade and Division were getting worried because they weren't getting their reports about what had happened to the DLI. Colonel Preston himself didn't know and he wanted to get information. He knew that his company was not very far forward, but he couldn't understand why he hadn't heard. So Lance Corporal Fearnley and myself were sent to try and make contact. We had to pass through this wood and we made contact all right. The company's headquarters was in a little house diagonally the other side of the wood. We had to move forward fairly quietly because we didn't know what the situation was. Anyway contact was made, we went back with our report and also the company had got in touch. *Private Charley Palmer, Intelligence Section, HQ Coy, 16th DLI*

In fact the Durhams successfully consolidated their crossing and next night moved on to keep up the pressure. As the Allied forces pressed

Pontoon bridge in mid-stream of the Volturno, 16 October 1943. IWM NA 7762

forward so once more the Germans withdrew, this time into their mountain fastness of the Winter Line itself.

The battalion was withdrawn from the front line and spent a few days of well earned rest at Carinola. Formal recognition of the battalion's achievements came with the announcement of medal awards on 31 October. The awards were haphazard and although this time Collins missed his just reward. Colonel Preston was awarded the DSO for his planning of the Vietri Defile operations, whilst Lieutenant Sherlaw received the Military Cross for getting through to Corpa di Cava. Sherlaw was pleased, but soon found that such rewards were not an unmixed blessing.

> I was very surprised, the biggest trouble with winning anything like that in a war is that people always then expect more of you. You have an awful job keeping up with your reputation. After that patrol I tended to become the bloke they sent out on patrol. It's a lot of rubbish really because you really aren't any better than anybody else at it – although the more you do you get better at it. But because you happened to have one good patrol doesn't mean you became an expert, you had one good patrol probably because you're born lucky. *Lieutenant Ronnie Sherlaw, C Coy, 16th DLI*

The battalion may have suffered heavy casualties but they also had a pride in what they had achieved together. This did not always make life easy for newcomers in the drafts posted out from England including many from the 70th (Young Soldiers) Battalion DLI.

> We got an officer there who'd come straight from England. He arrived in semi-darkness one evening and he wanted to know where his batman was and this that and the other. He was horrified with the service! He button-holed a bloke and said, "Bring my tea and shaving water in the morning!" The bloke said, "You can get your own bloody tea, mate!" That attitude! He said, "You're talking to an officer!" He said, "Well, I'm not a batman either, I'm a Corporal – and I've got my own job to do, I'm not running about after you! We don't do that in this battalion! The officer was going berserk and by pure coincidence the second in command was having a decko across the valley with some binoculars just above our heads. He came down and introduced himself and said, "We'll just have a little word..." I think he told him that a quite a lot of them didn't have permanent batmen and he was getting off on the wrong foot!" He didn't make it obvious to everybody but that was the general thing. *Driver Tom Lister, MT Section, HQ Coy, 16th DLI*

CHAPTER FIVE

The Winter Line

The Allies faced an increasingly difficult strategic situation in Italy as they approached the German mountain lines in November 1943. German resistance was determined and there was no great numerical supremacy for the Allies to exploit. As a diversionary theatre it was increasingly starved of reinforcements and war material as the 'Overlord' campaign exerted its sway. Nevertheless Alexander remained determined to batter his way through to Rome and twisted and turned to avoid having to return shipping and air units back to England for the invasion. This strategic vacillation might have been acceptable if Rome had been captured quickly, but it was obvious that this would not be the case.

The 7th Armoured Division and 46th Division reached the River Garigliano on 2 November. The Germans had flooded the coastal plain, blown the bridges and with guaranteed pin-point artillery observation from the hills, it was an almost impassable obstacle. Further inland lay Mount Camino, an imposing area of mountainous terrain towering above the junction of the Garigliano and Liri Rivers which was only one of several such features blocking the Allies' way through to Rome. Fifth Army Commander Mark Clark ordered 56th Division to storm Mount Camino and the attack began on 5 November. Although the Guards Brigade clawed their way onto the summit, they were isolated and forced to retreat in the face of intransigent German resistance.

Clark reorganised his forces and on 2 December launched another general offensive under the code name of Operation Raincoat – an ironic reference to the prevailing torrential rain. Once again 56th Division was to attack the blood soaked slopes of the main Mount Camino peak. This time they were supported by 46th Division who, by pushing forward into the Calabritto basin, were to secure a superior jumping off position. The Fifth Army still had only seven divisions to face five and a half German divisions secure in their mountain fortifications.

The preliminary bombardment was impressive as the whole of the British X Corps artillery was joined by the neighbouring US II Corps. Shells rained down on the German positions.

The night before I think there were 650 guns of our artillery firing on that mountain. Every gun was used, even the ack ack guns, the Bofors were put on their other role as an ordinary gun with tracer bullets pointing out targets for the big guns. The whole lot were firing: 7.2″, which were a huge gun; 5.5″; the 25 pounders and the Bofors. It was like bonfire night, the shells, the lights on this mountain. *Company Sergeant Major Les Thornton, Support Coy, 16th DLI*

The 139 Brigade had been given the role of capturing the spur running south from Mount Camino and forming the eastern rim of the Calabritto Basin. This spur rejoiced in the evocative sobriquet of 'Barearse Spur'. The attack force was to consist of the 2/5th Sherwood Foresters, the 2/5th Leicestershire Regiment and B Company of the Durhams. The rest of the Durhams waited for their turn at the sharp end in the village of La Murata.

This was in the depths of winter and there were feet of mud on the tracks. All the roads and tracks were very badly damaged by shell fire, any bridges or culverts, all that sort of thing had been blown by the enemy. So we had the greatest difficulty in getting our transport and things forward. Then we found ourselves in this little village where we were concentrating and we could see this mountain range ahead – Monte Camino – which was just a bare

Panorama of flooded countryside caused by the flooding of the River Garigliano, Sessa area, 5 December 1943. IWM NA 9519, IWM NA 9520, IWM NA 9521

escarpment. Hence the name Bare Arse. We assembled there in little platoon groups just basically waiting for our turn to go into the attack. There was a wind-up gramophone, with a 78 record or two there – that's the first time I'd heard the 'Intermezzo from Cavaleria Rusticana'. Then it was another song 'When it's Moonlight on the Colorado', and things like that. We played these for days, over and over again. *Lieutenant Russell Collins, A Coy, 16th DLI*

At 22.00 on 1 December the attack formations left the start line and pushed up into the Calabritto Basin. Although progress was made they were held up some 400 yards short of their objective.

It was night when we went up there. It was a terraced hillside. My section was on the top terrace. I had to dig in and we were under machine gun fire as soon as they heard us digging in. They were on the opposite side of this valley. A chap got hit in the stomach and he was in a terrible state. We dug in eventually and I was an odd man because I had an even number of men in my section, so they paired off to dig their trenches which left me on my own to dig one for myself. All I could do was dig along so I could just get below ground. The following morning they started to mortar us from across the valley. *Lance Corporal William Virr, B Coy, 16th DLI*

Calabritto village, 6 December 1943.

They suffered several casualties including their popular Company Commander Major Ballance. If anything, their situation deteriorated when they withdrew to some trenches previously occupied by the Germans.

> It came on absolutely bucketing down with rain, terrible weather. It just churned it all to mud, the slit trenches were half full of water, you were just sat in them, trying to get a cigarette going – but you couldn't. Then they started mortaring us, of course they knew the exact range for these trenches because they were the ones that they'd dug. They were dropping these bombs all round and luckily half of them were dud – they weren't exploding – whether it was because of the soft ground. A chap in the trench next to me, he must have sat up above the level, a bomb killed him. His mate with him was badly wounded. It was awful, I never did

like mortar shelling because they come straight down. You can be in a slit trench but it can drop right in with you, whereas a shell at least comes down at an angle. Mortar fire was worse to me. If you're under a long bombardment I think you go mad eventually, go off your rocker. Every man has a different breaking point and some go before others. So you could never point the finger at anyone because another half hour and it might be you. You tend to be on the brink and it takes all your striving to prevent yourself from going to pieces. I've been on the point of it a few times and I suppose everybody else had. When you feel like letting everything go – gabbling and screaming, gibbering away – just letting go. I just managed not to – till next time. You just curl up in a ball and hope nothing comes your way. I always lay on my left side and put my hands between my legs, my tin hat on the top and hope for the best. There was nothing you could do. *Lance Corporal William Virr, B Coy, 16th DLI*

Again they withdrew to escape the deluge of shells.

We pulled back then, a bit further back, on to an embankment just round the corner from the entrance to the valley so that we were out of range. I told the lads to dig into this embankment and I tried to get some tea. It was still raining. I managed to get a ration box as a shield, got a tommy cooker. After about three tins of this petroleum jelly I managed to get a mess tin of tea boiled. It's all powder you see, tea, sugar and milk powder. The lads meantime had dug a 'cave'. There was all roots stuck through from the top. I took this tea in and gave them some. I was just about to drink mine and a clod of earth dropped from the roof straight into it. It had taken me about an hour to get the water boiling! *Lance Corporal William Virr, B Coy, 16th DLI*

Although very few were aware of it at the time, all their suffering in the Calabritto Basin did have a rhyme and reason. The Foresters and Leicestershires, assisted by B Company, were successful in protecting the left flank of the main attack by 56th Division which was launched on the night of 2nd/3rd December. Barearse Spur fell and the division was soon established on the main peak of Monastery Hill which overlooked the whole Calabritto Basin.

Perhaps because of their success in the Vietri Defile operations, the Durhams were then asked to exploit this new position. A night march was planned, via Points 620 and 683 (between Barearse Spur and Cocuruzzo Ridge) already held by 56th Division, to attack the Germans on their left flank on Cocuruzzo Spur (Point 430 and 420) which formed the western lip of the Calabritto Basin. The plan was for C Company to take Point 430 at first light; A Company would then pass through them to take an intermediate promontory code-named 'Dick';

then C and D Company would surge through to capture Point 420. The battalion moved off from La Murata at 11.00 on 5 December.

> We started and got to the bottom of the mountain to wend our way up. I had my company headquarters with me and the Captain. I had my full kit on, and on top of my pack was a coil of barbed wire – Sergeant Majors had to do the work as well you see! Just a little way up this tall figure with a stick came bouncing down and says, "Good morning, Sergeant Major!" "Good morning, Sir!" I wondered what the hell he's been doing up there – it was the Corps Commander Lieutenant General Sir Richard McCreery – he'd been to have a look. Naturally he couldn't stay up there, you can't have generals being taken prisoner or killed. *Company Sergeant Major Les Thornton, Support Coy, 16th DLI*

It was tough going as they climbed up the mule tracks up on to Point 683.

> It was like climbing Snowdon, in later years. There were very steep tracks, and of course we were carrying full battle order, 48 hour rations, full water bottles and full load of ammunition. There was no possibility of any motor transport going up there so we had pack mules which took the heavy stores up. Going up this winding track all through the night, with periodic breaks of five or ten minutes each hour and so on. With the mules going along beside us, going up as quietly as we could and so by the morning we got up on the high ground. Unobserved, the enemy quite unaware, as far as I know. *Lieutenant Russell Collins, A Coy, 16th DLI*

They reached Point 683 at 20.00 and then laid up concealed behind Point 620. At 03.00, C Company went into the attack and despite opposition from their right flank were successful in taking control of Point 430. Behind the leading companies the rest of the battalion were slowly moving up. When the Germans became aware of what was happening the mortars started up.

> Then half way up it started, oh aye, down we got in the rocks – shellfire, mortars – my Corporal, if you see a dog in pain with his brown eyes looking up at you, that was him, terrified, absolutely terrified. We were all frightened. When it finished I says, "Corporal, you're no use to me, man, get back, go back down and report sick!" So I sent him down, he was absolutely useless, he had broken. I couldn't afford to take him up. *Company Sergeant Major Les Thornton, Support Coy, 16th DLI*

At first light A Company moved forward to try and take 'Dick'.

> We were given an axis of advance, A Company was being commanded by Ray Mitchell at that time. As we were going across there we came under a lot of small arms fire, and a lot of artillery fire. In fact the artillery fire was extremely confusing; it was all so

close to us, that we were never very sure if it was German defensive fire, or our own barrage supporting us, because the shells seemed to be falling all around. But the most conspicuous thing was the small arms fire and we suffered a lot of casualties, about 18 men in A Company, in the space of about half an hour, were hit individually, with bullets. The medical officer did a tremendous job, because he had brought his regimental aid post forward and set up in a sort of crofter's hut down on the leeside of the mountain. These casualties were taken down to him. *Lieutenant Russell Collins, A Coy, 16th DLI*

Behind them Support Company moved into position to provide covering mortar fire.

On we went right until we got to the top. The carnage at the top – there was Guardsmen hanging out of holes in the ground, there was Germans lying all over. There was still rifle fire. They were disposed of and we started our climb down to the valley. This barbed wire on my neck was bouncing up and down and it wasn't very comfortable at all, you believe me, especially going down. Eventually we got down to the bottom, it was getting light, on we went to where I had to put my Company Headquarters. It was just a little part of the valley, I went a little way and I saw two bodies lying on the ground – Sergeant Kennedy,[6] a friend of mine and his Corporal beside him – they'd been caught by German machine gunners just on top of the little knoll we were standing below, got it in the head. So we buried them there, a shallow grave, took their disks, put their gas capes over them and marked it so that the padre would come along later on, see them and they'd be moved. We halted there and waited for orders. *Company Sergeant Major Les Thornton, Support Coy, 16th DLI*

A Company were coming under considerable German fire as they approached their objective.

We were under this fire and of course we were keeping pretty close to the ground, because anything that moved was fired at, we were sort of cowering behind boulders, very low drystone walls and things. I spotted where it was coming from, about 80 to 100 yards on our right, as we were going across. We were going across from right to left, it was on our right as you would expect. A lot of fire was coming from there – like a crofter's small farmstead. I was so incensed really, very angry that some of my chaps were being hit. One very nice lad, Private Jimmy Baglin, was hit. Ray Mitchell was there wondering quite what to do I think. So I said "Well look, I think I'd better go and sort it out; will you let me go!" He said "Good Lord, if you want to – sooner you than me!" I said, "I'll take a little assault party round to the right flank," and he said "Well, all right and good luck!" So I set up a machine gun post to fire back at these people, to keep their heads down, while I moved with two or three chaps, Phillips my batman, Corporal Clayton was another of them, I picked about three or four men. *Lieutenant Russell Collins, A Coy, 16th DLI*

Collins had developed very firm views about an officer's role in action and he had the resolve to put them into action.

Rightly or wrongly, I led from the front whenever possible. I felt more confident that way. I felt it was my duty, to tell you the truth, I really felt I couldn't send somebody else there if I wasn't prepared to do it myself. So I nearly always led from the front. In the war the dominant lesson I learnt was the crucial role of the junior officer, because it was quite clear to me that unless platoon commanders led their platoons, nothing happened. *Lieutenant Russell Collins, A Coy, 16th DLI*

Collins arranged a fire plan to keep the Germans' heads down while the small party made their approach as covertly as possibly.

We went around to the right flank. One thing I've had nightmares about since was that I don't remember what order I gave them as to how they would know when to stop firing when I went in to rush the building – I don't think I gave any orders or fired a signal. Of course I wanted to get on with it. So I went positively, you might say impetuously, but anyway straightforwardly. As I ran into the target area on which our machine gun was still firing rapid fire, the bullets were cracking over my head, but I think they saw us just in time. When I got round to the side of the building, I saw that there was no ground entrance but there was an outside staircase. I rushed straight up the staircase and there was a door open at the top. I was aware of the danger of going into an open doorway, so somehow or other I established that there was nobody in the upper room. Then I looked over the sort of parapet, where I was standing at the top of this stairway and down behind was an extension to the farm building, a cow-shed or something like that. It was clear then that the enemy were all in there. Of course I was standing about eight or ten feet above them. I opened up with my tommy gun down through the slats of the roof and I ordered my other chaps around the side of the staircase to my left. So they were standing outside the door with their rifles at the ready and I was standing up above, firing down on this roof. What came out through the door was a white flag on the end of a rifle bayonet, because there was absolutely nothing else they could do. We shouted at them to come out with their hands up. They came out, something like 16 or 18 of them. I'm afraid that when we lined those prisoners up, if any of them had any cameras or anything like that, which we didn't want to fall into the hands of the people guarding the prisoner of

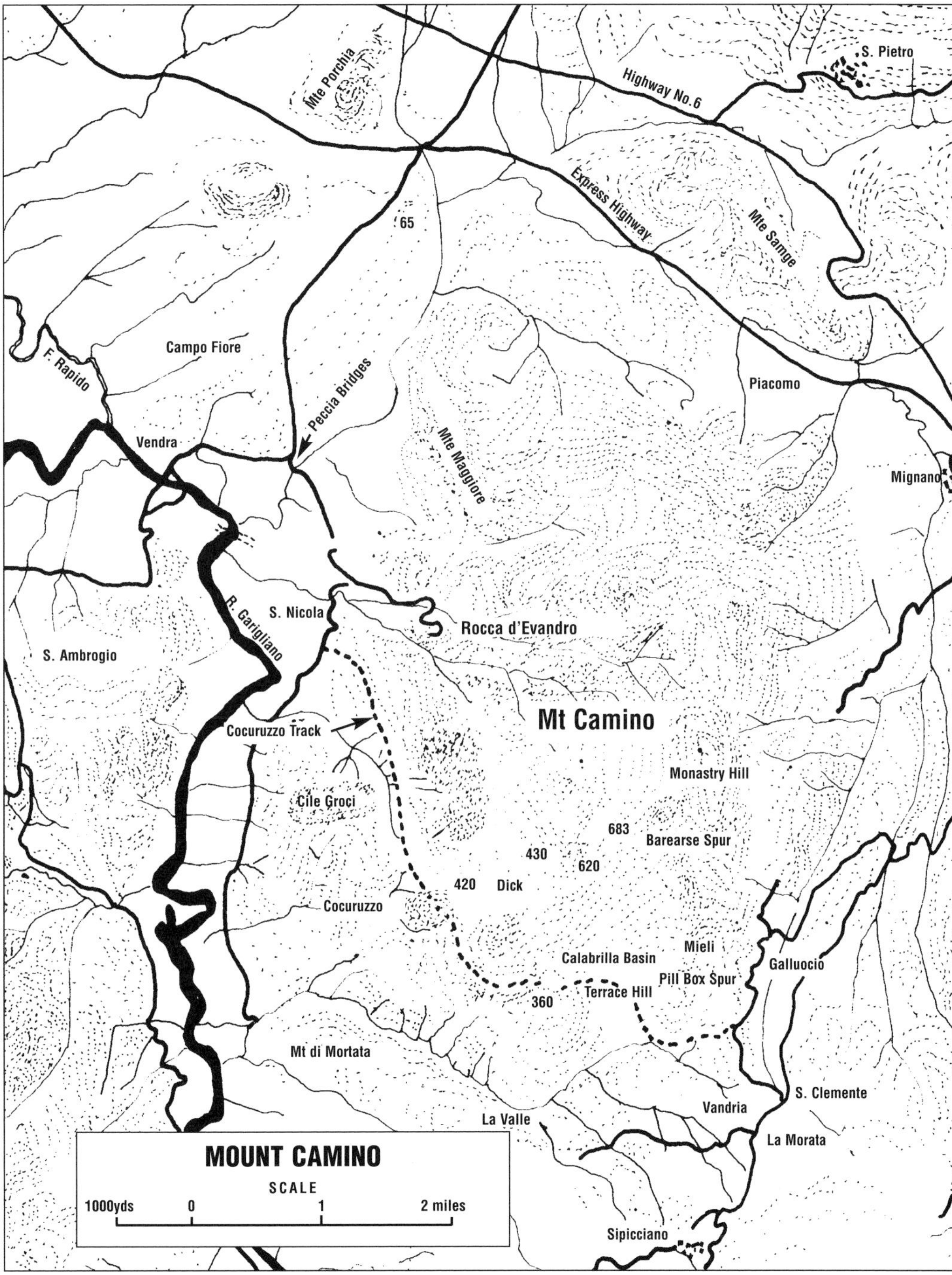

S. Pietro
Highway No.6
Mte Porchia
Express Highway
Mte Samge
65
Campo Fiore
F. Rapido
Peccia Bridges
Piacomo
Vendra
Mte Maggiore
Mignano
S. Nicola
R. Garigliano
Rocca d'Evandro
S. Ambrogio
Mt Camino
Cocuruzzo Track
Monastry Hill
Cile Groci
683
Barearse Spur
430
620
420
Dick
Cocuruzzo
Mieli
Calabrilla Basin
Galluocio
Pill Box Spur
Terrace Hill
360
Mt di Mortata
S. Clemente
Vandria
La Valle
La Morata
MOUNT CAMINO
SCALE
1000yds
0
1
2 miles
Sipicciano

war camps behind, we helped ourselves – we felt that we were more entitled to them than they were. Perhaps slightly reprehensible in some ways. Among them was a camera and I took some snaps there and then. Then we dug in, consolidated the position and had a brew up! *Lieutenant Russell Collins, A Coy, 16th DLI*

Consolidation was essential as soon as a position was captured.

The most important thing is the security of your own defended locality. You're responsible for deciding where the most likely threat is and setting up your weapons – light machine guns and so on; then deciding what regime of sentry guard you wanted. You just get a sense about it – I mean I was never attacked and over-run in all that time. It's really just a question of having a sense of how to set up these interlocking arcs that are mutually supporting and then having a good, responsible regime of keeping people on the alert all the time. I would give orders as to what the strength of the sentry guard was to be – whether or not there would be two men awake at a time or whether there must be half a section, or whether the whole section would stand-to. We always manned the machine gun, whoever was on sentry, would move into the position where the machine gun was and the others would be resting. We always had a stand-to at dusk and dawn, everybody stood to their posts with their weapons. These were theoretically the most likely times for an attack. You had to make sure that you gave people enough rest otherwise they would fall asleep at their post, and of course that's hopeless. Mark you, chaps who fell asleep got a pretty severe rocket, they weren't shot anymore, I mean you couldn't do that because people are only flesh and blood after all. But some people were more slack than others and they had to be made aware of their responsibilities. I was very strict about checking on them you just can't leave it to chance. *Lieutenant Russell Collins, A Coy, 16th DLI*

The 'Dick' position was firmly held with A Company in position to its right.

Although the attack had gone well, Major Ray Mitchell was furious that two of his stretcher bearers, Privates Millett and Davenport, had been killed by a German sniper. He resolved to interrogate the prisoners taken by Collins and his platoon.

We lined them all up and Major Mitchell was going mad, "Who's the sniper? Who's the sniper that had killed the stretcher bearers?" There was only one there with a camouflage suit on, he didn't look like a German at all, dark hair. Mitchell said, "Right, you're the sniper, go to the side!" And he pointed to me, Webley and Mason, "You three – aim your guns!" I thought, "Hey, we can't do this!" But this German was just standing not showing any

Two German prisoners of war captured at Mount Camino, 6 December 1943.
IWM NA 9471

fear at all, just standing, scowling, just glaring at us. Major Mitchell was looking for him to show fright and he wouldn't. I thought, "Hey, I don't like this idea at all". He said, "Get back in – shoot the lot!" I thought, "Oh God!" Everybody lined up with their guns. "Right aim, when I tell you fire, fire, now aim!" They were all standing, nobody moved. Then suddenly this great big fat one, right at the front, he must have been about 18 stone, he started crying. He got down and started taking all his photographs out of his wife, he was looking at them... But the other Germans were looking at him as if he was dirt. He was crying, "Whhrrrrrrrrr!" I don't think Mitchell would have shot them but he wanted somebody show fright. I think that's all he wanted in the end. He said, "Right, march the lot away..." *Signaller Tony Sacco, A Coy, 16th DLI*

During the night of 6 December elements of the 6th Yorks and Lancs moved forward and found the German opposition had evaporated. Next day the battalion moved forward into Cocuruzzo village and it became apparent that the German forces were withdrawing from the whole Mount Camino area. The first cracks in the much vaunted Winter Line had been rammed open. But time was passing...

The Mount Camino operations were just one part of Operation Raincoat as Clark's divisions tried to batter their way through. Although generally successful it had all taken too long. There was no prospect of an easy march through the Liri Valley as Mount Cassino and the Gustav Line barred their way. The Italian campaign was becoming a slogging match which tested endurance as well as military finesse.

One obvious option was to use the Allies' maritime supremacy to land troops behind the German lines, in effect to leapfrog down the coast of Italy. However there were two complicating factors. Firstly, a pre-requisite of landings was landing craft, and these were urgently needed in Europe for the D Day landings. Secondly, such landings were dangerous, for, although they outflanked the German lines, there were limits to how many troops could be landed in a short time. If the main front was not making sufficiently swift progress, then the isolated bridgehead could be attacked and destroyed in detail by the German reserve divisions. All these factors were under urgent and serious consideration as the Allies considered the gamble which resulted in Operation 'Shingle' – better known as the Anzio landings.

★★★★

Oblivious to this, the Durhams were relieved from the front-line and withdrawn to the villages of Rongolisi, Corigliano and Avulpi. They badly needed a rest but some found their slumbers cruelly disturbed.

The Colour Sergeant met me coming along and he saw we were absolutely shattered, "Come on, Sergeant Major, we've got some clean blankets!" I said, "You what, clean blankets, lovely!" So we went into this building and got down to it. Well – right outside the building opposite was a 7.2″ artillery piece, that was the biggest gun we had. They started to fire – our building went up and down like that!" I said, "Who thought of this place for a rest!" My God, every time it fired the blast was terrific, so we didn't get a great deal of sleep! *Company Sergeant Major Les Thornton, Support Coy, 16th DLI*

Later, on 15 December, the battalion moved into billets at Campo and St Vaglie where, besides their operational role of acting as a reserve force in case the Germans attempted to return to Mount Camino, they also provided working parties to assist the Royal Engineers in improving the Calabritto-Cocuruzzo track to allow road traffic. A group of new officers joined on 19 December and one of them was pleased to find a familiar face.

Another chap I saw was a man called Duffy who was a well built lad, a Major, MC, whom I had sent out as one of the draft officers some time ago. He was keen to get out and had been doing the Battle Schools and that was what he was best at – he was a bit wayward in other respects. Getting into trouble over larking on

British troops coming out of the line after fighting on Mount Camino, 11 December 1943.
IWM NA 9635

Alan Hay

Frank Duffy MC

and not having that sort of respect. He loved the Battle Schools and so he was a natural to get abroad. He was Company Commander and he said, "What are you going to do, Alan?" I said, "Well, I haven't been told yet!" He said, "Would you like to come to my company?" I said, "Certainly, yes – which company's that?" He said, "D Company – we'll look after you!" So I went to D Company. They'd just come out of the battle and we went to a little village called La Vaglie, which was the most God awful place you ever saw! *Captain Alan Hay, D Coy, 16th DLI*

The Durhams then relieved the 5th Hampshires from their front line positions to the north west of San Carlo. This was a relatively quiet sector but reconnaissance patrols still had to be sent out. Hay had had years of training and exercises in England but was keen and fully aware that he had a lot to learn.

Lieutenant Critchley, who came out with me, was to take the patrol. I was curious and I said, "Can I go down and see what the procedure is for them going out?" "Oh, yes!" I went down and I saw Critchley and his men. I said, "Don't worry, good luck!" They walked into the Germans and Critchley[7] was killed and one or two of our men – the new ones, first day out. I thought, "All the time we've been wasting in England, why couldn't they have brought one or two of us out, just to be there, to get the feel of things? Because it's a hell of a sight different going against the real enemy, particularly in small patrols where you get this nous, you get the feel and the smell of the thing. *Captain Alan Hay, D Coy, 16th DLI*

The battalion had great difficulty in digging in on the rocky, freezing slopes of Mount Maggiori on their next posting into the line. For Lieutenant Barnett, who had only just rejoined the battalion on 22 December after recovering from his wounds on Hospital Hill, it was not a happy return.

This was really the most horrible place I was ever in. We were on rock into which you could not dig. We had in the rear positions one or two clefts between rock which gave slightly better cover, but in the night positions on the forward slope we could only lie

Garigliano, Sessa area, 5 December 1943. IWM NA 9520

British Tommies asleep in their foxhole scratched into the surface of Mount Camino, 7 December 1943. IWM NA 9635

behind sangars – which are little piles of rocks in a circle which you try and take cover behind. We had to stay all night and we were shelled. These shells used to be dropping and not penetrating into the earth at all – they used to go with a clang instead of a bang when they exploded – and the ground was littered with these huge pieces of jagged metal each morning. It was really a hell on earth. *Lieutenant Gerry Barnett, C Coy, 16th DLI*

Not unnaturally, in these less than festive conditions it was decided to postpone the traditional Christmas celebrations until the battalion emerged from the line into billets at La Vaglie on 31 December. The Durhams then had a chance to really celebrate and they went for it with a will. It forms one of the most detailed entries ever to appear in the battalion war diaries!

The light snow, which had brought in the New Year, formed a fitting background. During the morning the Padre visited Battalion HQ and all the Companies taking services. Dinners, which were visited by the Colonel and Second-in-Command, can only be described as lucullan, and were served by officers and NCOs in an atmosphere of great joviality. Roast pork, some turkey, roast potatoes, cauliflower, Yorkshire pudding, stuffing and apple sauce, plum pudding and white sauce, formed the backbone of the menu. When the serious business was done, the diners punctuated their work among the nuts, fruit and beer, which followed, with cheers for everyone from the Colonel to the cooks. The Divisional Commander visited the Battalion during the afternoon and the Divisional Concert Party gave an excellent performance. Celebrations were carried on, after a light tea of mince pies etc, in improvised Officers' and Sergeants' Messes and in all quarters during the evening; and so ended a great day. *16th DLI War Diary 2 January 1944*

The ugly business of war awaited and on 6 January the Durhams moved up onto the lower slopes of Mount Maggiori. Next day B Company crossed the Peccia River that lay before them to provide flanking protection for a 2/5th Sherwood Foresters' attack that night on the hill of Cedra. The Foresters' attack stalled and on 9 January the rest of the Durhams crossed the Peccia and made a successful night advance of some 1,000 yards to Cedra. Next morning the sun brought with it a dense blanket of mist which covered the whole valley. Lieutenant Barnett and his platoon had spent the night in a group of farm buildings on a slight knoll.

We were roused very suddenly about dawn by one of the sentries who had seen some German soldiers right outside the building. I rushed out, as I was, I didn't even pick up my Tommy gun, I had my pistol on my belt of course. I rushed straight out and there they were a few yards from the door – a group of 6-8 German soldiers. There were then something like half a dozen of my men with me including my Sergeant and we ran at them. Two dropped to the ground in the ensuing melee and the others scattered and ran. It was at that moment that this delightful Sergeant of mine, a Yorkshireman with an unbelievably big moustache danced round us waving his rifle and shouting, "Try to take prisoners, try to take prisoners!" It was such a startling intrusion that I stopped aghast at him – and then I felt absolutely delighted that such a humane action could take place at a time like that. But it didn't stop us of course – there wasn't time to do anything about it. Two of the Germans had thrown themselves to the ground and were taken prisoner; the others were still running so I shouted to the men to fire and emptied my pistol myself in their direction – I didn't hit anything of course – you can't with a pistol! I snatched a rifle from a man, had a go myself and then they were all in cover, they'd all gone down the slope. All this was very quick and took only a few seconds of time – a minute at the most.

A recce patrol uses a bank for cover, 2 January 1944. IWM NA 10470

Almost immediately they'd gone to ground a German machine gun opened fire on us. For some reason I thought it was on the higher ground on the left on a knoll. I set off with a few of the chaps following me along this partly made road to look for it, thinking I was having a little bit of cover from the revetment on the left of the road where it was dug into the hill. I'd gone only 50 yards when the machine gun hit me. I realised from the wound I received that I'd made a mistake and it was on the right down on the lower ground. I was hit in the neck and because of my crouching position the bullet went through the right of my neck and out through my left shoulder taking a lot of my shoulder blade with it. The hole in the neck was very small but the hole in my back was fairly large. I didn't know that then of course. It was a curious experience – I had time to reflect on it – I thought I was dead at first because all the consciousness of my body went. I could see and I could think and that was about the limit of it. I knew I was folding up because I could see I was slowly falling to the ground, my body was collapsing. I thought, "Well, this is yet another interesting experience to add to the list!" I folded onto the ground and I was lying on my back with my knees sticking up. Then I found I could move my right arm. So my first thought was to push my knees down because they could be fired at. Then slowly some feelings returned. I couldn't move my left arm, that was paralysed. For some reason I thought I'd been hit in the groin – Heaven knows why, I wasn't – with my right hand I got my field dressing, but I couldn't open it, so I stuffed it inside my trousers thinking I was bleeding there. Then, very bravely, my runner and Sergeant rushed out to me and dragged me back along this road to where they'd half constructed a drain. A hole into a culvert underneath and they threw me head first down this drain and ran for cover themselves to the ditch, crawled into the drain and dragged me threw it and back to the buildings. I was just numb, I didn't feel any pain. The stretcher bearers got hold of me, took me into one of the farm buildings. I was wearing a new trench coat and a leather jerkin. Leather jerkins were issued in the winter but they didn't have enough to go round, so we used to take it in turns to wear it – it had been my turn that day. I asked the men cutting my clothing off to get a dressing on my back, to ease me out of the jerkin rather than cut it, because it was a precious garment. It probably had a hole in the back of course! Consciousness went then.... *Lieutenant Gerry Barnett, C Coy, 16th DLI*

Barnett had fought his last battle as he was evacuated back to England.

After a period of patrolling and minor skirmishes the Durhams were relieved and moved back across the Peccia to their former positions. During this time Lieutenant Russell Collins was awarded a richly deserved Military Cross for his actions on Cocuruzzo Spur. The boy had become a man.

> I don't think MCs came up very frequently for platoon commanders, they came up sometimes for company commanders who'd commanded a successful attack, but hadn't done anything perhaps too personal. I think in general they were well merited. The thing that sticks in mind is that I did many things which in my mind were equally meritorious and some of them even more hazardous which just weren't recognised at all. But one doesn't complain about that, it's the luck of the draw. I was quite chuffed about mine! *Lieutenant Russell Collins, A Coy, 16th DLI*

****

Meanwhile the Allied Command had finally weighed its options and decided, in a wild leap of faith, to launch a new landing by VI Corps at the port of Anzio. The intention was to cut the lines of communication behind the Gustav Line, forcing the Germans in theory to abandon their entrenched positions and retreat to the north or be encircled. This would allow the capture of Rome, still the ultimate objective. To prevent the German concentration of reserves on the Anzio bridgehead, the US Fifth Army was to launch their own frontal offensive on the Gustav Line and they began a series of staged attacks on 12 January. The British X Corps moved forward across the River Garigliano on 17 January 1944.

The Germans reacted violently to the Anzio landings on 22 January. Hitler ordered Kesselring to stamp out the threat posed by VI Corps, whilst the Gustav Line, far from being abandoned as the Allies optimistically hoped, was to be held at all costs. German units were withdrawn from Southern France, Germany, the Balkans and Northern Italy. A furious battle began as the Anzio beachhead was encircled by a ring of German steel. The British could not break out, but nor could the

British infantry crossing a pontoon bridge across the Garigliano, 19 January 1944.
IWM NA 10942

Germans sweep them back into the sea. For the next two months there was a grim stalemate.

In armies of hundreds of thousands, such strategic manoeuvring did not have an immediate impact on the fate of one infantry battalion. Fifth Army troops battered themselves senseless against the almost impregnable German bastions, but initially at least the Durhams were not involved and indeed had a period in reserve at La Murata, until 25 January. Then, in atrocious weather conditions, they crossed the Garigliano by pontoon bridge and moved into the Suja area where they were given the role of reserve battalion attached to 138 Brigade for the forthcoming attack on Mount Tuja. Taking cover where they could, the men cowered in shallow holes scraped out of the unyielding ground.

> When it was hard and frosty you can hardly dig in. It took a bit of doing. I found a nice little spot that was soft. I thought I was bloody fine! But when I got so far down it was bloody terrible – it smelt of shit – it had been a Jerry latrine! I got out of there and it took me ages to get it off my boots. *Driver Jackie Milburn, MT Section, Headquarters Coy, 16th DLI*

Gradually moving forward in the wake of 138 Brigade, they were finally required to move forward from the southern slopes of Mount Turlito on to Point 400 and Mount Siela. Collins recorded the event with a few lines in his diary for Saturday, 29 January.

> Moved forward to Hill 400. Had few hours rest, went forward with platoon all night. Infiltrated behind Jerry. Attacked at dawn, captured seven. Two Jerries wounded. One of my men killed, Mawson. Pongo wounded, bullet through lung. *Lieutenant Russell Collins, A Coy, 16th DLI*

This prosaic entry records the death of a fine soldier.

> Private Mawson, was a splendid little man, totally reliable though he wouldn't say boo to a goose. I think I recommended him for the Military Medal; I know I had it very much in mind to do so. A very interesting lesson I learnt from the war was that the calm, quiet, people like that, undistinguished people, you might think, not extrovert in anyway, were absolutely steady and reliable. Whereas other people who were showing great bravado, "My God, I can't wait to get at them!" often crumbled in an instant. I've seen this happen time and time again. The moment they're fired on they explode in a puff of smoke. *Lieutenant Russell Collins, A Coy, 16th DLI*

Collins and his men were attempting to work round the north side of a spur and on to Monte Siela using a rocky gully to climb the steep slopes.

> It was quite a deep patrol and we got into this gully. Well the Germans were in it, that was the trouble, they were covering it –

Out of the line and in rest billets. Russell Collins with men of 8 Platoon, A Coy. Over Russell Collins' left shoulder is Sergeant Jerrison and over his left shoulder is Private Mawson. Kneeling to the right of Collins is his batman Private Len Phillips.

machine guns certainly on one side and possibly on both sides. We were trying to make progress, but I saw that we had gone too far and were going to have difficulty in extricating ourselves. We came under fire – so we just had to get out of the gully as soon as we could. But poor old Mawson was hit and he couldn't move. It was a question then of whether anybody could go down and recover him or not. He was some thirty or forty yards from me to my left. I agonised as to whether or not I should go or send anybody to try and get him out – whether or not we should hazard more of us to try and get him out. You couldn't rely on the Germans, it wouldn't be any good taking a Red Cross flag or anything like that. If anybody else went down there they would have been fired on as well. So he was just unlucky, but still, that was that – Private Mawson died of his wounds and this caused us all great sadness.
Lieutenant Russell Collins, A Coy, 16th DLI

Next day, B Company was moved up to attack Monte Siela.

Our platoon was the reserve platoon, the last of the three platoons going forward. As the first platoon got amongst these positions all hell let loose. They threw everything at us. We had to just scatter where we were. There was a sangar, just one in all this hillside, a tree with this sangar built round it. The three of us dived into this sangar. There were rocks you could have got behind, but this looked handier. One lad threw a Bren gun in with us. We realised as soon as we got in that the Germans got a fixed line on it with a machine gun! So once we'd got in we couldn't get out! You could see where it was gouging the rock where he had it trained and clamped up so that every time he pulled the trigger it was hitting it. We were in there the biggest part of that day. We could hear the troops in front of us, quite a few were killed, Mr Coutt's batman, Jack Vile, he was hit in the pouch, he had some flares for the Verey pistol and they all set alight and burnt. Sergeant Makepiece[8], he was killed and several others, some were taken prisoner. One or two lads in front of us took their packs off and slid back. It wasn't a matter of running away, you were in a position where you couldn't do a thing about it. What could you do? The Germans had more or less done away with the first two platoons, if we'd got up and walked into it, we would have been wiped out as well. We were left there, we thought we were all there was left of the company. Our Platoon Commander, he was a little bit of a windy bloke really, he got his head down as well. He should have been the one to tell us. You could kid him into going back if you wanted – he didn't take a lot of persuading! He said, "Oh, I've been hit, I'll have to go back to the Medical Officer, you stay here!" A piece of rock had hit him thrown up by a mortar bomb – it wasn't much. *Lance Corporal William Virr, B Coy, 16th DLI*

Lance Corporal William Virr

The attack had failed and the remnants of B Company were withdrawn as German counter-attacks sought to re-capture Point 400. The German tactics were simple. As the defending army they had the choice of where exactly they would make their stand. Obviously they picked the very best highest sites for observation posts. In this way they could hold other surrounding peaks without troops just by all seeing observation directing inch perfect shell or mortar fire.

A grim stalemate was finally established and a routine developed for the men in their slit trenches.

The officers and NCOs inspected their men each day with particular attention being paid to their personal weapons. You had to have a proper regime of weapon cleaning. Small arms are particularly susceptible to malfunctioning due to mud, ingress of mud and grit. And of course they are most likely to get the ingress of mud and grit! So it's quite an important problem. *Lieutenant Russell Collins, A Coy, 16th DLI*

Many also insisted that the men maintain the best possible standards of personal appearance – whatever the conditions. This was not just 'bullshit' they really felt that it improved morale.

> I always made my people wash and shave, and they thought it was ridiculous sometimes, you know we had no hot water. But if we were going to move the next morning, or go on an advance or an attack, I always insisted that everybody got his mess tin, put a drop of water in it from his water bottle and washed and shaved. It had a tremendous morale boosting effect. *Lieutenant Russell Collins, A Coy, 16th DLI*

Yet at the height of winter, conditions were appalling.

> I went to sleep with just one blanket, laying in amongst these rocks. I thought, "It's raining!" and pulled my blanket over. When I wakened up, I was covered in snow! It makes you wonder how we survived the conditions. The weather was atrocious. *Lance Corporal William Virr, B Coy, 16th DLI*

Menaced as they were by German machine guns, mortars and artillery it was essential that swift, accurate artillery retaliation was available to the Durhams.

> There was a regiment supporting each brigade and a battery supporting each battalion. So in the division there were three field regiments and probably a medium regiment as well. They would all register so they could lay on a particular target at a moment's notice. If they were divisional targets they had the letter U, the phonetic name for U then was uncle, so they were 'Uncle' targets. If you had a concentration down on 'Uncle' target, my goodness, you knew nothing moved in that area. *Lieutenant Russell Collins, A Coy, 16th DLI*

When the location of a menacing group of German mortars or artillery was established it could well be an 'Uncle' target and usually this brought instant relief to the men stuck in the trenches. Smaller targets would be tackled by the battery specifically designated to the Durhams and the Durhams formed a particularly close bond with their artillery.

> We had such a close working relationship that must have been very rare in the history of the war, if not unique. The battery affiliated to us was 449 Battery, Royal Artillery, part of 70th Field Regiment – they were our battery. We became integrated, almost as if we were in the same unit. We knew them all extremely well, personally and I think that's why it worked so well. They were brilliant. *Lieutenant Russell Collins, A Coy, 16th DLI*

The liaison was carried out by the forward observation officers attached to the forward companies of the Durhams.

> The gunners had got all the maps, and had the ability to

compute and convert from one set of references to another. One would then give them details of the target and they could then compute from that the range and bearing from their gun position. They would then put down a round of fire, they'd say, "One shot fired." It may be eight or ten seconds before the shell arrived and then you heard a crump in the distance – you looked around and you couldn't see it, or it might have been quite close. In the very, very difficult and close country in Southern Italy, the gunners felt that we weren't always terribly sure where we were, because the maps weren't perfect, not like ordnance survey maps. It was a matter of speculation to a degree. *Lieutenant Russell Collins, A Coy, 16th DLI*

In these circumstance there was plentiful scope for accidents with shells falling short or not hitting their target. This could poison a relationship between gunners and infantry, but the Durhams and 449 Battery had a real confidence in both each other and themselves. Minor problems or disagreements could be overcome through the underlying friendship that existed between officers.

I could see quite distinctly through my binoculars an enemy machine gun post under a tree about 400 yards away. Well the gunners wouldn't have it that I knew where I was – but I did! The first shell they dropped was absolutely nowhere in sight. So I said "Well you'd better try again!" They tried again and got one closer. Now the drill is then, once you see a shell then, taking the axis of one's self to the target then, in relation to that, you say, "Go right, 200, go up 100", or whatever. I did that and of course it was a total fluke, rather like a hole in one at golf, but the next shell fell slap on the machine gunner under the tree. Of course the gunners were delighted and so was I – but it was a pure fluke! *Lieutenant Russell Collins, A Coy, 16th DLI*

The stalemate lasted into February, with the companies taking turns in the most dangerous forward positions. Patrol work was extremely dangerous in the tangled mountains where an ambush was easily organised.

One afternoon we heard firing ahead of us and the officer came and said, "Come on, with your section, we've got to go – the Company Commander's gone forward and looks to be in trouble." You could hear the small arms going. We got so far up and this officer said, "Can you tell where that firing's coming from?" I said, "Yes!" "Well get your Bren down and give it a burst!" I said, "I think we'd be best placed going further on, at the moment he doesn't know we're here, but if we get down and fire the Bren it will signal that somebody's here!" Anyway, we went about another 200 yards and we were spotted. Jerry brought his mortars down on us, so we had to get back to our positions. I've never been under shellfire like it before or after. He tossed everything at us that afternoon. We had a string of blokes went shell shocked – just lost their nerve – they were crying, laughing, crying one minute laughing the other. Just like babyish... I felt terrible but I got through it. We just had to crouch down in the slit trench because there was nothing else we could do. It was just pouring down. There was two of us in the slit trench and one shell fell that close to the bank side that it nearly covered us up. We just sat in the bottom of the slit trench and waited till it quietened down. It was just going through your mind, "When am I going to get out of this, is the next one going to come down here?" Our CO or the Company Commander had the presence of mind, as soon as the dark came in, he moved us about 300 yards further into the wood. And believe me the next morning he brayed hell out of the positions where we'd been before. *Corporal Tom Turnbull, B Coy, 16th DLI*

In these debilitating circumstances it is not at all surprising that morale began to slip.

They were sick, they were fed up. Normally in a war you are fed up, but you could see the difference in the men. They were tired, they'd been up in those hills for three weeks, so they hadn't really had a rest. None of us had had a real rest, not what you'd call a rest – just a couple of days when you knew straight away you were

Out of the line and in rest billets. Men of 8 Platoon, A Coy. Back row left to right: Corporal Clayton, unknown, Private Brown, Corporal Robe, Private Mawson, unknown. Front row unknown.

going back in the line. So it wasn't a rest, your mind didn't register it as a rest at all. The men were just weary, battle fatigue and war weary. Just fed up, they'd had enough, they'd been there too long. They'd been fighting since Salerno in September. *Company Sergeant Major Les Thornton, Support Coy, 16th Bn DLI*

The officers were aware of the problem

As for myself and my platoon, you know you can sense when everybody is at a low ebb. If it was necessary to detail somebody off to accompany me on a patrol then I had to think twice, "Well now who can still take this sort of thing?" *Lieutenant Russell Collins, A Coy, 16th DLI*

They may have hung back from obvious immediate danger but many of the men were still bound together despite the grim conditions. The Salerno mutineers who had reluctantly joined the Durhams in September were given their chance to leave. Not all now wanted to leave their new friends.

Johnny Preston kept his word, he gave them all a chance to go back, sent word round. One chap from our company he says, "Jimmy, they've sent for us, I've got a chance to go back to my own battalion in England!" "Ohhh," I says, "Good on you!" He says, "But I'm not fussy, I've got used to the lads here – I don't want to make another landing – I think I'll stay!" He got killed the next day! *Private James Corr, B Coy, 16th DLI*

It could be a cruel world.

Finally they had done their stint and on 14 February they were pulled out to La Vaglie. Here they rested – had chance to wash and shave properly, new kit and uniforms, concert parties and a drink or two. Rumours flourished as usual but this time they had a solid grounding in fact. It was announced that the battalion would not be returning to the line, but would instead be having a long period of rest and retraining. Not only this, but the whole of the 46th Division was being pulled out of Italy and sent to the Middle East. They were indeed lucky to go as they left behind the sanguinary battles to break through the Gustav Line, which increasingly came to rest on the need to capture the grim fortress of Mount Cassino. The Italian Campaign had stalled – and the capture of Rome remained a distant dream.

Chapter Six

Middle East Interlude

On 21 February the battle weary Durhams boarded the troopship *Sobieski* and set off for the land of the Pharaohs.

> It started to get warmer and warmer and warmer, of course all the spirits rose, the chaps were thinking, "Ahhrr, great this!" On the 27th February we arrived at Port Said and the contrast to the weather – sun, warm, even at that time, warm lovely weather and spirits were very high. *Company Sergeant Major Les Thornton, Support Coy, 16th DLI*

The Durhams moved to El Quassasin Camp located in the desert close by the Suez Canal. As 'front line troops' they had developed a natural dislike to those troops that also served but miles behind the lines. This antipathy proved to be mutual.

> We weren't received very well by the people there – the lads called them 'base wallahs'. There was quite a few scuffles went on, the lads were let loose. There was a bar there, there was beer there, so even in the Sergeants' mess there were quite a few arguments and scuffles with these chaps who thought that we shouldn't be there. *Company Sergeant Major Les Thornton, Support Coy, 16th DLI*

Several of the troops developed a keen interest in a thriving local Egyptian culture.

> Johnny Arab would come round and shout, "Horny books" and the troops would buy these books. The parson used to get very upset about it and I used to confiscate them when I came across

Group of Signallers taken in Cairo, February 1944.

them, but you couldn't do anything about it. There you were in the Spring of '44 and the troops had been away since the December of '42. Better that probably than the brothels. *Major Viz Vizard, HQ Coy, 16th DLI*

Almost immediately the men were sent on leave into Cairo. Here the troops behaved as well as might be expected, but this was not enough for some of the Military Police who pounded the streets in search of easy victims.

We had about three days holiday in Cairo. Everybody got pinched for not having gaiters on. That was the dress out there but we didn't have them. So Johnny Preston got the whole battalion on parade and he says, "Now, everybody that has been charged for being improperly dressed – I've decided to hang one of you and jail the rest of you for life!" He says, "They're stupid, bloody mad, they've got some on a charge for fighting – I've trained them for fighting! Cases dismissed!" *Private James Corr, B Coy, 16th DLI*

On 13 March the battalion moved to Kefar Yona near Tel Aviv in Palestine.

It was a new tented camp, everything was spic and span, eight

A Company officers and sergeants taken in Palestine, 1944. Front row left to right: *Lieutenants Marshall, Collins, Miller, and Tiffin.* Back row left to right: *Sergeants Green, Jerrison, Lieutenant Reeves, Sergeants Kalman and Price. On the return to Italy Lieutenant Marshall, Sergeants Green, Price and Jerrison – were killed. Lieutenant Tiffin and Sergeant Reeves were both seriously wounded. Lieutenant Miller was posted as liason officer to Brigade HQ. Sergeant Kalman was not long with them.*

man tents. The camp was surrounded by an expanse of barbed wire and immediately behind the barbed wire were these very lush orange trees with Jaffas. But there were notices all round the barbed wire, "Do not trespass beyond this point!" There was a supreme optimist at the entrance to the camp who had a pile of what must have been two or three tons of Jaffa oranges trying to sell them to the troops. I must say I don't think he sold any! The troops just went under the wire and everybody had a tent full of oranges! *Captain Alan Hay, A Coy, 16th DLI*

Ronald Elliott near Lake Tiberious, 1944.

Most of the troops were totally unaware of the simmering tensions between the Arab and Jewish populations. At this point various groups of Jewish insurgents were launching attacks on the Palestine Police and on symbold of British rule. On 24 March, the Durhams were put on one hour's notice to move to Tel Aviv to aid the civil powers and later that day they were ordered into the city. Over the next few days they were to assist in the enforcement of a curfew.

Our CO decreed with the Police that a curfew would be enforced from 5 o'clock each day. You have got to imagine that Tel Aviv had this beautiful beach, it was very busy, a normal people not at war, no signs of any war. To shut this down at 5 o'clock when everyone had to get off the streets! This is when our job started, we had to patrol. Nobody was allowed on the streets, they'd had plenty of warning, so we used go round with these patrols. There were cat calls and things thrown at us as we went round. In one particular area there was a leader, he wore a distinctive shirt, he was unmistakable and he was rousing them. They were on their balconies and he was a right rabble rouser. Now we weren't allowed to go into any houses so we devised a little scheme. We would send the truck round going slowly, attracting people's attention. It would get past this particular chap and it would be this, that and the other. And we came quietly with the jeep – we didn't nab him, he got inside his house – but we still

Company Sergeant Major May receiving the US Silver medal from Major Alan Hay.

went in and gave him a good what you call 'duffing up'. Of course there were complaints about it but... *Captain Alan Hay, A Coy, 16th DLI*

On 27 March there was a bomb scare when at 11.00 a telephone message was received that bombs had been planted in the District Commissioner's and the Income Tax offices.

I got a telephone call to go down to one of the government buildings in the middle of Tel Aviv. They'd cleared the building, the employees were standing outside being kept back by the police. I had taken a squad of men and the superintendent said, "There's been a report of a bomb being planted in here." I said, "Why in this building?" He said, "Well, this is the tax building – let's go in." So I had no option but to go in with him. There were cigarettes burning and you could see that people had come out in a hurry. So he went round, kicking wastepaper baskets, looking. There were a lot of rooms and we went round. After a while he said, "I don't think there's anything here." Well, it wasn't what I'd call a thorough search and I said, "Do you want an organised search by one or two picked men of ours?" "No, no," he said, "it's just one of these scares – they're starting to do this to disrupt life." He didn't think there was a bomb, they'd been getting these calls. *Captain Alan Hay, A Coy, 16th DLI*

The originators of these false alarms were not found. Eventually order was restored and the Durhams moved to Ar Rama near Lake Tiberius. Here they flung themselves into a programme of platoon and company training. This was followed by more exercises and training in Syria. On 4 June they returned to Kefar Yona and then on 18 June to El Quassasin Camp. This time the officers managed to fall out with the 'base wallahs'. Captain Jimmy Coutts provided one form of irritation for them.

Jimmy often seemed to be very angry, he was angry with life. A good officer, very good for an infantryman – aggressive, hating the Germans and hating anyone who was around to be hated. Very good company. When were at El Quassasin he had painted on his bivouac in black paint, "Base wallahs – hack 'em in the fork!" In big letters all across the thing. That summed up his outlook to base wallahs. *Lieutenant Dick Hewlett, B Coy, 16th DLI*

But it was the Durhams' behaviour in the local officers' mess which tipped the balance and they suffered the distinction of being banned.

It was mainly caused through drinking a drink which we christened 'Culloden Field'. This consisted of every drink on that row, everything on that row all in a pint glass. The base was a tomato juice and everything else went into it – it was a lethal concoction and we had everybody, including the padres, drinking it. *Lieutenant Dick Hewlett, B Coy, 16th DLI*

One night's enthusiastic drinking culminated in a wild impromptu game of 'rugby'. Even relatively senior officers were fully involved in the drunken revelry.

He was quite a lad Ray Mitchell, particularly when you were enjoying yourself in the mess. We knew we were going back to Italy. We started passing a cushion imagining it was a rugby ball, playing rugby and we were passing this cushion. It got very, very boisterous with the tackles and unfortunately there were one or two ladies in there. I think they took offence – and somebody sent

Officers of the 16th Battalion the Durham Light Infantry.
Back row left to right: *Ronnie Elliott; Brian Hill; 'Giff' Footer; Dick Howlett; Tim Marshall ; John Smith.*
Third row: *McVicar; Tom Periam; Arthur Pearson; Frank Flory; Bill Miller; Russell Collins; McKenzie; Ken Mitchell; Dai Dodd.*
Second row: *Jimmy Coutts; Laurie Johns; Gordon Harris; Pat Casey; Woody; Ray Mitchell; Geoffrey Lindley; Tom Reynolds, Henry Harris.*
Front row: *'Doc' Jones; Alan Hay; Frank Duffy; Dennis Worrall; Lieutenant-Colonel Preston; Captain Pritchard; Harry Mynheer; Bert Newman; Maurice Richardson.*

> for the Military Police! We ended up out side and Mitchell was there with his khaki drill shirt torn. The MPs came up and said, "Get in the van!" to him. He said, "I am an officer! I am a Major!" And he put his hand behind his shoulder and pulled his shirt round so they could see his epaulettes and there surely was a Major! *Lieutenant Lionel Dodd, Mortar Platoon, Support Coy, 16th DLI*

The Mililary Police departed thwarted, but the Durhams had gone too far in the generally quieter backwaters of the Canal Zone.

> We were banned for very unruly behaviour. They probably had

good cushy jobs and were there for the duration of the war. They didn't really understand that for infantry officers things were a bit different. *Lieutenant Dick Hewlett, B Coy, 16th DLI*

There then came a complete bombshell for all ranks as they found they were to lose their much respected leader on the very brink of returning to active service in Italy.

Colonel Johnny Preston said goodbye to us. We don't know why. He was a great colonel, we all got on well. He brought out soldiering in us that we obviously didn't have. He was great and when he gave his orders it wasn't in a profound military sense – he chatted to you. I know he was the same with other company commanders, when you had a particular job to do he would say, "Don't be suicidal, do what you can, you've got a few more battles to fight – don't make this one your last one!" He was encouraging in that way, he was very humane. He understood, "No good dashing in to lose more troops than need be." *Captain Alan Hay, A Coy, 16th DLI*

Dick Hewlett

Preston sent a last message to the battalion which he had commanded with distinction since taking over after the Battle of Sedjenane in March 1943.

On 24 June I was suddenly ordered to Italy. I had no time to say good-bye to the Battalion which I had the honour to command for 15 months. None will dispute the fact that the Battalion proved itself to be most efficient both in and out of battle. Our successes in Italy speak for themselves. We would never have done so well unless the Battalion fought as a team. This it did, with everyone doing his particular job and doing his best. Don't forget the old motto, "It all depends on me." I wish to thank every Officer, Warrant Officer, Non-Commissioned Officer and Man for their unfailing loyalty to me as their Commanding Officer. They made me a proud and happy man. Leaving you all made me feel very sad and I wanted to take you into action once more. You are all in great heart and I know you will have even greater success in the future. God bless you all and Good Luck. *Lieutenant Colonel Johnny Preston*

By now there were ever-increasing rumours that they would soon be returning to Italy. Soldiers are great fatalists and most seem to have accepted their imminent departure calmly.

We were expecting it, and it was quite a relief really to find that we were going back to Italy rather than face the Second Front with new dimensions as it were. New commanders, new chiefs, new everything. In soldiering you get a comfortable feeling about something, it's not always pleasant but you know the people about you, you know your commanders, you get to know the German habits – what to expect. We knew Italy and it wasn't bad fighting. If you're going to have to fight you may as well go in knowing something about what to expect. *Captain Alan Hay, A Coy, 16th DLI*

There were however hidden stresses behind the outward facades that they wore to preserve their self respect in the face of their comrades.

I don't remember being particularly apprehensive on this occasion. We had to go somewhere and we knew we'd had a good four months break. It was quite an interesting move to go back. Yet I think I must have been subconsciously apprehensive about it for I was taken ill with a very severe gut ache shortly after we returned to Italy. It was never really fully diagnosed and was presumed to have been some bug that I'd picked up in the Middle East. But I've wondered since, whether – being quite frank about it – whether it was some subconscious mechanism, telling me that I didn't want to go back there again. But I can't say – I know that I was suffering from a high temperature and very intense stomach pains. So it was on my records and it was only in recent years, that I've really begun to reflect on this. But it might not have been that at all. It might just have been some unidentified bugs. It does mean that I was actually in hospital in Rome for a few weeks. Every time that I seemed to be better and got up out of bed, my temperature would soar again. *Lieutenant Russell Collins, A Coy, 16th DLI*

Russell Collins

The Durhams had plenty more fighting ahead of them.

Chapter Seven

Gothic Line

In July 1944 the 46th Division returned to Italy to join V Corps under the command of General Keightley. They were now part of the 'new' Eighth Army which had been commanded since January 1944 by General Oliver Leese.

The situation had at long last moved on after the desperate battles of attrition against the Gustav Line. Time and time again the Allies had thrown themselves forward without success, until one last supreme effort breached the line in May. Mount Cassino finally fell and the Allies broke through to capture Rome on 4 June – six months late. The Germans were in headlong retreat back to their next defence line – the

Mount Cassino, strongpoint on the Gustav Line, finally fell in May 1944 with Polish troops taking the Monastry ruins. The way to Rome was open and it was captured 4 June. Allied troops in front of the Vatican. The Germans had not attempted to defend the city but had fallen back to their new defensive positions north of Florence – the Gothic Line.

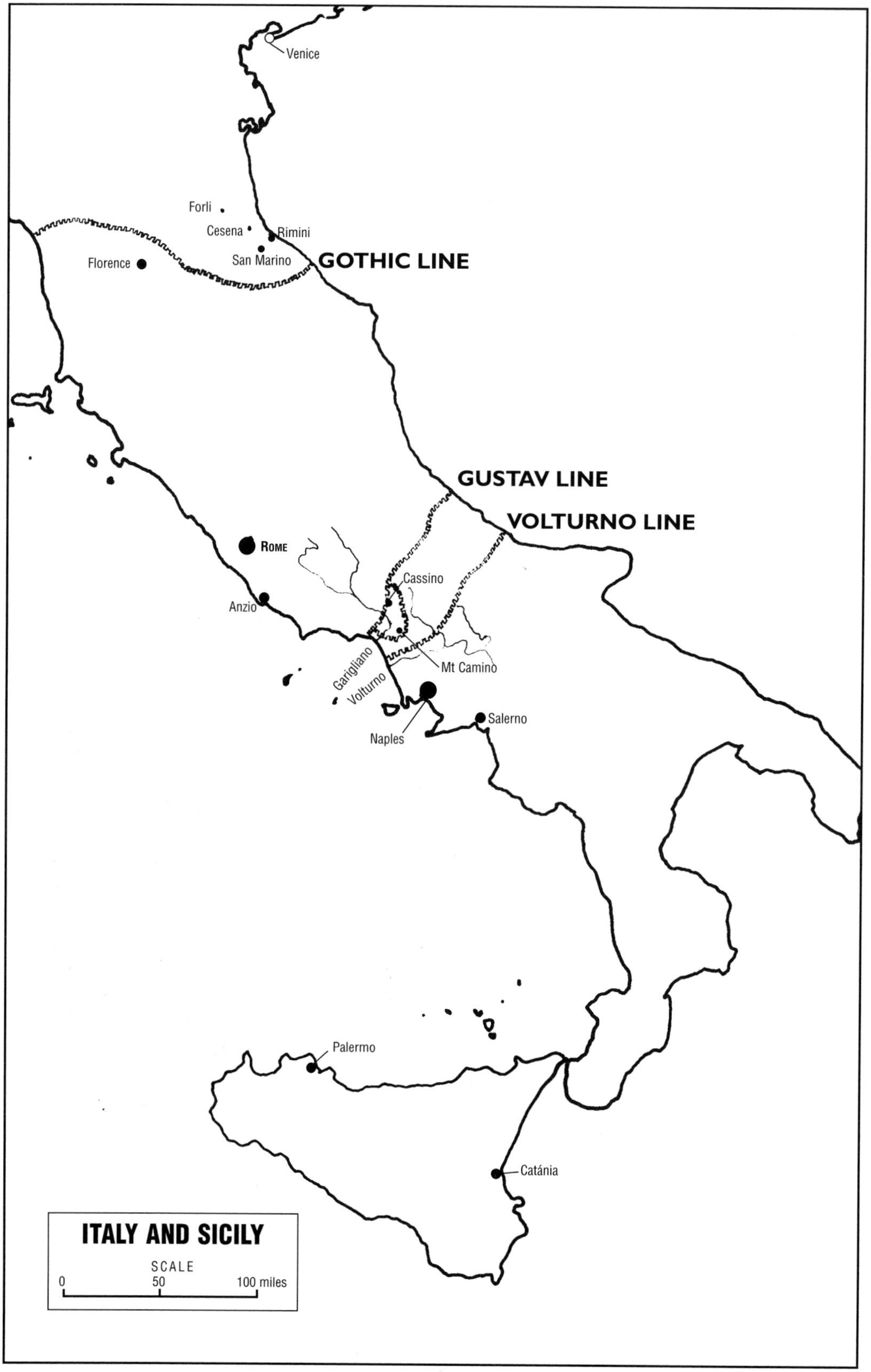
Venice
Forli
Cesena
Rimini
San Marino
Florence
GOTHIC LINE
GUSTAV LINE
VOLTURNO LINE
Rome
Cassino
Anzio
Mt Camino
Garigliano
Volturno
Naples
Salerno
Palermo
Catánia
ITALY AND SICILY
SCALE
0
50
100 miles

Gothic Line which extend from Pisa to Rimini. Just two days later the Normandy Landings captured the headlines and Italy was reduced to the inside pages once more. Had it all been worth it?

The question of what to do next surfaced once more: the British still had their eye on a push forward and into the Balkans; the Americans, now indubitably the senior partners, had always been sceptical. In strictly strategic terms the Americans were probably right, but Churchill almost certainly had half his mind on the post-war European geo-political situation. Control of the Balkans might be crucial if any disagreements arose between the Western Allies and the Soviet Union. This time the Americans got their way. Although the landings in Southern France, code named 'Operation Anvil', were no longer really necessary after the Normandy breakout, they were still to be given priority. The landing craft and no less than seven divisions were withdrawn from the Italian Campaign and assigned to 'Anvil'. With these resources, a series of seaborne landings, combined with a resolute frontal pressure could have destroyed the whole German Army in Italy. Their loss prevented a proper exploitation of the victory that had been won. The opportunity was lost and the Germans were successful in stabilising their front.

Unfortunately the Germans were masters of defence and the Gothic Line reflected their skills. Yet the Allies did not settle for containment in Italy. Alexander was ordered to attack once more with the intention of reaching the industrial and agricultural regions of Northern Italy. As before he was to divert all possible German resources from the developing offensive through North West Europe – but he only had 21 divisions to face no less than 26 German divisions. Only their near complete air superiority, with all its ramifications, allowed any thought of an Allied offensive against prepared positions. The main attack was to be launched by the Eighth Army along the Adriatic Coast and timed to begin on 26 August. It could fairly be said that the Allied plan lacked subtlety.

The Durhams landed in Italy on 3 July and initially moved to San Secondino before moving on to the evocatively named Bastardo near Assisi. They were put through an intensive programme of training designed to 'bed down' the battalion and ready them for the battles that lay ahead. Route marches, tactical exercises, river crossings, street fighting, weapons training and various specialist courses all sought to bring the men up to peak efficiency. One exercise, code named 'Trigger', was scheduled for 25 July.

> We were taken down to Perugia, which was quite some distance south from where we were, to man a route because the King was

paying a visit. We travelled nearly all day in these vehicles, red hot it was, lined this road, in the mid-day sun. They came along with water-carriers, sprinkling it on the road to keep the dust down. We would have been damned glad of having something to drink! The King came along, old George, he was dead white, he had these very white milky knees, with a blanket over him and it was red hot. The officers were saying, "Hip, Hip, Hooray!" And everybody was saying, "Hooray......" The lack of enthusiasm must have been quite noticeable even to the King. We were right up to our noses in it by then and the thought of having to go all that way just to go and say "Hello" to the King – nobody was at all charmed! That was supposed to be a morale booster!
Signaller Ronald Elliott, D Coy, 16th DLI

Back row left to right: *Ronald Elliott; Les Brown; Webberley.* Front row: *Mason; E Scriven.*

The training carried on until on 22 August the battalion started to move up into the line, reaching their concentration area at Isola di Fano on 26 August. Next day they crossed the River Metauro into the Isolo del Piano area and on 27 August their assault on the Gothic Line began. The 2/5th Foresters and 2/5th Leicestershires initially took the lead for 139 Brigade, and the battalion moved up behind them consolidating the

Churchill tanks move forward north of Isola del Piano, 28 August 1944.
IWM NA18088

gains made. Already the trickle of casualties was under way.

> We were shelled, at first sporadically, sometimes more heavily. People got whittled away, that's one thing looking back on it. How your platoon got whittled away without any particular action. A couple of casualties whilst being shelled or mortared; two or three blokes standing on a schu mine moving through a field. A lad on my left screaming out – he'd stood on a schu mine. People were always frightened of getting their balls blown off. This was this fellow's main shriek, "How's me balls, Oh God..." He was all right as it happened, he was badly cut in the lower thigh. They were nasty things. A fellow used to drop off here and there, no serious casualties but fellows with shrapnel wounds. Even in two or three days you lost four or five men. *Lieutenant Douglas Tiffin, D Coy, 16th DLI*

On 28 August the Durhams took the lead and launched an attack on the small town of Petriano.

> We had tanks with us. It was rather like these pictures which I always suspected were posed, pictures of people marching behind tanks with their bayonets fixed. But however that is what in fact we

M10 self-propelled gun passing a column of 2/5 Sherwood Foresters on the road to Petriano, 27 August 1944. IWM NA 18123

did! We were behind the tanks and it all looked a bit like a posed picture. There wasn't any resistance in Petriano itself but there must have been the odd sniper here or there because as we were walking up behind these tanks you could hear the odd whine and ricochet going off. We advanced cautiously into Petriano, taking the necessary steps, doing it all by the book very carefully. It could have been very heavily defended, as it turned out it wasn't! That was a great relief and I think everybody was a bit too relaxed. *Lieutenant Douglas Tiffin, D Coy, 16th DLI*

The Germans launched a furious storm of shell and mortar fire into Petriano.

We'd only been in Petriano half an hour before they started knocking hell out of the place. Shelling – 88s – the flat crack of a high velocity weapon – they shelled Petriano very heavily, knocking down buildings, there were a number of casualties. A lot of us, including my company commander Frank Duffy, we were in this stone house with a very thick wall, cellars underneath. We weren't in the cellars we were just relaxing. I was leaning against the wall, Frank Duffy was on my left. Further to his left there was a door which led into a bedroom. We were tired and we had our packs on which we just rested up against the wall. In came this chap who remarked to Frank Duffy and myself that there was a bed there, "Why don't you go rest on that?" Both Frank and myself said, "Oh, can't be bothered, we're all right where we are!" Three minutes later the room, the bed and

A signaller of 2/5 Sherwood Foresters operating his 38/14 Set, 28 August 1944. IWM NA 18090

everything else disappeared in a cloud of smoke – a direct hit by a shell, we were no more than a few yards from it. Frank Duffy simply got up, obviously dazed and shocked, muttered something like, "I'll have to go back..." He'd obviously taken more of the blast – I'd taken only a comparatively small amount. What struck me so forcibly is that if in fact we'd laid on this bed we would have been dead. *Lieutenant Douglas Tiffin, D Coy, 16th DLI*

Major Duffy was evacuated with concussion as a result of this incident. In the middle of the turmoil was their imperturbable Brigadier.

We got shelled quite considerably and I was so impressed with Brigadier Block who simply ignored shells as though they were just flies. He didn't even go through the motions of brushing them away! He didn't have a tin hat on he just strolled around doing good to people's morale. He was a brilliant Brigadier. *Lieutenant Dick Hewlett, B Coy, 16th DLI*

A report came in to the company headquarters that there were a fair number of casualties lying in the road further along the village.

Somebody said someone would have to go and pick them up. The road was being shelled. I thought, "Well, I must do something about it." One of the chaps in my platoon, a fellow called Tuck – who was a little bugger, a very bad disciplinarian, but quite an intrepid fellow in many ways. He said, "All right, I'll go and pick them up! I'll get a jeep." I thought, "Well, I'd better go with him!" We got in this jeep which he drove very badly and I subsequently learnt that he couldn't really drive. He drove it along this village road which was being quite heavily shelled, a rather hair raising experience. We picked these fellows up who'd been badly hit by shrapnel. *Lieutenant Douglas Tiffin, D Coy, 16th DLI*

That night the Durhams moved forward across the River Apsa to take the ridge that lay just beyond. This was done without further casualties and it became apparent that the Germans had retired to the Gothic Line proper behind the River Foglia. As they went they emulated the Russians' scorched earth policy.

They used to kill everything like, rather than leave it, because the Italians had packed in then. He wouldn't give them an inch, he used to kill the cattle, as he went back. There was always that smell, sickly smell of death wherever you went. *Private George Bland, Carrier Platoon, Support Coy, 16th DLI*

They also sowed their deadly seed in the ground.

We had our jeep to move forward and we hadn't gone a dozen yards when the thing went up on a mine. One of the section was sitting on the bonnet and he was blown off. I was sitting next to the driver but there were sandbags in the seats so that lessened the impact to a large extent. But when I got out I could hardly walk. I

Bren Gun carriers of 16th Durham Light Infantry lined up ready to cross the River Foglia, 30 August 1944. IWM NA 18122

could hobble. So they sent both of us back, we were the only two that were affected. Lance Corporal Harry Senior died that night.
Private Charley Palmer, Intelligence Section, HQ Coy, 16th DLI

Tiffin and his platoon had a terrifying experience when they wandered into a German minefield.

We found ourselves in a minefield. Goodness knows how we got there! Suddenly we were surrounded, all round us except for the way we'd come in. We hadn't suffered any casualties. Now, we had to get out, so we had to go back the way we came in – that's not to say that we'd laid a white line or anything. If they were the heavier tank mines they may not have exploded but these places were full of schu mines. So it was simply a case of retracing our steps a couple of hundred yards through this minefield. We walked back in single file and 'Muggins' went first! That was my job, everybody expected me to apart from anything else. And that was one of the most terrifying, or numbing experiences that I can remember. We'd walked into the thing but once you knew you were in a minefield that was a different matter. As they say, "We proceeded cautiously back!" Fortunately without any casualties.
Lieutenant Douglas Tiffin, D Coy, 16th DLI

Many of the men were terrified of the threat posed by mines. B Company also faced a minefield.

It was marked, just one strand of wire and these signs, skull and crossbones with "Achtung Minen!" It was obviously a minefield. The first section were wondering, "What are we going to do now?" The Foresters were supposed to be sending a guide, they must have made their way through somewhere. He hadn't arrived, so the Company Commander said, "Push on!" The first section ducked under the wire and gingerly walked through to the other side. The next section followed and they hadn't gone two yards when one of them stepped on a mine. They were mines with a wooden box with pegs in which held the top half from dropping onto the bottom half. The weight of a man would break the pegs and allow the top half to go down, ignite the charge and blow your foot off. They stepped on one of these and Lantern lost his foot. One was killed, something flew up and hit him in the throat and another lad was wounded. We called for the stretcher bearers, two of them came, they ducked under the wire – and they stepped on one. So that was another lad – he had his foot off as well. We managed to get them back out and the Company Commander called the first section back. Well if you have seen chaps walking on eggs – you imagine! This Corporal didn't know where to put his feet but the other lads knew where to put theirs' – they put them wherever he had put his! They all came back and didn't set another mine off. Mines was one of the things I dreaded most – there were that many ingenious ways of setting them up. 'S' mines especially,

Sherman tanks near the River Foglia, IWM NA 18397

The 'S' Mine standard German anti-personnel mine. It had a precast TNT filling and two alternative methods of ignition: SM Z35 push igniter and Y adaptor fitted with two ZZ35 pull igniters. A ball-bearing filled canister shot into the air and exploded scattering its lethal contents through the advancing infantry. TAYLOR LIBRARY

> they were a shrapnel mine, you stood on that and it jumped about five feet in the air and then exploded with about 350 ball bearings inside. You'd really no chance, you stood on one of them and that was it. With a mine if you stood on it that was it – you'd lost your foot or lost your life. *Corporal William Virr, B Coy, 16th DLI*

Some mines were laid by the Germans with the cruel intention of literally emasculating the advancing Durhams.

> They had a thing we called 'The De-bollocker'. A small pipe about nine inches long, they put it in the ground, unscrewed the barrel and put a bullet in. It was on a small platform, they put it in the ground at an angle. When you stood on it the bullet fired, up your leg – and that was why it was called the 'De-bollocker'!" *Sergeant Edward Grey, Pioneer Platoon, Support Coy, 16th DLI*

A further risk was the German snipers.

> We were rather badly exposed to snipers. We were on a low piece of ground where there was no cover and we were hit by snipers. We caught a sniper up a tree, a fairly bare tree, fairly visible actually. A very young German and we had to fill him full of bullets before he'd give up – I think he had 30 bullets in him before he died. He was a really militant Nazi. They were very incensed at

the damage he had done sniping at people. *Lieutenant Dick Hewlett, B Coy, 16th DLI*

On 30 August the Durhams crossed the River Foglia and after a series of tactical switches the next battalion objective lay in the small town of Mondaino and the high ground of Monte Gridolfo. There was no doubt that they were now running into well prepared defensive systems.

They'd had a lot of time to prepare this. Their Todt organisation had built concrete emplacements, they had tanks that were sunk into these emplacements so that you couldn't really pick them up, they were nicely camouflaged. They had fields of fire for their small arms and here we were in broad daylight marching up. *Major Alan Hay, A Coy, 16th DLI*

As Major Hay gazed across the open ground that lay between them and the heavily defended town on the towering ridge, he was extremely reluctant to proceed further without proper support. Colonel Denis Worrall however was under heavy pressure from Brigadier Block to make immediate progress.

The CO came forward and he said, "I want you to take those buildings." Which happened to be a place called Mondaino which

German sniper of the Fallschirmjäger *(paratrooper) engaged in his deadly trade.* TAYLOR LIBRARY

Front line of one of the German defence positions. IWM MH 6374

was in the distance, about a mile and a half. I said, "Well what is the plan, where are the tanks, what about the artillery fire?" He said, "Oh, they'll be coming." I said, "Well, we'll wait till we get some support!" Then he went away. We advanced a bit further and we took some prisoners. We were then waiting for support, this was just after mid-day and I got a message from the CO, that we were to advance immediately. I said, "Well what about the support, I can't see any support." He said, "That'll be coming." So we waited a while, nothing came. Then he ordered me, he said, "The General said you must advance immediately!" I thought it was absolutely stupid, broad daylight! We were in a bowl. When we were looking at this target the Colonel said, "Our friends the Leicesters are there." I said, "Colonel – they're Germans – look!" He said, "No, they're our friends the Leicesters!" This was his first mistake. The Leicesters on our left had not taken their objective and they were still heavily engaged plus one of our companies. The Hampshires on the right had taken their objective, our C Company was too far away to give us any support and I wasn't in charge of them. So we all had to do this, I was threatened, I assumed I'd get court marshalled if I didn't. But this was entirely unknown to me – a commander threatening.... I said, "Well this is suicide!" He said, "The General said you must or you will be in trouble!" *Major Alan Hay, A Coy, 16th DLI*

This left Hay with no choice and he briefed his platoon officers for what he knew to be a suicidal attack.

We were entirely on our own at this stage. I gave Lieutenant Marshall some buildings just short of Mondaino and there were some old buildings on our right that I gave to Lieutenant Hood. I brought up the third platoon with my company headquarters. I discussed it with them and said, "Well this is it, we've got to go!" *Major Alan Hay, A Coy, 16th DLI*

The power of military discipline can be illustrated by the fact that Hay was ordering his men to their deaths – just as Worrall had passed on the orders from Brigadier Block to him. Block himself was only 'following orders' from Major General Hawkesworth who had dictated that the 46th Division must 'BURST the Gothic Line.' A Company were just pawns on the Gridolfo Ridge battleground.

So we advanced over this open country. There were one or two vines to shield us a bit. We hadn't got very far. There was road just underneath Mondaino, not much of a road. They were going forward to these lower buildings on Mondaino and they were immediately under machine gun fire coming from the left. Tim Marshall got quite a few of his platoon across the road to the first buildings. Hood got to the buildings on the right. I was following up. When I saw Marshall's platoon in trouble I took my third

View from former German Gothic Line machine gun post.

IWM NA 18330

To ensure perfect fields of fire the Germans demolished houses and felled trees on approaches to the Gothic Line.

IWM NA 18329

A typical German field of fire on the approaches to the Gothic Line.

IWM NA 18333

Churchill tanks in the hills above the river Foglia, 30 August 1944.
IWM NA 18123

Self propelled gun on winding mountain road near Mondaino, 6 October 1944.
IWM NA 18392

platoon to support them. But the casualties were alarming. The Gothic Line had been prepared specially for this. They had their lines of fire, they had machines set and it was just chaos. I got forward, I said, "Where's Mr Marshall?" They said he's down here. By the time I got to him he'd been killed. I said, "Get out to the right to the other buildings." I got quite a few of them out. We rested up, counted the cost, tended the casualties. We'd lost almost a platoon. I looked at the situation, still no support, no sign of tanks. My wireless set had been knocked out by that stage and I was almost glad not to have a word with the Colonel. We re-assembled and I got Hood to go round to the right behind these buildings and we were going to attack them from the side. By that time we were only one good platoon which was the one I'd taken over. Just then two aircraft from the Desert Air Force came in quick succession and each dropped a bomb on what we were going for – which was super! *Major Alan Hay, A Coy, 16th DLI*

Unfortunately it later became apparent that Hood's platoon had been too close or even on the target and took several casualties from the bomb blasts. The remnants of A Company achieved their objective but were now in a parlous state.

We were still under fire from these machine guns on our left. The right was clear because the Hampshires had got that. C Company who were watching all this had no orders and when I saw Major Mitchell later he said, "We had orders to stay there and we were far too far away give you any small arms fire support – we had nothing else." We were in the first buildings where the first bomb had hit. Of course there were still Germans in there, wounded, that we hadn't time to look at. But this bomb had really done quite a lot of damage. At that time we had to count the cost. I had lost one platoon officer, I didn't know I'd lost the other one. I got the chaps in some sort of defensive positions. Getting behind these brick walls in the ruins, just to protect ourselves from this machine gun fire. There was certainly more than one machine gun. But they had us in their sights. We were near enough to the Germans for them to be shouting at us to give up, surrender. We were very low at that time, we had chaps who'd been wounded and couldn't be attended to, the stretcher bearers were doing what they could. The Sergeant Major was extremely good, he was rallying them, taking command of the spare ones. I said to him, "I must go round to the right where I sent Hood's platoon to see how they are doing." I found Hood had been killed and I am quite sure a lot of the casualties were caused by this bomb. *Major Alan Hay, A Coy, 16th DLI*

Hay was furious that he still had no effective support.

We were on the objective, this was the main attack, we weren't

Grave of S C 'Tim' Marshall in Italy.

there alone. Generals, all sorts of people, must have seen what we were doing. You think you are alone but all sorts of people are there watching the battle as it proceeds. This astonished me that we were allowed to go on without support. I said, "Well, we'll just wait, they'll obviously wait until night time to reinforce us." I went round the men and eventually the count of fit men was 27, about 90 went in. *Major Alan Hay, A Coy, 16th DLI*

As darkness fell they were extremely vulnerable to a German counter-attack. Hay decided to take the initiative to try and forestall the inevitable.

We'd come to expect if you got onto a place the Germans were bound to counter-attack. They know there are not many of us, they're going to counter attack. So I said to the Sergeant Major, "There's only one thing to do, let's go for these machine guns, it's dark now, we know where they are." I led this little composite company of 27, my runner was Wood, we'd lost the wireless set, and I was going for this machine gun. I had a grenade in my hand when suddenly I saw the tracer fire coming from another position and I was hit on the temple. My first thoughts were, "Have I pulled the pin out of the grenade!" If you get hit I think you're concussed, but I was still thinking and I said to my man Wood, "Are you all right?" "Yes!" I said, "Well I've been hit, I don't think I can carry on." I was trying to get my first aid field dressing out and I couldn't get the plastic wrapping off it, obviously I couldn't see very well, I didn't know how bad my wound was. But I was still thinking and I saw the two Germans get up from the machine gun, only 20-30 yards away, so I said to Wood, "Are the others near?" He said, "I can't see anybody." I said, "Well get up and run – I'll follow you!" He got up and ran and I ran – I don't know much about it after that. I remember meeting up with the Sergeant Major somewhere down the line and I said, "Were there many casualties?" He said, "No, nothing further." So I think the two of us, myself and my runner must have been well forward of the others. I said, "Well, make the men safe, any reinforcements come up?" He said, "No." The next thing I knew I was in some dressing station. I was demanding, they said, to see the CO. *Major Alan Hay, A Coy, 16th DLI*

Lieutenant-Colonel D H C Worrall

Over the next fifty years, rightly or wrongly, Alan Hay never forgave Colonel Denis Worrall for the events of that afternoon at Mondaino. Yet this action was just one of many which meant that by the night of 31 August the 46th Division was firmly established on the Gridolfo Ridge. Someone was responsible for this success, just as someone was responsible for the severe casualty lists. It is now difficult to apportion blame accurately. Forced decisions, bullying by superior officers, lack of time, a confused situation and over confident situation reports from other units – all these factors could, and often did, cause tactical blunders in the pursuit of non-negotiable objectives. While Hay had every right to blame Worrall from his own perspective, we, with hindsight, can see that Worrall probably had a thankless task.

On the morning of 1 September D and C Companies attempted to move forward.

> We were ordered to go up and reconnoitre a white house and, if possible, occupy it. We picked our way through vineyards and I was leading the platoon. About 10, 20, 30 yards in front of me I saw a movement. I suppose instinctively I just rushed forward because I was so close. I had a Tommy gun which was a very effective weapon at this sort of thing and I opened fire. To my surprise after some shouting and screaming, one or two people had been hit, getting in amongst this, there was a platoon of Germans, about 15, 16 came out with their hands up. Why they hadn't fired on us – probably they hadn't seen us because the

vineyards were fairly full of leaves. They got such a shock to find people charging around and spraying them with bullets that they put their hands up and came out. It sounds like something out of *Boys' Own Paper* but they did, literally say, "Don't shoot Tommy, don't shoot Tommy, don't shoot Tommy!" That's what they actually said and out they came. This Warrant Officer or Sergeant came up to me saying, "Don't shoot!" Because they were still obviously apprehensive that we weren't going to ask any questions and keep on firing. He pulled his wallet out and showed me his wife – "Frau"– and children – "Don't shoot, don't shoot!" He had a lovely Luger, so I took it and stuffed it in my belt and I thought, "Well there's a good souvenir!" *Lieutenant Douglas Tiffin, D Coy, 16th DLI*

Tiffin and his platoon occupied the position they had captured from which they had a clear view of the white house which had been their original objective.

There were five or six Germans haring back. We had our Bren gun and I suppose they were a couple of hundred yards off. We were firing at them – and we didn't hit them. I suppose in all the best books you would have done. It was quite a clear target. *Lieutenant Douglas Tiffin, D Coy, 16th DLI*

Tiffin saw possibilities in the situation, for he could see that they had caught the Germans on the hop. He sent back for reinforcements but none came and soon the position began to deteriorate as the Germans steadied themselves. It became obvious that behind them the company must be in difficulties.

Then somebody came up and said, "You've got to pull back!" I said, "OK!" I went up to the forward section to bring them back. Moving round to get myself at the head of the platoon. I thought I was under cover, I was fairly careful, I thought, but they must have had a line of fire, they must have come round us a bit. The next thing I knew I was hit, I felt as if a sledge hammer had hit my left thigh, with excruciating force. I shot down the bank down amongst the vineyard. I didn't lose consciousness or anything. What I do remember is finding my leg across my body. The bone was completely shattered so the muscles contract and the leg comes across. The first thing I did was wiggle my toes because I thought the leg was off or it was a goner. However I could wiggle my toes. I had enough medical knowledge to know that if you can't wiggle your toes it's a goner. But everything was working. Two or three of the blokes came round. I told the Sergeant to take the platoon back as we'd been told to. We pulled the leg straight. It wasn't bleeding all that much, it missed the femoral artery or else I would have been dead in two or three minutes. I suppose that's only a millimetre either way. I suppose I'm the luckiest man alive.

Douglas Tiffin

We stuffed it with a couple of field dressings, put two entrenching tools on and bound it up. That was that. Then I did feel a sort of blackness coming over me, obviously it was loss of blood and shock, but I thought, "You're going to die, you're dying!" You laugh now but I thought, "No, I mustn't, I mustn't!" The blackness came over and it went away again. This was about 11 o'clock in the morning. I was too badly wounded to move. I had some water, two or three people left water bottles. The platoon all went back, two blokes said, "We'll stay with you!" One of them was this fellow Tuck the other was Askill. There we were stuck in this vineyard. Time went on. The Germans were shelling and mortaring the road which was just at the bottom. I saw two of our tanks, they passed right in front of us, Tuck was trying to attract their attention, but it was hopeless. They soon came back again because there was a lot of shelling on the road. A lot was falling in the vineyard, you could hear the fragments whistling through. Tuck said, "I'm going to go back, get somebody up to get you out, Sir!" So off went Tuck. He didn't come back. Tuck subsequently told me that he couldn't find anybody who would go forward – it was considered too dangerous – he did his best I'm sure. I lay there until dusk fell. *Lieutenant Douglas Tiffin, D Coy, 16th DLI*

Tuck tried to get help but no-one would come back with him as the Germans were patrolling almost up to Mondaino and Tiffin was lying almost a mile further forward.

All of a sudden you could hear Jerry voices, they'd put patrols out nosing their way forward, they passed within a few yards of us. You could hear them whispering. We were tucked into a vine, we tried to cover ourselves with leaves and things. It was pitch dark by this time – midnight. What I really feared was that if they saw us, they'd shoot first and ask questions afterwards. Anyhow they never saw us. It was quite a terrifying experience. After midnight the patrols stopped – one or two o'clock in the morning – they started shelling again, very heavily. Along the road, but they were falling in this vineyard. The vineyard came down to the road and where it met there was a ditch. The shelling really was bad and it was a matter of luck whether you were hit or not because you could feel the shell fragments whining through vineyard. I said to Askill, "We'll have to get in that ditch, we're going to be hit!" It was twenty yards away and I dragged myself down there with his help. It was excruciatingly painful. People say, "That is impossible!" It isn't impossible if it's a matter of life or death. By this time it was three or four o'clock in the morning, so I'd been out there getting on 16 hours without any medical attention. But I was still conscious. It was obviously getting near dawn so Askill said, "I'm going back, I'm going to bring somebody up if I bloody well drag them up!" So off he went. That was perhaps the worst part of it, there I was on my own. Now if he didn't come back, what the hell was I going to do? Even if I was found by the Germans and I didn't get shot and they treated me decently – which I'm sure they would have done – one fear I somehow had got fixed in my mind was that I didn't think they had medical treatment as good as ours and that they would probably amputate my leg. I lay there with all these thoughts for maybe an hour and a half and I was beginning to get annoyed. Suddenly I heard voices and there was Askill with two stretcher bearers from the Leicesters. They said, "Come on, get on! This bugger's practically dragged us down here at rifle point!" Which he had! *Lieutenant Douglas Tiffin, D Coy, 16th DLI*

Together they got Tiffin back to the Regimental Aid Post. In all he had been lying out with no medical attention for around 18 hours and as a result of his severe wounds he was to spend the rest of the war in hospital.

Later that day it became apparent that the Germans had withdrawn and contact was for the moment lost. A Company supported by tanks took up the pursuit and captured Saludecio. By 10.00 on 2 September they reached the village of Il Poggio.

We didn't see many Germans and the following morning we all gathered at the church at the far end of the village. The village main street was a pile of rubble really. I was taken short and all I could do was go back up the street, there was nobody there and squat down in this rubble. I was squatting down and this door opened and two Germans came out and put their hands up! I've never felt so silly in my entire life, pulling my trousers up and trying to sound authoritative! One of them had a pistol and gave it to me. I was trying to fasten my trousers up at the same time! *Corporal William Virr, B Coy, 16th DLI*

Such amusing moments occured even in the midst of the death and general mayhem which surrounded them. Lionel Dodd was still laughing over one incident 55 years later.

Harry Mynheer was a great man for presence of mind. We were near a bridge in some little village and it was being shelled. There were semi-detached houses with a passage going through to the back of each place and we were in this passage. Harry and I were in there and several civilians had taken shelter. One of them was a great big strong Italian and as the shelling increased he started to have hysterics, "Oh mama mia..." Of course Harry, with his great presence of mind, decided what to do – so he slapped this great big Italian round the face! Well it cured him – because he drew back his right hand and he gave Harry such a blow in the eye! It did quieten the Italian down because he realised the enormity of

German 150mm heavy howitzer with a destroyed Sherman in the background IWM MH 6365

his offence of striking a British officer! How I kept a straight face!!!
Lieutenant Lionel Dodd, Mortar Platoon, Support Coy, 16th DLI

B Coy ran into the Germans again on Serra Ridge. A brilliant action was co-ordinated by Captain Arthur Pearson who led B Company and the Carrier Platoon up onto the ridge where 29 German POWs, one 88 mm gun and a Mark IV tank made an impressive haul. Unfortunately their left flank was exposed as 56th Division had not been able to keep pace and B Company suffered more casualties in trying provide a link between the divisions. Nevertheless, as the rest of 139 Brigade moved forward to cross the River Conca, their grip on the sector was firmly maintained until 4 September when the whole of the 46th Division was relieved by the 1st Armoured Division.

The 46th Division had played a vital role in shattering the Gothic Line and in just 12 days had severely degraded no less than three German divisions and advanced 25 miles in country which has been fairly described as ideal defensive country. It was a truly magnificent feat of arms.

Yet as the Durhams moved into Saludecio for a well earned rest they could also count the awful cost in human lives and suffering. During the short period from 27 August to 4 September the battalion had suffered 137 casualties. The men were exhausted and most of the beneficial effects of the six month break from action had been dissipated.

While at rest the battalion began to get increasing numbers of drafts who had formerly served in the anti-aircraft units of the Royal Artillery. The ever increasing air domination exercised by the Allies meant a corresponding reduction in the need for masses of anti-aircraft units and many had been disbanded for retraining as infantry. The Durhams, although not immune from a little schadenfreude over the fall of the once mighty 'gunners', tried to make the new drafts welcome.

> We tried our best to make them feel at home, tried to keep them together when they came to us so that they weren't broken up. They weren't very pleased about being 'down graded' to infantry. Oh yes, they felt that as part of the ubiquitous artillery they were superior – the 'right of the line'. They didn't feel very happy about coming to infantry and we had to make them feel at home as best we could. We did this by pep talks and so forth. They couldn't understand what the Durhams were talking about for a long time. It was always that language problem but little by little they settled in. They picked up the idea pretty quickly and they settled in. After all later it was a question of survival so you learn very quickly then.
> *Major Viz Vizard, HQ Coy, 16th DLI*

For some of the new NCOs the situation was undoubtedly difficult. They were good, well trained NCOs but they had no infantry battle experience.

> It was a strange thing to us – they were infantrymen and we were artillerymen. It's hard to explain. We knew that they knew what infantry was about and we didn't – we had to find out. Most of those lads and NCOs had battle experience as infantrymen. We came there as artillerymen. I won't say we weren't made welcome, mixed in fine with them, but for myself I always knew that somehow I'd got a lot to learn. I was never sure whether I was doing the right thing and of course they would realise that. That was a snag, being an NCO and learning, where they already knew. You always had it in the back of your mind, you were checking up, "Would this be right?" And it wasn't easy to find out from anybody else. *Sergeant Tony Cameron. A Coy, 16th DLI*

They would soon learn as the fighting escalated yet again.

Chapter Eight

Gemmano

After all too short a break the Durhams moved up from Saludecio to Gemmano ridge just south of the River Conca on the night of 10 September. There had been much heavy fighting over the last few days. The ridge was made of up of several interconnected hills of which the most significant was Hill 449 connected by a saddle to Hill 414 which lay immediately west of the village of Borgo. They were to relieve the 2/4th King's Own Yorkshire Light Infantry in the villages of Gemmano and Villa. The same night a German counter-attack had thrown the 2/4th KOYLI and 6th Lincolns back from their hard won positions on Hill 449, captured Hill 414 and infiltrated into the northern section of Borgo.

The Headquarters, C and D Companies of the Durhams moved into

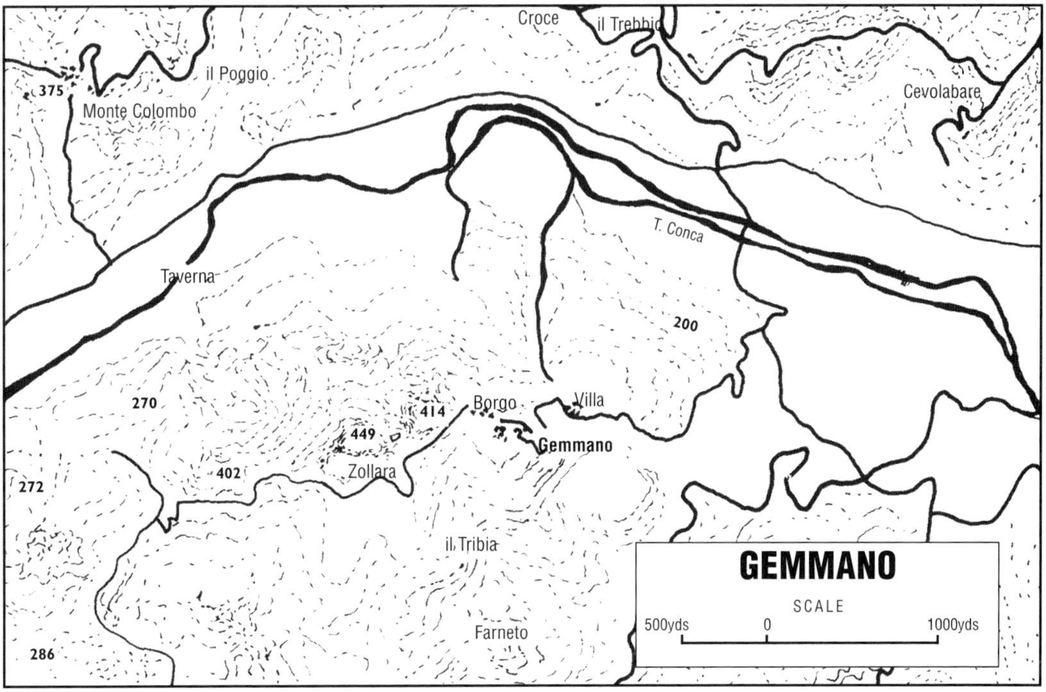

View of Gemmano village from a British observation post, 14 September 1944.
IWM NA 18623

Villa whilst A and B Company passed on up the hillside to the village of Gemmano itself.

> We were moving up when the shelling and bloody mortaring started. It was heavy, it was real nasty, the bloody place was alive then. We just kept on moving up you know, you halt now and again, move a bit, then halt a bit and then move a bit. They were stonking away all the time, mortar shells. We'd already lost one or two blokes and I passed 'Shack' on the road. I knew it was 'Shack', I could see him lying there, I knew he would be dead. There was nothing I could do about it, I had to just keep moving with my section, following the next section. We moved up practically right the way into Gemmano. We were mortared nearly all the way. Bloody nervous! There's no doubt about it – anybody who says they weren't is telling bloody lies, but you kept going. *Sergeant Tony Cameron, A Coy, 16th DLI*

The shelling was unrelenting and covered the whole area. Early on Dick Hewlett had his own miraculous escape.

> We stopped at this barn and brewed up and I was having a cup

British infantry on a rough footpath leading up the lower slopes of the Gemmano hills, 13 September 1944. IWM NA 18556

Mortar Crews firing on Gemmano, 8 September 1944. IWM NA 18476

of tea sitting on the ground at the door. A private from the Headquarters Company was sitting beside me. A mortar bomb landed right in front of us not 15 yards away. We both fell back, forced by the blast. He was literally blown to bits. His legs were broken, his arms were broken, everything was broken. All the contents of his cup of tea went all over me and I thought, "Oh my goodness, its blood!" But it wasn't, it was tea. I thought I must have been hit, I thought, "Oh my God, it's the end of my war!" I couldn't believe it – it missed me – he was as near as touching me and he was blown to bits. I didn't get a scratch, I couldn't believe it, most extraordinary. There was straw on the floor of this barn so there was a horrible mess of tea, blood and straw. *Lieutenant Dick Hewlett, B Coy, 16th DLI*

The Germans mortared and shelled the whole area incessantly throughout the next three days, assisted by excellent observation from the summit of Hill 449. On the open slopes there was little natural cover. At first Hewlett's platoon took shelter in a second barn. They found it was already occupied.

This cow was stopping us getting into the barn and we tried to push it further in and it just wouldn't. When the shelling started we thought, "We've got to get some cover!" So I said, "There's only one thing to do – kill this cow!" We shot it, put quite a few bullets into it and as it started to die we pushed it further in so we could all get into the barn. Then somebody had the bright idea of brewing up, they had a primus stove or something, which they put on the cow's back as a reasonably flat surface. And we got a cup of tea! *Lieutenant Dick Hewlett, B Coy, 16th DLI*

The villages themselves were the best refuges.

When we got into Gemmano we moved into the buildings and the particular building I moved into was opened at one side where it had been hit with shell fire from the Jerries on the hill opposite with a big black cross on it. You could get down into the cellar and get a bit protection there. They were big old fashioned strong walls and where there was a hole in the wall you could observe through there the Jerry position. You couldn't see much of them but you knew they were firing from there – you could see the flashes. We were stuck in that building quite a while – four or five days. We went to pick some grub up, they had transported some up near us at the bottom of the hill. And 'Shack' was still lying there, my mate, still lying there on the side of that road. By then he was black.... There was nothing you could do about it. *Sergeant Tony Cameron, A Coy, 16th DLI*

Some of B Company took shelter in a cellar of a ruined house.

There was shells landing all the time, clouds of dust coming in and nothing you could do. You kept hearing cries above, "Stretcher

Shattered ruins of Gemmano, 15 September 1944. IWM NA18560

The village of Gemmano after it had been taken. Dead Germans killed by the barrage amidst the ruins, 15 September 1944. IWM NA 18562, 18624, 18561

bearer! Stretcher bearer!" A chap was laid there, he'd just been covered with a gas cape. His lips were protruding through it just as though the gases out his stomach had dissolved the cape. There must have been people buried in some of the ruins because it stank, a terrible stench. It had been going on for a while and it was hot weather – the bodies soon putrefied. We were there about two days. *Corporal William Virr, B Coy, 16th DLI*

The villages were slowly smashed to pieces by the rain of shells.

I've never seen a town flattened as much in my life. We were stationed at the bottom and there was a road winding up. When we actually took it I was sent up with a message to headquarters. This road, there was tin helmets like flat plates. There was German bodies lying all over the place. Young lads with khaki shorts on. The smell of death in the place. *Private James Corr, B Coy, 16th DLI*

British troops patrol through a ruined street in Gemmano, 15 September 1944. IWM NA18641

Other men were forced to dig in as best they could into the unyielding ground. It was hard work indeed.

I dug in to the side of the hill. We had pick axes with us as well as entrenching tools. I dug into a bank and dug down. After about six inches going down I hit rock and it was really a question of hewing through it with your pick axe. Anyway I got it out, put the rock we'd dug up on the outer side to give us extra protection. Another section commander in my platoon was a young Scotsman who'd come from the artillery. I thought I'd go and have a look round and see how the other chaps who'd not been in battle before were doing. I saw this Jock Corporal with another chap, they were sitting in a slit trench which couldn't have been more than 18 inches deep. I said to him, "You want to get that bloody trench deeper, Jock!" He said, "Well, we've got rock down here!" I said, "Here's a pick axe, dig through the bloody stuff – but get your head down boy!" I gave the same sort of advice to three other slit trench pairs and I went back. Then all hell opened up and it continued all through the night. We really did get blasted. At first light I got out of my slit trench and had a look round. The Jock Corporal and the chap with him hadn't bothered to dig down any deeper, they both had their heads blasted off. There were a few others dead. *Corporal Kenneth Lovell, B Coy, 16th DLI*

The shelling went on for days and nature can only be postponed so long.

We were in this position where we were being heavily shelled with mortars and artillery. Naturally we wanted to go to the toilet sometime and there was no toilet around! The shelling died down and I decided to go outside near a tree to do what I wanted to do. Well, I got my trousers down and started – and so did the Germans! There I was, lying flat on my stomach with my behind facing the sky and I daren't move. I had to remain there until the shelling ceased. Then I finished what I was doing and went back to my company headquarters. It's a laughable thing now but it was serious then. *Company Sergeant Major Les Thornton, C Coy, 16th DLI*

Even amidst the death and destruction there were incongruous sights that could cause a man to question his sanity. Fresh from his clash with a cow, Hewlett now faced another set of farmyard friends.

Sergeant Jerrison

I happened to meet Sergeant Jerrison, he was A Company, I think, and I was asking him for information. It was fairly quiet, he was standing to attention as he spoke to me. There were chickens all over the place, one was on each shoulder and one on the top of his steel helmet. The chickens needed company and you couldn't push them away, they came back, I don't know whether they wanted food or they just didn't want to be shelled by themselves! A strange thing. They were standing on top of him and it didn't seem to worry him at all, extraordinary sight. I thought, "This is something we're going to laugh about one day!" *Lieutenant Dick Hewlett, B Coy, 16th DLI*

Unfortunately Sergeant Jerrison never got the chance for he was killed on 12 September.

Lieutenant Colonel Denis Worrall decided to make the perilous journey up to Gemmano to see what the situation was himself.

Colonel Worrall's own jeep was out of commission and his driver was trying to do something about it. He told the Captain Quartermaster that he would have his and grabbed me to drive it. He'd got the reputation of 'Mad Worrall' and I suppose in a sense I was lucky. He said, "Drive up to Gemmano!" We got round the corner all right at the bottom, got half way up the hill and there was a sudden shower of mortar bombs. It wasn't a very wide road, there was a deep ditch on the left hand side and I stopped the jeep, which was the natural thing to do, and dived in the ditch. He played holy hell with me, "Get back in the jeep, drive on, I'll tell you when to stop!" He got into the ditch with the idea of digging me out and we got back on the road – and the entire windscreen had disappeared and there was water squirting out of the radiator. But it went and he insisted in going on. I got behind the remnants of a house at the bottom end of the village and he pressed on – he threatened me with God knows what. In fact some time after he said I'd probably done the right thing, but in the heat of the moment he'd been very annoyed. *Driver Tom Lister, MT Section, Headquarters Coy, 16th DLI*

A Bren Gun carrier passing a burnt out Sherman on the approach road to Gemmano, 14 September 1944.
IWM NA 18659

Whoever they were, whatever they did and wherever they hid, it seemed to be only a matter of time before one of the innumerable mortar shells smashed into each one of them.

They opened up again that night. We had an almost direct hit on the trench. The huge lump of rock that we had dug out was blown in on top of me and pinned my legs. The Bren gunner, he got a chunk of shell or mortar fragment through him – he died. I was sort of pinned there with his dead body on top of me. By a lot of hard work I eventually managed to get out from under this slab of rock. I found Mr Hewlett and of my platoon, there were about five of us alive and unwounded. One or two were really screaming bomb-happy. We didn't know what had happened to the other platoons so Mr Hewlett said to me, "Go and have a scout round, see if you can find the Company Commander and let him know what the position is here." We were under very heavy mortar fire the whole time. Just below us there was a spring or well and chaps were going there to fill up their water-bottles, but the Germans must have had it really pin-pointed. They were warned not to go there but they still went down to get water. I must have seen a dozen men killed there. *Corporal Kenneth Lovell, B Coy, 16th DLI*

Whenever an attempt was made to get across the saddle from Hill 414 to Hill 449, it was met with devastating fire from machine guns firing on fixed lines. Lieutenant Frank Johnson of A Company took a battle patrol out between the lines. Alongside him was Sergeant Cameron who was increasingly aware that he had precious little infantry experience to justify his rank.

I don't know really what we were supposed to do except that we had to clear this farmhouse down in a dip towards the Jerry. We were on one hill, Jerry was on the other hill, he must also have been down in the valley as well. Frank said it would help if my section gave defensive fire on this farm track on the bottom of the Jerries' hill. I had a section, with my own Lance Corporal and a Corporal in charge of the Bren. We moved out and went a round

View of Hill 449 with walled cemetery below it at Gemmano, 15 September 1944. IWM NA

The Cross on Hill 449, 15 September 1944. IWM NA 18654

about way and came along this farm track between our positions in Gemmano and the Jerries' positions on the hill top where there was a big black cross. It was quiet so I told my lads, "Right, line up here, get the Bren down there!" Frank had said, "Now, you'll hear us move into that farmhouse," which was right in the dip. There was a lot of bangs and cracks went off, you could hear grenades exploding. I said, "Fire on the farmhouse!" We started firing and then the bloody Spandau machine gun fire came at us. We were on the track and they must have had fixed lines somewhere on the hill. I rolled back over, it was only about a foot high on the path against the hill, I never saw where the other lads went of course, everybody dispersed, luckily nobody was hit! I lay there for quite a while, I had a Tommy gun hugged in on me and the Spandau bullets were hitting along the track, I could practically see the splashes of dirt. When they stopped I lay there, no idea where the rest of the platoon was or anything. I didn't know whether to follow Frank, but in any case I couldn't because there was no-one to follow him with! I didn't know which way he'd gone so I went back the way I'd come. I got back on my own and there was half my section still there – where the other half went I don't know. They must have done the same as me, doubled back and the other half disappeared. That was at the time that infantry were like that – they were lads who'd been right up Italy, they'd had a belly full of that and at the first real thump a lot of them used to disappear. After that experience I thought, "Well I can look after myself better as a Private – it's no good me being an NCO when I can't control these blokes. I'm in a bloody spot looking after myself, never mind looking after them. I'm going to be a Private and I'll know what I'm doing for me!" So I asked to revert right back to Private after Gemmano – I preferred to learn from scratch. *Sergeant Tony Cameron, A Coy, 16th DLI*

D Company made several attempts to get across the open ground without success. As the shells continued to pour down on them, morale, not unnaturally, began to suffer.

I said to Les Brown over the radio – which I shouldn't have done – that we were in a hellish position, it was absolutely impossible, we weren't serving any useful purpose and we were just being chopped to pieces, it was quite panicky I guess. The next day it all started up again. Mortar shells were raining down upon us. There was a bloke dying on one side of this path, nobody could do anything for him, or nobody did, he was just bleeding away to death. People were being wounded, there was just this rain of mortar shells, fairly regularly almost incessantly. After one particularly bad spell of bombardment there was a panic and people rushed away. Even I got involved in it as well, Jackie Wells and I. We had the set with us on our backs at the time. We thought that we'd pulled out so we all ran out. The beauty of the position we were in was that if one followed the stream out of where we were, you eventually came out into the river plain which was part of the English occupied area. That was a natural escape, once you got out there you were safe. This is what we liked – to know our line of retreat. We ran out in panic and eventually when we got out into the clear I grabbed somebody running past us and said, "Where's Company Headquarters then?" He said, "They're still in there!" I said, "You mean to say we're not all out?" He said, "Oh no, just a few of us have come out..." So I looked at Jackie Wells and said, "Look, we've got to go back there.." So he said, "Yeah,

German position on Hill 449 after its capture, showing the view over the approaches and the walled civilian cemetery, 15 September 1944. IWM NA 18653

Sergeant Dabner, killed at Gemano, September 1944.

OK!" After a stream of bad language! So we went back in again. It was just as bad, 'Giff' Footer who was I think acting Company Commander gave us the thick end of his tongue, he played bloody hell, said, "Where the hell have you been?" So we said, "Well, we've been temporarily deserting but we've come back again!" Very shortly afterwards we did pull out and were relieved because quite clearly tactically it was a waste of time, we were doing no good, as a military position it was useless because there was nothing we could do about anything. *Signaller Ronald Elliott, D Coy, 16th DLI*

While the Durhams suffered on the bloody slopes of Gemmano, other units were gradually encircling the German positions. By 15 September they were forced to withdraw to Montescudo.

For the Durhams Gemmano had been a peculiarly unsatisfying battle, combining the maximum of suffering with the minimum of

British troops descending the rocky slopes of Gemmano after the battle, 15 September 1944. IWM NA 18640

directly effective action. They had been under continuous mortar and shell fire for over 72 hours. All ranks had been under incredible stress and it was beginning to show.

> I don't ever remember anybody saying, "I won't go!" But it got to the stage where you were saying to a Platoon Commander, "I think you'll have to take a couple of your sections this time!" And he would say, "Oh God no! I've been out so many times..." You'd have a long job persuading them. It was better doing it that way than it ever was saying, "Never mind what you think – you're going!" If you could get them to say, "Oh well all right, it's my turn – I'll go!" It's much better. By and large I was always able to do that. *Major Ronnie Sherlaw D Coy, 16th DLI*

For some it was all over.

> We had to bury, there must have been about twenty – not only Durhams, there was Germans, there was Italians. They'd caught them in a cutting. I'd never been on a burial party before, it scared the death out of me to tell you the truth! I think there was about ten of us on the burial party. The Medical Sergeant was there and the Padre. We had to collect them, pull them out of this ridge, put them on a stretcher, fetch them up, search them, get all their stuff out – pay books and identity discs, the padre collected them. I'd seen dead lying before, like, but when you come to pick them up, blokes that have been lying out in the sun and the rain two or three days, you know, the smell was terrible. They were rancid, man, their blood was dried on their faces. We had to pull them up and fetch them up a bit of flat field. As we were fetching them up this bloke kept rolling off, I don't know if he was a Panzer Grenadier but he must have been about 6' 3" and about 14 stone. This bloke from Houghton le Spring said, "He's trying to get away, get hold of him!" We took them off the stretcher, laid them on the blanket, put the blanket around them and then tied them up round their ankles, round their waist and round the neck. The army blanket doesn't cover your full length. We had a jeep with us and a three tonner. They lifted all the blokes on this truck and the smell.... There was a bloke in the three tonner sitting on top of them. I wouldn't get on the truck, I got on the jeep, there was about 10 of us hanging on to the jeep. We went to the 56th Div

cemetery – they wouldn't have now't to do with it, "No, no, they're not our blokes, try somewhere else." We tried another cemetery the 78th Div and they were the same. Then it was getting to tea time. We got a burial place in the finish, but they more or less kicked them into the ground, the graves were that shallow, like. The MO Sergeant said to me, "Din'nae be frightened of them, lad, they're dead man!" It was just the idea of lifting them and the smell seemed to be on your hands for weeks after. It was horrible, I was scared stiff to tell you the truth. *Private George Bland, Carrier Platoon, Support Coy, 16th DLI*

After a short rest the Durhams were ordered forward to the village of Serravalli on 21 September.

There was only about 20 of us left in the platoon. We were moving in file up this road and we came under fire from this village at the top of the road. Everybody hit the deck straight away, we pulled back down the hill and then there was only about 12 of us left, because there were a few hit on the road. We pulled back, re-organised and we were moving forward to take farmhouses to the right side of the village. In the distance you could see the peaks of San Marino. We formed up in line, headed up the hill across open fields for these farm houses. The platoon Sergeant, Frank Bousefield, passed me and as he passed me he said, "Tell the Platoon Commander I've been hit, I'm going back!" When the firing really started heavy we moved up within 50 yards of these white houses and there wasn't many left, I didn't see what happened to them. The section Corporal in charge of the Bren, he had a Tommy gun, he was standing up against a tree, I was lying down with a rifle. I could see Frank Johnson, the platoon commander 10 yards in front of me. The

Letter in response to Hewlett's notification to a Middlesborough family of the death of one of the 'Durhams'.

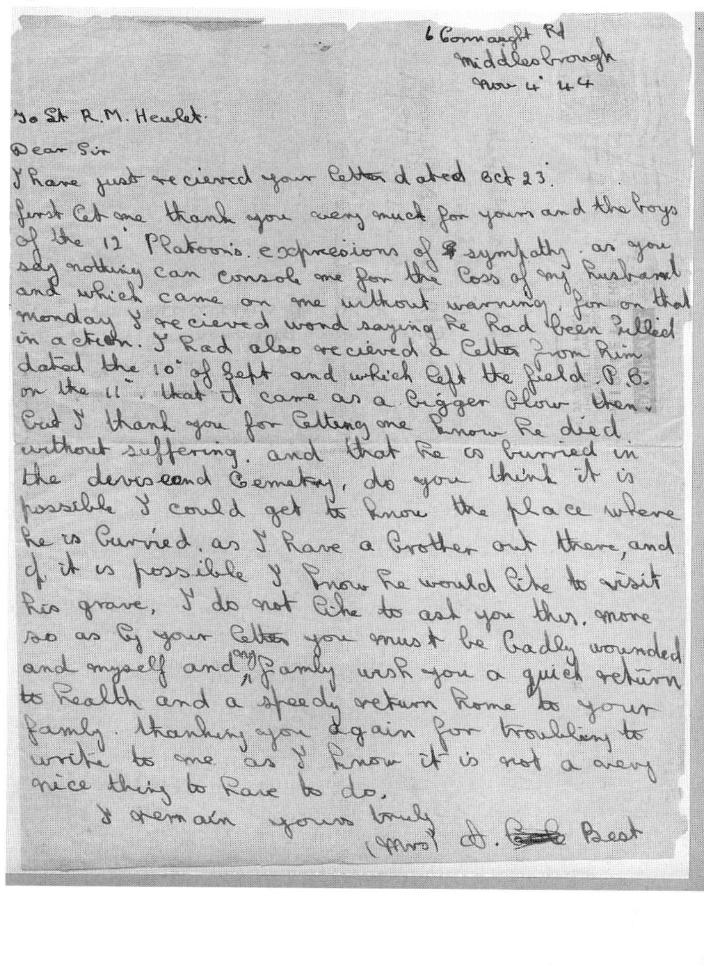
6 Connaught Rd
Middlesbrough
Nov 4' 44

To St R.M. Hewlet.

Dear Sir

I have just recieved your letter dated Oct 23'.
first let me thank you very much for yours and the boys of the 12' Platoon's. expressions of sympathy. as you say nothing can consol me for the loss of my husband and which came on me without warning, for on that monday I recieved word saying he had been killed in action. I had also recieved a letter from him dated the 10' of Sept and which left the field P.O. on the 11'. that it came as a bigger blow then. but I thank you for letting me know he died without suffering. and that he is burried in the devisonal Cematary, do you think it is possible I could get to know the place where he is burried, as I have a brother out there, and if it is possible I know he would like to visit his grave, I do not like to ask you this, more so as by your letter you must be badly wounded and myself and my family wish you a quick return to health and a speedy return home to your family. thanking you again for troubling to write to me as I know it is not a very nice thing to have to do,

I remain yours truly
(Mrs) A. ~~[illegible]~~ Best

section Corporal got a mark across the head, red, he goes down, but he started crawling away so I knew he was all right. I looked up and Frank's still going forward, so I jumped up to follow him. They started mortaring then and I looked round and I couldn't see no-one else. I shouted to Frank, "Frank, there's only the two of us!" Well he couldn't hear me, the mortaring had bloody started. He got down behind a burnt haystack. I thought, "That's bloody silly, that's not going to stop nowt – a heap of burnt straw!" It was 'BANG BANG BANG' bits of stuff flying all over and that's the last thing I remember.... When I came to I was lying there, no sign of Frank, no sign of nobody, but it was quiet. I'd been hit by mortar fragments. I was in a state of bloody shock – and I was sore – I had no idea where I was. *Private Tony Cameron, A Coy, 16th DLI*

While he was unconscious, A and C Companies supported by tanks successfully attacked, the Germans withdrew and the objective was consolidated. Even in this short skirmish the Durhams lost four killed and 14 wounded. Towns captured from the Germans were not safe environments.

We established our aid post in a house which was very comfortable. However, the following day the Company Quartermaster Sergeant brought us our rations, with a little extra for the wounded and sick. We waved farewell to him and said, "See you tomorrow." The jeep he was travelling in went upon a mine, he was killed and some officers hurt as well. The poor Sergeant was back in the Aid Post – dead and nothing could be done for him. We were all very shaken, for we ourselves, and an ambulance, had passed over that mined area a number of times. *Medical Officer Captain Jones, HQ Coy, 16th DLI*[9]

From Serravalli the battalion pushed on passing through the independent state of San Marino.

I went into the Ducal Palace where the men-servants were dressed in puce coloured velvet with knee britches and there were halberds on the wall. I actually saw a German officer's equipment lying around. They cleared out in a hurry – they'd been there – guests of the Duke. The old fellow hurried forward and said how glad he was to see us – which was lies of course! It's always lies – they're never pleased to see you. It's just another invading unit as far as they're concerned. *Major Viz Vizard, HQ Coy, 16th DLI*

By now the battalion had been reduced to three companies as C and D Companies were combined under the command of Captain Sherlaw. River followed river. The Marecchia was crossed on 24 September, the same day they emulated Caesar in crossing the Rubicon. Considerable fighting followed in the area around Camerano as patrols probed for the German positions.

Lieutenant Collins who had recovered from his debilitating illness had returned to the unit and was probing forward with his platoon when he had a lucky escape on 26 September.

> Alan Hay was my company commander and I was his leading platoon, and we'd gained our objective, a farmhouse. I'd made it secure and I'd found in the back room a bit of a camp bed. I thought, "Right platoon headquarters here!" I set myself up in there and I had this bed all ready, everybody else had their blankets just to lay on the floor. Then Alan turned up with his Company Headquarters, "Ah," he said, "Thank you very much, very nice Company Headquarters you've found for me!" Of course there was nothing I could do about it. So he pinched my nice billet! He said, "You can stay here – but anyway thanks for the bed." He set himself up on this bed and said, "Well, we're all right here, unless a shell happens to fall in that doorway!" We all laid down on the floor – and it wasn't long before a shell fell in the doorway! Poor old Alan, because he was upon the bed, he was the only one above ground and a shell splinter went through his hand. But that was a shell splinter that really had my number on it; but he'd rubbed it out and put his own on it! *Lieutenant Russell Collins, A Coy, 16th DLI*

As the battalion continued to take casualties by the 27 September it had been reduced to two companies only.

The pattern of the fighting was becoming clear. Although the Eighth Army was making fairly steady progress as it battered its way forward, it could not achieve a breakthrough. The results were disproportionate to the efforts being expended. Hamstrung by a lack of fresh reserves, the same battalions were thrown into action time and time again. Seemingly endless, miserable rain poured down on them making all forms of movement difficult and restricting the use that could be made of air support. The Germans were implacable and obviously resolved not to give an inch without a vicious series of counter-attacks. All in all a true Gothic horror.

In possession of Hill 449.IWM NA 18652

CHAPTER NINE

Casa Ricci

Russell Collins

On 28 September D Company, which had been temporarily combined with A Company, was given the task of attacking a group of farmhouses occupied by the Germans on the summit of Casa Ricci Ridge. Major Ronnie Sherlaw commanded the joint company and one of his subalterns from A Company was Lieutenant Collins whose reputation was sky high throughout the battalion.

> Collins was a right character, 'Winkler' was his nickname. 'Winkling' was the operation whereby you winkled Germans out of prepared positions. He really was a very good officer indeed, very dare devilish. *Signaller Ronald Elliott, D Coy, 16th DLI*

They moved off up a track leading towards the farmhouses which had the code name of 'Johnson'. Tanks were in support to give covering fire. This was not necessarily seen as a bonus.

> What a racket they make – as a matter of fact I used not to like fighting with tanks because one relies so much on a sort of sixth sense – you can just hear and feel if there is any movement, or any shells approaching and you can take evasive action. Being in the close neighbourhood of a tank is very like being blind; you're deafened and so you just lose the capacity really to exercise that sixth sense. I always felt very vulnerable if I was anywhere near a tank. *Lieutenant Russell Collins, A Coy, 16th DLI*

Nevertheless they did offer the advantage of highly concentrated mobile firepower if it could be directed properly. However there were also practical difficulties in getting them to do what was required once combat was under way.

> It was exceedingly difficult as you can imagine at junior level. At command level they had radio nets but at individual foot-soldier level it's extremely difficult. The way we had to try and communicate was very difficult but it worked. They installed a telephone on the outside of the tank, behind the turret, communicating to the commander inside. We were meant to run up behind the tank pick up this phone, crank the handle and then we were supposed to be able to talk to the crew inside. But even if the tank commander had his head stuck out, it was very difficult, the noise prevented one really communicating by shouting, so it was jolly difficult. *Lieutenant Russell Collins, A Coy, 16th DLI*

Infantry awaiting at the start line for the signal to begin an attack along with Sherman tanks. TAYLOR LIBRARY

Overall then the Durhams were ambivalent about their armoured support.

> As we set off from our start line, there was a tremendous amount of mortar fire and shelling. We went over open ground in open order and fortunately at that stage didn't have any casualties. We reached some out-buildings of a farm about half way to the objective. I'd got the artillery FOO to put down a lot of smoke on our left because that was where the fire was coming from. I was hoping that when the smoke was down we could advance. We set off and we got another big stonk during which a small piece of shrapnel went into the back of my leg. The difficulty then was that we were on a hill and I found that I just couldn't walk up the hill.
> *Captain Ronnie Sherlaw, D Coy, 16th DLI*

Sherlaw handed over command to Collins who pushed on up the hill.

> I was told to take over. The assault was launched by then and we had to get on with it. The idea was that the tanks would fire smoke canisters and put down the smoke screen to protect us as we actually charged the buildings. Now as we faced the two buildings, we were approaching the one to the right of the road, in fact the whole of our force was. So perhaps we were coming in by the right flank a little bit. I led the men right through this smoke area but the tanks were still firing these smoke canisters. They were things weighing about five or six pounds and dropping on you from perhaps a hundred feet in the air – it could have been very nasty. But I mean there was nothing for it but to press on,

luckily nobody was hit by them. We burst through and got into the right-hand farm house. The enemy had gone into the rear rooms, but we were able to get into the rooms nearer to us and I secured the first, the nearer building. *Lieutenant Russell Collins, A Coy, 16th DLI*

Once captured it was a race against time to consolidate the position.

That was the first stage. Then everybody would move forward, including company headquarters and the signals and you would dig in. Because the first thing that would happen is you would be counter-attacked. Maybe counter-attacked immediately or counter-attacked subsequently – but you would be counter-attacked. *Signaller Ronald Elliott, D Coy, 16th DLI*

As part of the D Company headquarters Elliot and his small team of signallers moved forward up the hill as fast as they could go carrying their wireless equipment.

We got a message back that company headquarters had to come forward to 'Johnson'. On the way there was this hollow by some trees and there were a lot of people there. I think it was what we called at the time 'Chinese trouble', which was this problem about bomb happiness and shell shock cases – genuine or feigned or whatever. People who instead of going forward had come back. We were having signs of people reacting to having to go into action by opting out as it were. A fair number of them anyway. Us two signallers and the Company Sergeant Major were going forward past these people – there wasn't much one could do about them. We moved on up the hill up towards this 'Johnson' feature. Shells and bullets stormed down upon us, a rain of fire, we dropped to the ground. It seemed to go on for a while so we just came back again to this hollow which was in an area which obviously couldn't be seen because there wasn't any firing at that point. We were then confronted by Ronnie Sherlaw, he had a wound on his leg, in an absolute fury. Playing merry hell with us and the Sergeant Major for not going up, and tending to bracket us with these other layabouts – these cowards or worse than that. We took great exception to this because we had seriously tried to go forward and had been prevented. But as far as he was concerned he thought we were just larking about not going up front as we ought to be doing. Anyway he was on his way out himself because he was wounded and Lieutenant Collins was in charge. *Signaller Ronald Elliott, D Coy, 16th DLI*

Sherlaw's temper did not improve on being evacuated by jeep.

We had these frames to bring wounded down on the jeep where you couldn't get a truck or an ambulance. I can remember one in particular was Major Ronnie Sherlaw. He was wounded in the leg. He was just on the roadside waiting for somebody to pick him up.

They bunged him on and he wasn't in such a terrible state I don't think, but he forcibly reminded me the first chance he got after he got back to the battalion recovered from his wounds, that he'd suffered more from my driving than he did through being hit in the leg! He said he'd had a headache for a fortnight after bouncing his head. The jeeps wasn't particularly well sprung and it was a bad, narrow road, strewn with boulders, You were making the best pace you could in case you got stonked. So you tended to put your passengers last and yourself first! *Driver Tom Lister, MT Section, Headquarters Coy, 16th DLI*

Elliott and his party made another attempt to climb the hill to 'Johnson'.

We then attempted to go forward again. Part of the difficulty was that there were vineyards with wires strung out mines. It was bloody impossible to travel through these with the wireless set aerial. We dropped down two or three times because of the fire and eventually we all came to the conclusion that, "Look, if we're going to get bloody killed we'll have to get killed! So we stood up and walked through it and of course, as would happen, we came through unscathed and got there. We arrived at 'Johnson' where the wireless set was in absolute dire need because they were being counter-attacked by upwards of 50 Germans with tanks and self propelled guns. *Signaller Ronald Elliott, D Coy, 16th DLI*

As quickly as possible they set up the wireless. Signallers saw themselves almost as non-combatants, but they had a vital role in such circumstances.

We were operating with a two man operation to a set halfway between ourselves and battalion headquarters so it was a pretty dicey sort of operation. We had problems all through the day of never being sure whether the communications were intact or not. Our job was to preserve and protect that position because without us they would have been finished. We had to direct artillery fire onto areas where in fact the Germans were, either infantry concentrations, the guns or tanks. *Signaller Ronald Elliott, D Coy, 16th DLI*

Having secured the farmhouse buildings on the right, Collins sought to complete the capture of the 'Johnson' buildings. The tanks would obviously be invaluable and this time, using the wireless net, he was for once able to establish contact with the tanks.

I left some of the troops there in that first building and went across the road to try and sort out the situation in the other building. It was on a slope and somehow we got up a staircase. The Germans were all concentrated in a downstairs room and looking down the stairs they were obviously in the room which was just out

of sight to me, I could see the doorway to it, but I couldn't see in. They were down there and we were in the upstairs room. It would have been very foolhardy to go down those stairs, so we lobbed down the odd grenade. Then we communicated by radio with the tanks. We made a little plan that we would get out of there and the tanks would blast the building. So I gave orders for all our chaps who were in and around this building to withdraw to the other building, to clear the way. When we went across to the other building, we could see the aspect of the left hand building which the tanks were going to fire at. They started firing and as soon as they started firing, a man came and appeared at the upstairs window. I felt it was one of our chaps who had been left behind in there. One of these sort of nightmarish visions, which I've never been able to rationalise or get out my mind since – he was waving his arms desperately – but the next shell went through the window and that was the end of him. That picture is engraved on my mind.
Lieutenant Russell Collins, A Coy, 16th DLI

The tanks rumbled forward

The tanks then started to move forward and tried to gain the crest, get a view over the crest, they like to fire from a hull down position. A tank came up, and when it got about level with us it

A direct hit on a Sherman with the usual result – they tended to burn.
TAYLOR LIBRARY

became just exposed. The German 88 anti-tank gun only a couple of hundred yards ahead, got it with a direct hit right on the front of the turret. We had a birdseye view, because it was only about 15-20 feet from us just outside the window. That shot went straight through the turret, it must have killed the commander, then the hatches went up at the back and the rest of the crew baled out quicker than you can say 'Jack Robinson' – very wisely in case it blew up. They were back down the hill like scalded cats. *Lieutenant Russell Collins, A Coy, 16th DLI*

The other tanks met a similar fate.

Two or three of the tanks were destroyed and the other one pulled out. There was always this difficulty with tanks that they don't like to go forward, because they are afraid of infantry, and the infantry don't like to go forward in case German tanks are around. So you always have to protect each other and sometimes you haven't the opportunity. *Signaller Ronald Elliott, D Coy, 16th DLI*

Although they now controlled the objective the whole position was extremely tenuous.

We put around such defences as we could, but the right tactic would be to exploit beyond the objective to anticipate the counter attack. Although we had gained the objective, we were really very insecure there. They were massive buildings and they weren't on the very top of the hill. Obviously the Germans hadn't given it up, they'd just withdrawn to re-group. There was a sense of foreboding, that the Germans were going to counter-attack again, they hadn't given up, they hadn't withdrawn and we were very exposed there. I put out such machine gun posts as I could and observation posts. Our gunner OP was a chap called David Purnell, he had the whole thing under observation, he controlled the battery and he did it extremely well. But I remember him coming up on the blower to me, we had reasonable radio contact then. He was asking what protection we had because he was planning supporting fire. "How close could our shells fall? Were we sufficiently protected?" I just had to use my judgement about that, but he actually made the calculations and directed the fire. When the Germans did counter-attack they just arrived in numbers, mainly from the left hand side as we looked forward beyond the building which we'd evacuated, so they got back into there. *Lieutenant Russell Collins, A Coy, 16th DLI*

Only grim determination and brilliant support from the gunners kept them in place.

The Germans attacked us throughout the whole of that night. We hung on, communications came and went but we always managed to get through and brought down artillery fire when it was needed. They fired phosphorus bombs at us, 88mm guns, mortars, the lot. There was hand to hand fighting. *Signaller Ronald Elliott, D Coy, 16th DLI*

Nevertheless on one terrifying occasion the Germans managed to get in the main building occupied by Collins and his men.

Then they actually got into the building that I was in and the Italian family were still there in the building. There was an ordinary standard doorway about eight feet high and a kitchen dresser blocking across it. I became aware suddenly of a great excited conversation going on on the other side – I could hear an Italian woman's voice and a German man's voice. So I got hold of a chair and got up on it. I looked over the top of the dresser and there, about eight feet away, was this very large German officer, with his steel helmet, haranguing this poor woman as to where the British were. So it was a question of what to do. I had no option really, I wasn't going to draw attention to my presence. I drew my pistol and fired at him. You always have to aim a little low, I tried to fire at his head but I got him in the throat actually. He fell like a sack of coal, the woman screamed and they hid under the table. I called to one of my soldiers, "Give me your Tommy gun!" I put that over the top and tried to make sure that I'd finished him off. He fell partly behind the door, so I then had to fire the Tommy gun through this rather thick door. A rather brave German soldier,

German troops observing the effect of their fire on the advancing Allies. TAYLOR LIBRARY

German assault gun ready to shell Allied positions. IWM MH 6376

only just visible around the doorway, dragged the officer away out of sight, and so that was that. That was how close the contact was there. But in fact as their numbers were coming up, David Purnell brought down this divisional concentration of fire all around us. Really it was very good infantry and artillery co-operation, because I knew exactly what our situation was and was able to convey it to him. Anyway the attack was repulsed and the main thing that broke it up was the artillery fire. We were really hanging on quite honestly by the skin of our teeth and were really pretty insecure. *Lieutenant Russell Collins, A Coy, 16th DLI*

Elliott was fully aware of the dreadful situation they were all in.

This was about the worst period, the period when I felt we were in most danger and we were certain that we would be killed or captured. Part of the difficulty was that we knew the dispositions of all of the brigade and even the division at that time and we couldn't think of where they could find anyone to relieve us, because obviously we had to be relieved. We'd held our position but we had come to the end of our tether and numbers were going down. *Signaller Ronald Elliott, D Coy, 16th DLI*

Finally a vital message came over in code.

Then my signaller was trying to receive a message on the radio from the Intelligence officer and he couldn't make head nor tail or it! So I took over the handset and the Intelligence Officer, 'Giff' Footer, was saying, "Peter, Mike; for figures six nine, read four three." Now it didn't mean anything to the signaller but it did to me! All units, for convenience of identitification of their vehicles, had a code number. The code number of our vehicles in the 16th Battalion Durham Light Infantry was 69, and the code number of the Divisional Recce Regiment was 43 and I knew that. 'Peter, Mike', is just of course pm, in other words this evening. So what he was saying to me was, "This evening you're going to be relieved by the Recce Regiment." So that was very good news indeed. *Lieutenant Russell Collins, A Coy, 16th DLI*

Ironically the 46th Reconnaissance Regiment were badly delayed and did not arrive on the 'Johnson' position until early next morning.

We hadn't realised that this was a possibility, so all that we were worried about then was whether we could last until they actually came. But they came, things were quiet at that moment in time during the night, the Germans had pulled back a bit, or at least weren't taking any particular action apart from the odd shell. *Signaller Ronald Elliott, D Coy, 16th DLI*

Dis-engaging a front-line unit in close contact with the Germans was a highly risky undertaking and had to be done in stages.

The first elements of the Recce, a couple of troops came up. I

Tanks and infantry moving up to support the attack. TAYLOR LIBRARY

couldn't help feeling rather sorry for them, because it was a rather precarious position. But you know we had gained it and we had hung on there. I showed them the position and the problems. I started pulling out some of my chaps, sending them back. *Lieutenant Russell Collins, A Coy, 16th DLI*

It was then that Signaller Elliott got a severe scare.

The Captain of the Recce troop came up, Winkler Collins showed him the position and told him where to put his people. He came in to see us and he said, "Well this is the signal terminal if you want to put your set in here, the Recce officer said, "I haven't got any signal set..." I looked at Jackie Wells and he looked at me, "Jesus Christ! We're going to get landed here..." But Winkler said this set belonged to the DLI, it was on the DLI network and therefore he would have to take it with him and he couldn't leave it – for which we were devoutly grateful. *Signaller Ronald Elliott, D Coy, 16th DLI*

Finally 'Winkler' Collins, his duty done, could make his way back to safety.

I was the last one left, which is the right and proper thing. I set out and by then I was absolutely on my uppers and exhausted. I just staggered back down the hill on my own, wondering how I was going to get back to the rallying point when along came a jeep. I recognised Harry Craggs, the Battery Commander of the battery that supported us. Dear Harry Craggs, he stopped and hauled me aboard and so we got back to the rest area. I collapsed and slept the clock round, absolutely exhausted. Unfortunately, when I eventually came to, the first thing I was told was that the Recce Regiment had lost the feature soon after we'd handed over. They'd come to it, they hadn't got the feel of it, they hadn't a cat in hell's chance really, at night. So it was very bad luck on them. Whether we would have been driven off if we'd stayed there – who knows? *Lieutenant Russell Collins, A Coy, 16th DLI*

The whole battalion had been relieved and was on its way for a well deserved period of rest and recuperation in the small town of Verruchio. Free from the imminent danger of death the men could begin to live again.

The first morning you lay in bed – I say bed, wherever you slept – till about 9.00. You got up, went down for breakfast, about 09.00-10.00. Then you started to getting your clothes exchanged, getting fumigated, baths, showers, medicals – FFI – fit and free from infection – free fag issue they used to call it, inspection for what they called mobile dandruff! Then we'd get up into the village and get drunk! *Sergeant Tommy Chadwick, C Coy, 16th DLI*

The men were by no means fussy about exactly what it was they were drinking.

The men very seldom got any beer. The only time they got anything to drink really was if they got into a village and the inhabitants had a wine cellar. Very often they did. We went into this barn place and there was a little Italian lad in a barrel stamping. I said, "What's he doing?" Of course the Italian explained that he was pressing the grapes with his feet. The mud on the floor was terrible. They just turned the tap on put a glass underneath and drank it – it wasn't even fermented it was just pure black grape juice – but they would drink it! *Company Sergeant Major Les Thornton, C Coy, 16th DLI*

Next on the agenda was women and here too many men were less than discriminatory.

They wanted a woman if they could – they were all human. They probably hadn't seen a woman for six months, and naturally if they had the chance they would. Half of the company lined up for one woman. *Company Sergeant Major Les Thornton, C Coy, 16th DLI*

Wine, women and song – the traditional amusements of the battle frazzled soldier – tried and trusted methods of forgetting the horrors they would be returning to in just a few short days.

> The lads had the time of their lives. The ladies of the town started off at five lire and a bottle of wine was a couple of lire! The boys were having a high old time until the Yanks came in and prices went up suddenly! We were compelled to see a photographic exhibition showing the ravages of venereal disease. They were pretty ghastly photographs, not the sort of thing you want to see immediately before lunch. The infantryman's view is, "Sod it, I may get killed tomorrow so why not!" But I think it put a lot of the lads off their nookie for quite some time and it made a lot more take precautions – they no longer rode 'bare back'! *Corporal Kenneth Lovell, B Coy, 16th DLI*

Less excitingly, rest periods also offered a chance to catch up on correspondence with family and friends back at home. Mail was absolutely vital to the maintenance of good morale. Even the most banal exchanges of views and news from loved ones could alleviate some of the mental scars of battle fatigue. But for a tragic few, those longed for letters brought even more despair.

> All mail outward had to be censored. I used to get a packet every day of mail to sign off before the post Corporal would take it – he had to have an officer's signature. There were some heart rendering stories of infidelity, quite a few pretty dreadful GI problems. What we saw was not the incoming mail, but the mail going back from the man to his wife. I used to give the parson a list of men that I could see were having, or were likely to have, severe trouble. He would make it his business to 'bump into them' and then develop a conversation to see what could be done. In fact he had contacts and he did at times write to fellow vicars and curates and ask them to call round and see what the score was. But there were a lot of very sad cases. They used to get very depressed. When I saw what they were writing home I used to make it my business to go down the lines and have a chat, "How are things?" This and that and so forth. He knew I'd read his letters so he would tell me and I would say, "Well, are you sure it's as bad as that?" "Yes," he'd say, "It's no good, its all over..." And we'd talk about this. He'd say, "Are you married?" I'd say, "No!" "Have you got a girlfriend?" "Yes" "Is she all right?" I'd say, "I don't know, I hope so..." Then I'd say, "Have you had a word with the padre?" "No!" "I wonder if you'd do that – have a word with the padre – nothing to lose!" *Major Viz Vizard, HQ Coy, 16th DLI*

On a slightly less serious note, various specialist personnel were plying their trades.

We had a battalion sanitary man, a Lance Corporal Hall who was responsible for the commanding officer's latrine and checking up on the latrines of the companies when we were out at rest. The commanding officer came round inspecting one of these positions where we were at rest and he sent for Lance Corporal Hall and said, "Corporal, the men are not using the toilets! It's all in the hedge-rows." Lance Corporal Hall, being the man he was, said, "Sir, I've inspected that, it does not belong to our men! It's Eyties!" After that we called him, "The Connoisseur." *Company Sergeant Major Les Thornton, C Coy, 16th DLI*

Meanwhile Signaller Elliott was suffering a reaction to his experiences on Casa Ricci Ridge. Fortunately a fellow signaller spotted the tell-tale signs.

I think Les Brown probably put in a good word for me, that I had just about come to the end of my tether. I was nervy and on edge. Very hysterical at times. A bit distracted. You become conscious that you've been pushed a wee bit too far. It was a continuous thing you see. I had had a couple of pretty bad experiences and this one was about the culmination of it. So I was pulled out and sent on a week's rest in Rome. *Signaller Ronald Elliott, D Coy, 16th DLI*

Chapter Ten

Fear

By the middle of October 1944, many men, like Signaller Ronald Elliott, found that they were approaching the edge of their personal limits. This was a very real phenomenon which eventually afflicted almost every individual and unit continuously in action. In the First World War their fathers had called it 'shell shock' but to most of the Durhams it was being 'bomb happy'. A jokey term for a very real and awful condition. Even decorated individuals with fine active service records found that it was becoming harder and harder to motivate themselves to go into battle time after time after time.

> You see there's this thing, I think you must call it 'battle fatigue'. I'm sure that I'd reached that point myself at the very end. At the very end, I was beginning to feel that, rather than saying, "Come on chaps follow me", I was rather saying, "Now look, I'm going to put my headquarters here, and you go there and you go there." Which many people had done from the beginning – but that was not my way. The thing that really weighed on my mind – it's sheer rationality really – was the number of officers and soldiers who'd been killed, wounded or missing from the start of the Italian Campaign to the end. Bear in mind that I was a platoon commander in the front echelon the whole time. I mean I used to regard a company headquarters as a place of comparative safety. So you reach a point "Come in now, your time is up." You just waver and think, "Well, this just can't go on." Everybody else that I could think of had been killed. There was nobody who had survived as a platoon commander as long as I had and it weighs on your mind in the end, that your turn must be just around the corner. *Lieutenant Russell Collins, A Coy, 16th DLI*

As the capture of each ridge or valley led only to the next obstacle, without any end in sight, those of the Durhams lucky enough to survive, realised that their luck could not last for ever. Fear waxed and waned in the short term, but in the longer term it could just grow and grow until it destroyed a man's morale, almost as comprehensively as the smashing fragments of a German mortar shell would destroy his body.

> One was just afraid. One was afraid all the time. Fear in this sort of context is not just a mental thing, it's a physical thing, you really have almost like indigestion, someone gnawing at your insides all

the time that you are in action because of fear – or even the thought of going into action. This is what you have to live with and that really is the quintessence of bravery, not doing something remarkable at any one time, but continually having to go in. What happens ultimately is that everyone is conscious that if you're continually being pushed into action – people are killed, your friends are killed and it's a state of attrition – eventually it will be you that will be killed because of the sheer inevitability of it all. This is the thing that gets you, you keep getting pushed forward, seeing people go, having to live with the fear. Ultimately there comes a point where you can't go on any more. *Signaller Ronald Elliott, D Coy, 16th DLI*

It is precisely this sense of self preservation that military training is intended to counter. Ingrained discipline, the repetition of the parade ground, the tactical exercises on the barren moors of England – all these are intended to bolster the morale of the soldier when he faces his enemy for the first time. As fresh drafts arrived from the transit camps to join the battalion, the veterans eyed them up. Conventional notions of the 'what made a hero' had lost their validity and boastful characters were looked on with caution. What could they be hiding behind that blustering facade?

You could tell them when they came in, "Wait till I get out to them Germans, I'll show you what I'll do to them!" I says, "Another bomb happy case!" Mind I was right – I always was. The ones that came out saying what they were going to do and what they weren't – they were trying to make themselves confident. But they were the first ones to go. *Private James Corr, B Coy, 16th DLI*

The quiet types sometimes seemed to withstand the pressures better.

We had one little chap, Jakeman in my platoon. He was a chap of 30, maybe 32, looked a lot older, he was the sort of chap you could imagine coming home at night and saying to his wife, "May I have my pipe and slippers, dear?" Then sitting down by the fire, lighting his pipe, reading his newspaper, being waited on by a dutiful little wife, chintz curtains – that sort of chap! Anybody less like a soldier than Jakeman I don't think you could ever meet – and yet Jakeman went through the whole campaign as stoically and gallantly as any of us. *Corporal Kenneth Lovell, B Coy, 16th DLI*

A 'bad hat' who surrendered to his yearnings in brothels and bars out of the line could be a trustworthy soldier in action.

My chaps used to come back and they were the worse for wear and the provosts used to throw them into a truck and bring them back to the guard room. Next day they used to come up in front of me and I nearly always found that the fellows who were the biggest offenders were the best soldiers. The ones with the long conduct sheet were the best fellows when you were in action. They were the ones that were still there. *Major Viz Vizard, HQ Coy, 16th DLI*

The officers assessed the overall makeup of their platoon – the men whom they would lead into action.

There would be 30 odd. As I got to know them better there would be 10, 11, 12 people you could rely on in practically any circumstances. There would be another 10, 11, or 12 who, if everybody else was doing their duty, could be relied upon to follow suit. Then there were 5 or 6 who were not particularly reliable. *Lieutenant Douglas Tiffin, D Coy, 16th DLI*

Whatever their personal make up and character, every action – no matter how trivial as recorded in the battalion war diary – required the men involved to once again screw up their nerves for action, seeking to tread a fine balance between dull morbidity and hysteria. For most it was the anticipation of what was to come that preyed on their minds.

Everybody was nervous until they got under fire and then it just left you. The time before was the worst. They'd say to you, "Look here, we're going in at 11 o'clock tonight!" Well, them hours after they told you were the worst hours. I would rather they just came to us at five to eleven and said, "Right you are, you're going in lads!" But they didn't, they told you beforehand. That was the worst part of it – the waiting – everything went through your mind. The loss of a limb was the main thing, we all had a dread of that, everybody said they'd rather go straight out. But once you actually got in, it was just self preservation. *Private James Corr, B Coy, 16th DLI*

But when the battle was over and even when they emerged alive, the very evidence of victory only pointed up their own frail mortality.

One of the nastiest jobs I can remember is that there were two Germans who had been blown to pieces. There was nothing except bits and pieces all over, which had to be gathered together and buried under the stones. That was all we could do. We found their pay books and photographs and these were sent back to the Red Cross and despatched. Immediately you sort of think, "Well, it could have been me – it could be anybody!" After all it doesn't matter how good a soldier you may be if you come under fire from a distance – the enemy doesn't know who he's killed. It's not a personal battle. *Private Charley Palmer, Intelligence Section, HQ Coy, 16th DLI*

As they surveyed the shattered corpses and pondered on what might lie before them it was not surprising that many men developed a peculiar affinity with their German counterparts.

We all respected the Germans as marvellous fighting men.

The ordinary German soldier had the respect of the average British soldier – he was seen as a 'marvellous fighting man'. TAYLOR LIBRARY

> There were the elite ones and some of them were bastards like the SS or the Gestapo type, but the ordinary German soldier was someone like ourselves. He was having to do the job. In the war situation, in action, it's rather like a triangle or lots of triangles. With some poor individuals at the very point of that triangle in the forefront of the battle. And behind them is all the back up, all these base people and all the generals – who are all pushing this poor bugger forward in fear and trembling – he's the one that is going into action. And the same is true of the other side. At these points, although they have to fight one another, they have a lot more in common and they have a lot of respect for one another. They are people put in the position of having to fight each other because of pressure from behind. So in a sense we detested rather more the hierarchy of the army establishment that were pushing us forward, than we did our immediate enemy. *Signaller Ronald Elliott, D Coy, 16th DLI*

The sheer stress and unyielding anxiety of daily existence was a boon to cigarette manufacturers. Non-smokers took up the pernicious weed, smokers became heavy smokers and heavy smokers were truly desperate men in search of a fag.

At times cigarettes were more acceptable than food. If it was very bad heavy shelling and food couldn't be got up, it was far easier to get 5,000 cigarettes up to a section than dragging food up in adverse conditions. Of course the smoking took the hunger pangs away, so it did help. This is where I started smoking properly – because everybody smoked. There's no doubt about it – it is a 'relaxer' especially if you're a bit tense. The cigarettes did help. *Sergeant Tommy Chadwick, C Coy, 16th DLI*

For some, drink or cigarettes, could not bury their feelings deep enough. They sought any way of avoiding a return to the front line.

You'd get a fellow walk up to one of the regimental policeman and he'd belt one of them straight on the chin – flatten him! The object of the exercise was to go in the nick, because it's better in there than it was 'up there'. But they got wise to that, so what they used to do was bundle him on the truck and get him up there. Then when he came out the first day he was on rest – try him and then bang him in the nick! *Sergeant Tommy Chadwick, C Coy, 16th DLI*

In extreme cases men could not wait in an agony of suspense for some unknown, but horrible fate, and chose to end the tension themselves.

A lad shot himself through the foot. I didn't see him do it, but I saw him come in after it had been done and one of the lads says to me, "He did that himself – I seen him!" It wasn't common, but there were cases of it. It was bad enough letting them do it to you without doing it to yourself! *Private James Corr, B Coy, 16th DLI*

There was some sympathy for men that lost their nerve and certainly the primitive brutality of the First World War executions was avoided. Every front line soldier was at the point of a pyramid even within the battalion and it was senseless to try and force a man into a situation where he could not cope and would almost inevitably let his friends down. Where possible, attempts were made to accommodate such men in administrative positions in the B Echelon or Headquarters.

We're not all built the same. I'm not talking about bravery or anything of that nature, some cope far better than others – whereas some lads just couldn't take it. A good Corporal or Sergeant would note these lads and when they came out of the line, either try and get the medical officer to talk to them, or LOB them – leave them out of battle. But numbers were so thin on the ground that it was hard to do that and you were taking lads back in who were sometimes a liability, they were that frightened from the outset. Sheer fright, freezing! If you said, "Move!" they couldn't move some of them, they just sat there or ran the other way and lay down somewhere. I know in the First World War people were shot for less but it was ridiculous because they just couldn't cope, their physical attributes didn't allow them to cope with the situation. You dealt with it sensibly, tried to find them a job as a dining room orderly back at battalion headquarters or gave them some mundane job working with the ammunition men or helping the Colour Sergeant with the food and supplies. Everybody understood it, I think a lot felt like doing it at times. *Sergeant Tommy Chadwick, C Coy, 16th DLI*

Most men tried their level best to avoid showing their feelings to their comrades. They worked out their own strategies for avoiding a breakdown.

I was on the point myself, several times, when you felt yourself giving in, losing it. I suppose everybody else felt the same at various times. Anybody that didn't must have been made of stone. You had to get a grip of yourself. Partly it was the fear of showing yourself up. In my case I thought of what my father would think about me, he went through the First War and I thought, "What a disgrace it would be!" It helped pull you together. I had a New Testament that my Aunt sent me and I used to open that at any page and read whatever it said and try to apply it to the position I was in! When we were going into the line I used to tie my bootlaces into about ten knots. I thought, "Well if I come out all right I won't mind untying all those knots! And if I don't, it doesn't matter" Silly things like that. To try and boost your own morale. *Sergeant William Virr, B Coy, 16th DLI*

The more successful a man was in fending off his inner fears, then the more catastrophic could be their eventual breakdown. To their friends, there was often no visible warning of their impending mental collapse.

A lad was singing his head off. 'Chat-a-Nooga-Choo-Choo' – it was his favourite song. Just then some Jerry planes came over. They were going to bomb the artillery in the next field, we knew they weren't coming for us, they were going for the 25 pdrs. He just started running towards the Jerries, screaming at the top of his voice! We brought him down and dragged him back. We had to hold him till the ambulance came and practically put him in handcuffs to get him in the ambulance. He was just away with it. In a split second just like that his nerve went. As fast as striking a match he was away! *Private James Corr, B Coy, 16th DLI*

Corporals and Sergeants were the glue that tried to keep the section and platoon together in the face of these pressures. They were all too aware that they could not take on the Germans alone. They may have issued orders, but if they were not obeyed in action then they were helpless.

You got out of them the way you treated them. We always said, that when you were in action with blokes, you would have been in a right pickle if you'd come too much of the heavy hand with them. If you'd been on a patrol and things got sticky they would have left you – but if you were all right with the lads they were all right with you. They knew that you were their NCO and you were responsible for them, but at the same time they sometimes looked after you. *Corporal Tom Turnbull, B Coy, 16th DLI*

Most of the NCOs were popular with their men and had developed an effective way of communicating with them based on a mutual respect and common purpose.

You can't compare wartime NCOs with peacetime NCOs. It's a totally different discipline, a totally different ball game altogether. If they were in barracks they most likely wouldn't have had a clue how things were run. But with the experience they'd gained in the job they were doing at the time they were very good. The lads that I had the pleasure to serve with had that tact of man management. There was no, "Corporal, Sir!" and spring to attention – it was Bill and Joe, up to Sergeant, then you called him 'Sarge'. A different discipline in action, it's got to be tempered. By the same token, reaction to orders has got to be immediate or you don't live to tell the story. It's a totally different discipline than one gets in barracks or a training establishment. *Sergeant Tommy Chadwick, C Coy, 16th DLI*

However, part of the reason for that popularity could be that they had a reputation of being careful with the lives of their men. This could be contrary to military efficiency and was sometimes a shock to raw young replacement soldiers who had not faced the grinding realities of war.

The patrol commander, he might be a Lance Corporal or Corporal, would brief you and say, "Well, we'll see what it's like lads and if it's a bit dodgy we're going to pull back a bit. Don't worry, we're not going to stick our necks out!" They were working lads and they're doing their bit, but they're taking the minimum of chances – which is understandable. With hindsight I can understand them, the war wasn't going to go on for ever, they weren't going to stick their necks out and get killed when they thought it was a bit unwarranted. Especially on fighting patrols, because the chances were if you were caught you wouldn't come back – you were out-numbered. Secondly a lot of these fellows were getting battle weary, especially after Gemmano, which knocked them all for six. So their outlook was different from mine, mine was excitement and wanting to get involved, where they'd gone through that period. They always say the first time in is the best, because you don't know what's coming and every time you go back after it gets a little bit worse, because you realise what you're going into. *Sergeant Tommy Chadwick, C Coy, 16th DLI*

In maintaining morale the role of officers was absolutely crucial. Many of the men understood that their company commanders could not usually lead the charge from the front. Tactical control had to be maintained or there could be no effective response to changing circumstances. However, when things went wrong, there was sometimes extreme bitterness against officers who were rumoured to stay on the 'start line' and left their junior officers and NCOs to take all the risks in an attack. Given the extremely localised perspective of the front line infantryman in action, this sort of criticism was occasionally misdirected, but it cannot, and should not, be ignored. Without going into personalities, it can be taken as a general statement that most of the men felt strongly that their officers should be visible.

> If you're in a tough spot and your officer has told you what you are to do, you expect him to be in the near vicinity. You don't want to be looking behind you for some miles to see whether he's there or not. He has to be part and parcel of what's going on. *Signaller Ronald Elliott, D Coy, 16th DLI*

Inexperienced officers often found it extremely difficult to make the old sweats they commanded follow them. Sometimes the contempt was coruscating.

> He was a very smart young man but he'd been transferred over from the Royal Artillery so he'd done no infantry training. Consequently when he took over the platoon he was forever on about, "Fix bayonets!" and this, that and the other. Of course the old soldiers just told him where to go, because you just didn't fix bayonets and charge. But he'd read it up and he was trying to do everything by the book. Weeks later he was into the groove and he was a first class officer. *Sergeant Tommy Chadwick, C Coy, 16th DLI*

It was their job to lead men into action, to cajole, to persuade, to threaten and ultimately to force men into line if the situation was desperate. Even an inspiring officer like Collins could have problems with his men.

> Some people are just scared out of their wits from the start and they just can't take it. I've had men who have refused to go forward, refused a direct order. I had to threaten to shoot them, because of the effect on the others if they didn't go forward. And they've said "Well, you can shoot me if you like, but I'm not going forward." You just leave them there, you can't shoot people in cold blood. But they would perforce be got rid of. Either the Regimental Police or the Medical Officer would have them – they would go sick. *Lieutenant Russell Collins, A Coy, 16th DLI*

Not every officer had the self restraint to cope with these life or death confrontations.

> He came to me and said, "Sergeant Major, I can't go up the

line!" I said, "What do you mean you can't go up the line?" He said, "Well if I go up the line I won't come back." I said, "Don't be silly, you have as much chance as anybody else!" He said, "No, I won't come back!" I said, "Well, come on, get in front of the Major then!" So I took him in front of Major Pat Casey from Jarrow who was my Major at that time. He said, "Look son, who's going to do your job? Your mate?" You're going up the line and I'll take you up with this!" He held his pistol up, "You'll go up!" That lad went up and he was killed by shellfire the next day. He had a premonition, you see, that he was going to go and whether you believe it or not – he did! You ask yourself, "Should I have sent him up or sent him sick?" But when you lose men then every man is necessary to do a job of work. *Company Sergeant Major Les Thornton, C Coy, 16th DLI*

This was not an isolated incident. Major Pat Casey may have been a Company Commander with considerable experience in battle, but he himself was probably suffering from extreme stress and finding it difficult to control himself when faced with a reflection of his own doubts and insecurities. In these circumstances the inadequacies of others acted like a red rag to a bull.

I went to Major Casey with a despatch and he was in a little room in this farmhouse. "Right!" So I gave him his despatch and he said, "I'll only be a second, stand there!" Then he says to this lad, "You're going into action! I'm telling you, never mind you're feeling bad, you're going in!" And he started whipping him across the face. The lad straightened up, "All right, Sir! All right! I'll go in, I'll go in!" Casey said to me, "What's your name?" "Corr, Sir!" He wrote it down, "What Company?" "B Company!" "Right, you'll be wanted as a witness!" I thought he was going to charge the lad, like, you see. I couldn't say now't, "Right, Sir!" About a fortnight later Casey sent for me, "You're wanted – Major Casey wants to see you!" So I goes up, "Yes, Sir!" He says, "You remember the incident? Well I put myself on a charge but the Private has not pressed charges. He says he was in the wrong and I was right to do it and he thanks me very much because he's a good soldier again." But he had put himself on a charge for striking a soldier – I thought he was going to charge the lad. But the kid wouldn't press charges, he went into action and he was all right, he came round. Casey had slapped him round. *Private James Corr, B Coy, 16th DLI*

Officers had their own demons to taunt them.

Every instinct you have under those circumstances is either to hide in your hole and not come out, even to look, or more than ever to run away. That's what any sensible person would do if circumstances weren't making him stay there out of pride or whatever – certainly not bravery! It's your duty to your comrades, it's an over-used word, not to desert. Unless someone tells you to get out of your hole and go somewhere, you won't go. I didn't go anywhere unless somebody told me to go and likewise I had to show the way to my juniors and get up and go – to tell them to come with me. *Lieutenant Gerry Barnett, C Coy, 16th DLI*

Not all officers were able to withstand their inner demons. Some just catastrophically lost their nerve in action. In these circumstance their men looked at them with an almost dull eyed curiosity.

We were in a farmhouse and the officer was out on a patrol. I was on guard outside this farmhouse and I heard this shouting and screaming so I went to investigate. It was our lads coming back and they were dragging him back. Major Stringer said, "Come on, pull yourself round, Lieutenant, pull yourself round!" Slapping him across the face. We gave him a couple of hot cups of tea. They shifted him the next day. *Private James Corr, B Coy, 16th DLI*

The officers who had the biggest responsibilities were the youngest and most junior in rank – the platoon commanders.

The hardest rank for commissioned officers was platoon commander. Because he takes the big patrols out, he does everything forward. His Company Commander is back at company headquarters. So the three platoon commanders were up with the three platoons, they take the rough edge, there's no doubt about that. A very, very tough job. Plus he's got to have the platoon tactics, for if he decides to make an attack on something. He's got to do it all. The thing that people didn't bear in mind when they criticised a lot of our officers – they weren't much older than us the platoon commanders. So they had a hell of a lot of responsibility for 21 and 22 year olds. I've a lot of admiration for them – a terrific amount – they had a lot on their plate. *Sergeant Tommy Chadwick, C Coy, 16th DLI*

As Lieutenant Russell Collins had found, the better they were, the worse it got.

The turnover of platoon commanders was incredible. If you were at all good as a platoon commander and lasted any time at all, before very long they would take you and make you a company commander. But quite often they were killed or captured or didn't last the course for one reason or another. I wouldn't like to say what the turnover was – but it was quite horrific. *Signaller Ronald Elliott, D Coy, 16th DLI*

They rarely lived to get the promotion they had deserved. Several officers came out from England and were immediately appointed as Majors in command of companies.

I must have been a pretty naive and simple minded soul. There were people who hadn't got a fraction of the experience, or success that I had had. Yet they were promoted to command companies or to go to Brigade Headquarters. The thing was, I was so much younger than most other people, I was still only 21. But no, I don't remember any great feeling of resentment. *Lieutenant Russell Collins, A Coy, 16th DLI*

Even the bravest found it was all getting too much for them.

I've a feeling that even the first time I was wounded that I was getting a bit sick of doing little patrols at night with half a dozen men. It was quite unnerving. Initially they didn't worry me too much, but as time went on, and the more I did, the more I was apprehensive as I went out. It's like all of these things, once you set out, you get on with it, but the apprehension before you set out is always just that little bit unnerving. I think at the time I got that second wound I was a little bit on edge. But it was nothing that a fortnight off didn't put right and I was in quite good form, I know, after that. It never got easier, it never got easier.... I don't know

As the fighting in Italy entered its final stages men found that it was becoming harder and harder to motivate themselves to go into battle time after time after time. TAYLOR LIBRARY

anybody who didn't find that the repetition of action didn't affect them one way or another. The funny thing was it very often evidenced itself out of the line rather than in the line. People got involved in excesses of one kind or another, they started being silly over drink, doing daft things. Stress just got on top of them. If you were never wounded you never got a rest! It's a strange thing but the wound gave you two or three weeks out of the line and improved you. *Major Ronnie Sherlaw, D Coy, 16th DLI*

Once wounded, most men, like the Salerno mutineers, saw it as their right to be returned to their own unit. If they had to be in action, then they would rather be with their friends than strangers.

I think the majority of people I came across who had wounds were a good deal more concerned about getting back to their own battalion than anything else. You made relationships in an infantry battalion which were quite unique. Somehow or other, to have to start again, to make the same sort of relationship, was something you didn't want to face up to. *Major Ronnie Sherlaw, D Coy, 16th DLI*

The front-line soldier was alone in any crowd. As they had no guaranteed future it was inevitable they found it difficult to connect properly with anything 'real' from their former civilian lives.

Certain things didn't register. You were in that little world of your own. It just seemed as if it was somewhere you'd always been and the rest of the world, your home, England, just seemed as if it didn't exist. In the front line you were a different species. *Sergeant William Virr, B Coy, 16th DLI*

As many teetered on the edge of mental collapse in the face of dangers we can barely imagine, just how did they manage to keep going in the face of it all?

There are all sorts of influences, not bravery, not even fear of court martial really in a sense. More a fear of loss of self respect. You think that you are a man, that you ought to be able to do this, and you would be less than a man to yourself if you didn't. You didn't think of King or Country or anything like that. It was also respect for your mates that were with you, you were supporting one another, you did it for them. You did it perhaps sometimes for a commanding officer for whom you had a high regard, he was doing it, he was there with you and you were part of it, you were supporting him. One reason why not many officers were shell shocked was that it was useful to have some responsibility. If you had some responsibility for others this gave you an extra determination not to let them down. *Signaller Ronald Elliott, D Coy, 16th DLI*

And so most of them fought on.

CHAPTER ELEVEN

Balignano

In the late afternoon of 9 October, the Durhams moved out of the Verruchio sector to relieve the Hampshires of 128 Brigade who had succeeded only with difficulty in crossing the River Fiumicino and capturing the Montigallo Spur. Early next day, 8 Platoon of A Company was given the task of patrolling forward to the village of La Crocetta at the foot of the Balignano Spur. It was obvious that the Germans were alert.

> I'd taken a bit of a gamble in going across a rather open space in open formation. We had all our heavy weapons and when we were in the middle of this open space the Germans opened up with artillery fire. It was a very, very alarming moment – shells falling, concentrated on a given area – and there we were. It's an exceedingly terrifying thing to be lying there, just cringing on the ground, really hoping that the ground will open up – the shells are falling within feet all around. You just think, "My God, the next one is going to land on me!" But somehow or other, miraculously, I don't think anybody was hit, there was a little lull in the firing and we got back under cover again. My chaps were beginning to say "Well, we're not going to go out there again." I had the greatest difficulty in persuading my chaps that we had to go on after that. I promised them we would go around a more secluded way. Which we did and so we got on. I didn't see any mines – we just carried on and got to our objective up in the village. We were rather shattered to hear later on that our Company Headquarters followed us up and poor old Ray Mitchell, the Company Commander trod on one of these things and had his leg blown off. But the whole of my platoon had gone up the same track – so his number was on it and not mine. *Lieutenant Russell Collins, A Coy, 16th Bn DLI*

Ray Mitchell

Mitchell who had been a keen footballer responded to his misfortune with a splendid demonstration of sang froid.

> "Bugger it, I shan't score any more goals with that foot!" *Major Ray Mitchell, A Coy, 16th DLI*[10]

It was decided to push on to Balignano Spur as soon as possible. Major Stringer, who had taken over command of B Company on 27 September, was given the task of capturing the feature.

We had an 'O' Group and Denis Worrall said to me, "Laurie, I want your company to go into the attack at 19.00 hours. You will have artillery support and you will be able to call for artillery support once the operation starts." This was a company attack and I had supporting me a platoon from another company commanded by 'Winkler' Collins. He was possibly one of the finest soldiers in the battalion who'd already got a Military Cross. He was attached to me because the feature I would have to attack was very large. It had to be a frontal attack although I did ask Collins to go round on the right flank, go up that way whilst my company went forward. You had a Battalion 'O' Group then you had a Company 'O' Group. I was going to attack with two platoons forward and one platoon in reserve, with Winkler Collins going round the right flank. 'H' hour was to start with a barrage at 19.00. The two platoons were to be divided by the sunken road. I was going to have a creeping barrage in front of me. I didn't have a Forward Observing Officer with me but I was told that the FOO would be at a vantage point and could call for extra fire with a Verey Pistol. *Major Laurie Stringer, B Coy, 16th DLI*

Laurie Stringer

Collins was shocked to be included in Worrall's plan.

We'd had a fairly taxing day, and then it was announced that B Company was going to put in an attack on this Balignano Spur, but they had to be re-enforced by an additional platoon. And guess whose platoon was deputed to re-enforce them? Mine! I felt that was really decidedly unfair and I thought Colonel Worrall had really taken advantage of us a bit too much. I said so to the B Company Commander, Major Laurie Stringer, I protested and he upheld my protest. He went and complained to the Colonel. But Colonel Worrall wouldn't hear of it and he said "No, his platoon has got to go!" When I told the lads that we were going to have to do this attack, there were groans all the way round, because we'd been the leading platoon all day. Then one of the older soldiers in my platoon, a man called Corporal Vick, a very nice, quiet gentlemanly man, a section commander, took me on one side, and said, "You know, Sir, I don't think I can go on, I've had enough. I don't think I can make it, we've had so much ..." I said "Well, I know the feeling, Corporal Vick, I feel just the same, but I've also already represented to the CO that we ought to be relieved of this and they've said, 'No we've got to do it', so we can't let the side down now – we must go ahead." He said "Well, all right!" And so off we went. *Lieutenant Russell Collins, A Coy, 16th DLI*

Lieutenant Stanley Waymark, a newly arrived officer took the left hand platoon, Sergeant Reading commanded the right hand platoon, while Lieutenant Dick Hewlett's platoon was held in reserve. Hewlett had been out in the Middle East since 1940 and was imminently due to return to England.

Because I was due to go home to England, having been abroad much longer than anybody else, they were going to try and keep my head down for the last week and I would be reserve platoon on the attack. Later they would see if I could be assistant transport officer to keep me out of the line of fire. *Lieutenant Dick Hewlett, B Coy, 16th DLI*

So the attack began. At 19.00 they fixed bayonets and started advancing up the hill. Almost before they started, Hewlett nearly blotted his copybook in the most dramatic fashion.

I was towards the rear in the middle, with Laurie Stringer. I had a Tommy gun and – guess what – it didn't work – in fact trying to make it work I very nearly shot Laurie Stringer. I chucked it away and got my pistol out. *Lieutenant Dick Hewlett, B Coy, 16th DLI*

Major Stringer and Lieutenant Hewlett followed the two leading platoons approaching under the cover of a heavy artillery barrage on the top of the hill.

The barrage was pretty colossal, it was a pretty heavy barrage. It was moving and we got to within about 20-25 yards of it. On the way up the hill we took quite a lot of German prisoners. They came out of their slit trenches with their hands up. I remember feeling, "Oh well, that's not too bad!" We took a substantial number of prisoners initially. They were an embarrassment because you've only got one objective and that is to get to the top of the hill and deal with the opposition there. But they had to be dealt with, so I told two or three men from Hewlett's platoon to round up the prisoners and take them back, get them out of the way. We had to carry on the action. *Major Laurie Stringer, B Coy, 16th DLI*

The German defensive fire began in earnest as they concentrated on B Company toiling up the hill towards them.

We were under small arms fire and nebelwerfers. Terrifying,

high trajectory mortars which the Germans had recently brought out. They made a whizzing, terrifying noise and their explosive fire was quite substantial. They were on the reverse slope and they were coming right over. I say this with very, very great humility, when you are leading men in action you cease to be concerned about yourself and you are worried solely about your men. To say that I wasn't frightened would be an exaggeration, no human being would like to be in that set of circumstances, but I didn't let it worry me, because I was concerned about managing the men that I had under command and trying to keep the casualty level as low as possible. The job had to be done and I was going to do it to the best of my ability. *Major Laurie Stringer, B Coy, 16th DLI*

As the attack developed 'Winkler' Collins was sceptical about the frontal nature of the plan adopted by his superiors. His experience thus far had convinced him that a flanking manoeuvre would be likely to achieve more success with fewer casualties. The village of Balignano lay on the ridge along the crest with a church on the right at the end of the street. Here Corporal Vick[11] fought his last battle.

We set off on the due signal and made our way forward and up, around to the right heading towards the church. There was a tremendous lot of shooting on the central part of the attack but there was no direct opposition where we were – which was obviously the better line of approach. When we got within about 50 yards of the church, I deployed some of the heavy weapons, the anti-tank projector because that's quite good amongst buildings and machine gun positions to give covering fire. I sent one section, led by Corporal Vick because he just happened to be there, to lead the assault on the church and if possible to get in. He got up there and just walked in the church door – he was shot – that was the end of him. The poor chap – whether it was the stress – he just forgot his drill at the moment. Instead of taking some precaution, a quick look round the door and throw a grenade in, he just walked in the doorway. Of course they were waiting for him inside and they killed him. *Lieutenant Russell Collins, A Coy, 16th Bn DLI*

Meanwhile B Company was struggling up the Balignano slopes. They were not progressing evenly, split as they were by the sunken road which ran up to the village.

It looked to me that we were having success on the right hand platoon, Sergeant Reading's platoon on the other side of the sunken road. Yet we were beginning to find the opposition stronger and I called for more artillery fire with my Verey pistol. Quite a heavy 'crunch' came down on to the top of the objective. It was splendid. I couldn't see what Collins was doing, there was a lot of heavy undergrowth and he was well away at the church end of the spur. Mine was more open, there were haystacks, I got up to them and I saw some Germans go into the haystacks and I fired into them. We made progress and I was feeling reasonably happy. Then from the left hand platoon one of Waymark's men came to me and said, "Mr Waymark has been hit, Sir." "Carry on, carry on, you can't do anything about it." Seeing success on the right, I thought, "Now one of the principles of war is that you reinforce success where you can and not failure, well this is the time when I ought to launch my reserve platoon to support Sergeant Reading." So I got the message to Dick Hewlett and he went into action on the right hand side. *Major Laurence Stringer, B Coy, 16th DLI*

Lovell was in Hewlett's platoon.

I led the chaps to go across the sunken road and from the top of the sunken road, I suppose it was about 10-11 feet high, I jumped down straight into a trench with three Germans in it. They got their hands up before I got mine up, so I took three prisoners. It was a machine gun post covering the advance up the sunken road. If we'd gone up the sunken road, because of the confined space, we'd have really had very much heavier casualties. *Corporal Kenneth Lovell, B Coy, 16th DLI*

Hewlett led most of his platoon off to the right as directed by Stringer who himself carried on up the hill.

There was a machine gun firing towards us from over on the right. Laurie Stringer said, "For God's sake take your men and go and silence that machine gun!" So we had to climb up out of the sunken road onto the hill. We were running, hopefully in the right direction, perhaps slightly more to the right than we should have been, but going towards the first bit of cover one could see, small trees and bushes and things. I had difficulty in keeping my men together because there were vineyards on it with wires stretching out. Peoples' small packs got caught in the wires and I was concentrating on trying to help them to disentangle them and get them in a state where they could be firing their weapons. This slowed the progress down but there was good deal of haste. As any infantry officer will tell you, the most difficult thing in the world is to get your men to fire back once they get fired on. One is inclined to sort of freeze up so that you can't do anything – but the only thing to do is to fire. It doesn't matter where you fire. It was whilst doing that that I got hit – it was like being hit by a double-decker bus. The weight of a bullet is unbelievable when it hits you, you can't shake it off. It hit solid bone, like a sledge hammer right through the knee joint. That was real agony, the bones were broken and it was hanging off at the wrong angle, any move was agony – as you can probably imagine. I said, "Don't leave me here, dump me down in the sunken ditch!" *Lieutenant Dick Hewlett, B Coy, 16th DLI*

Assisted by his batman, Private Roger Appleby, Hewlett was helped back to the sunken road. Here Appleby commandeered two of the German prisoners to help carry Hewlett back to safety.

> They found this door or old shutter and that's what they put me on. Then the mortar bombs started and Appleby was hit as were the two Germans prisoners carrying me. They dropped me immediately. *Lieutenant Dick Hewlett, B Coy, 16th DLI*

Dick Hewlett

Meanwhile the remnants of Waymark and Reading's platoons had got tantalisingly close to the summit. However the attack was breaking down.

> By this time we had got up fairly close to the crest of this feature, within 50 yards of the crest, when the enemy counter-attacked from the reverse slope and from the left hand side of the feature. They had a machine gun firing in enfilade, I was beginning to have a lot of casualties and the situation was beginning to look serious. The whole advance had been stopped and we were beginning to fall back. I could see we were having heavy casualties so I gave the order to withdraw. To describe that situation now in cold blood is very difficult. It was pretty chaotic. I had actually got up to the top of the feature and I came down the sunken road. *Major Laurie Stringer, B Coy, 16th DLI*

Collins was still marooned out of contact over on the right flank.

> Suddenly I became aware that everything was very quiet. I listened and looked to my left and I couldn't see anything. I'd had no message over the blower, but it became apparent that the company had withdrawn, aborted the attack and gone home. I'd got no message and there I was with my solitary platoon on the edge of the village. It was no good being there on our own. So then we returned to the start line. *Lieutenant Russell Collins, A Coy, 16th DLI*

As they fell back down the ridge the situation was a mixture of chaos and panic. It is not surprising that no two accounts agree as to exactly what happened. Dick Hewlett, for one, found himself in an awful situation as he lay in the ditch by the sunken road.

> Things eventually went quiet, it went pitch dark and I was just completely alone. I could hear Germans walking round looking for

their own wounded and I thought, "Oh my God, they're going to find me, I'm going to end up a prisoner of war unless I die from lack of blood first!" I was losing quite a lot of blood, I might well have been unconscious, lying to the right hand side of this road. *Lieutenant Dick Hewlett, B Coy, 16th DLI*

Stringer was coming along the sunken road.

Some way down it I almost kicked someone. I saw that it was Dick Hewlett. I stopped and I could see that part of his leg had been shot away. He was still conscious and he said, "Leave me, Sir, leave me, leave me, leave me!" *Major Laurie Stringer, B Coy, 16th DLI*

In his confused state, drifting in and out of consciousness this was not what Hewlett really wanted at all!

I can't remember why I said that – shock I suppose. I must have been mad, if I said that! They had difficulty in carrying me because I was in such agony with any movement of my leg. They decided to tie my legs together with my own boot-laces which kept the whole thing more or less solid. Lieutenant Dick Hewlett, B Coy, 16th DLI

Stringer, with the help of Sergeant Major Clark, managed to get Hewlett back.

I didn't leave him. I lifted him, I was strong then, I lifted him and put him my shoulder and I shall never forget, the blood went right the way through my clothing, my vest and onto my body as well. The Germans weren't coming down towards us but they were firing from a distance of about 50-60 yards. I carried him, he was screaming with pain, I carried him for about 50 yards and then he became too heavy. Fortunately I happened to see my Sergeant Major and there was an old Italian outhouse there, with a door. I put Dick Hewlett down on the ground and we lifted him onto this barn door and we carried him back to the start line. Major Laurie Stringer, B Coy, 16th DLI

Lovell and his men had also been forced back down the hill. He found Appleby.

I found Private Appleby who was Lieutenant Hewlett's batman. He was in a terrible state, he had a great big hole at the base of his neck and he told me that he and a couple of others had got Lieutenant Hewlett, using a door as a stretcher. Whilst they were carrying him down, a mortar bomb had dropped near them and he'd been badly wounded. He didn't know what had happened to the others. He just wandered... I broke my field dressing out, stuffed his wound and did the best I could to staunch the blood but it was almost impossible, it was such a gaping wound. There appeared to be nobody else on the left side of the sunken road. I had about four other men with me so we decided to go back to the bottom of the hill and find out what was going on. We carried Appleby back and as we got back to the house that we'd occupied Sergeant Winterhausen our Pioneer Sergeant came along. I said, "Can you get Appleby back to the Regimental Aid Post?" This was about a mile in the rear. Evidently he did, but Appleby died virtually on the doorstep of the RAP. *Corporal Kenneth Lovell, B Coy, 16th DLI*

Hewlett was also taken back to the RAP where his leg was examined by Doctor Jones. The bullet had smashed into the femur of his left leg just above the knee joint which had been shattered. He was in a bad way and tormented even further by the onset of severe dysentery. In these circumstances the tender ministrations of the padre did not help his mood.

I was lying on a stretcher by then. Padre Meek was letting me drink a cup of tea and with the best intentions in the world he poured tea that was too hot. I couldn't swallow it and it went all down my front – scalding hot tea all over me – as a blessing and a comfort! *Lieutenant Dick Hewlett, B Coy, 16th DLI*

Hewlett was in hospital for the rest of the war.

Stringer was fully aware that the action had not been a success.

My company had been cut about quite a lot, 20 or 30 wounded and 8 or 9 killed. Collins actually got up into the church area and eventually had to retire as well because of this German counter attack. I think Russell thinks that if we'd handled it better we might have got the feature the first time. He thinks we might have done the whole operation as a right flanking attack rather than attacking from the front. He thinks we might have had a greater degree of success and he might well have been right. *Major Laurie Stringer, B Coy, 16th DLI*

CHAPTER TWELVE

Cesena to Cosina

On 11 October the Germans were found to have retired from Balignano Spur and B Company occupied it at first light. The baton as front runner was passed to 138 Brigade who over the next few days made considerable progress through Longiani, Moniano and Magliotti to the lower slopes of Monte Romano.

Meanwhile the Medical Officer faced a slightly unusual challenge to his abilities in an army of men.

> The fighting had moved on and I was asked by the Italians to visit a lady who was in labour. Fortunately it was her fourth and she did most of the 'delivery' herself. The placenta took a long time to be delivered and it had me worried for I had no 'blood' or anything should difficulties occurred. However all was well. The local farmer was very grateful and we were given a chicken which was enjoyed by all. *Medical Officer Captain Jones, HQ Coy, 16th DLI*[12]

The 139 Brigade then took over again on 15 October, moving forward to open the way for an attack on Cesena. The Durhams were initially moved up only in reserve, relieving the 2/5th Leicesters in Celincordia early on 19 October. They were assigned the task of launching the assault on Cesena itself.

The first stage demanded the capture of the Monastery of Madonna del Monte, situated on a hill overlooking Cesena. C Company were given this task, assisted by the tanks of the 10th Hussars. Signaller Ronald Elliott was attached to Headquarters Company and he was given the task of accompanying the tanks into action. At first he was delighted.

> They had decided that co-operation between tanks and infantry wasn't particularly good, which was not untrue to say the least! So they decided to have a company signaller in a tank on the company network to provide immediate communications with the troops that were attacking. Because Jackie Wells and I were spare, we went into the tank in this attack on Cesena. The interesting part about that was that we'd always thought as infantry that the tanks had this marvellous life because every evening they pulled back to some sort of reserve position and laagered up, had food and got their heads down. We thought that was great. The poor old

infantryman tends to get stuck up where they were. I was in this tank and the communications side of it didn't work particularly well, they were pretty bloody, but it didn't really matter in the event because the battle went quite well and the tanks and infantry co-operated as they tended to do by some form of hand signal! The part that really intrigued me was that I was more afraid inside the tank than I would have been outside the tank. You were more conscious of shot and shell; the shrapnel pinged on the side of the tank; it was claustrophobic; it was noisy. You felt as though you were the focus point particularly of any likely attack and that you were vulnerable inside. Outside I guess you probably felt that you had a fair bit of room in which to be evasive, but you felt specifically in the line of fire inside this tin can. It put me off tanks!

The 16th DLI entering Cesena, 20 October 1944. IWM NA 19638

The infantry hadn't a great deal to commend it but on balance I preferred it to a tank man's life. *Signaller Ronald Elliott, Signal Section, HQ Coy, 16th DLI*

Still assisted by the tanks the Durhams now moved on the western suburbs of Cesena itself. B and C Companies moved down one of the main roads each with a troop of three tanks in support.

We moved forward. In a lot of Italian towns the houses are built right onto the road and there are no gardens on the side. So the houses were cheek by jowl on to the road itself. We moved forwards under a certain amount of desultory machine gun fire from a distance. We were walking along and the tanks were in the centre really. We were just slightly ahead of the tanks on either side. I was walking along by the side of the tank. I got to within 60-70 yards of the 'T' junction in Cesena itself and suddenly from the other side of the 'T' junction a Spandau opened up and fired on me and my chaps. There were no gardens, we were really sitting ducks. The tank commander saw what was happening – but I had got to within 25-30 yards of the 'T' junction, there was no cover on either side and I said to my Sergeant Major, "Follow me, Sergeant Major!" My idea was to run round into the main street, then get into the house through the front door – it was the only cover I could possible get. Sergeant Major Clark, instead of following me, he crouched up against the wall and stayed there and the Spandau picked him up and killed him without any trouble at all. Meanwhile the tank commander of the leading tank had seen what had happened and his cupola swung round and he fired an HE shell at this house where this Spandau was firing from and the whole of the house came down into the road. It was a fantastic thing. So that finished that particular machine gun – it could have been two. But there was a lot of machine gun fire coming from other directions at this stage. I ran round, got into the main road, ran across the garden into the front of this house on the left hand corner. If you go to the house today you will see machine gun bullet holes all the way round the entrance to the house – how they didn't hit me I shall never know. I flung myself at the door and fortunately it gave way. When I got inside the house I was met by ten screaming hysterical women! So, without being dramatic about it, imagine the situation. I was expecting a German counter-attack at any moment and I had these women to deal with. They were absolutely hysterical. Just a little way down the passage there was a cellar of some kind so I put my arms round all these women and I pushed them down this cellar. This all happened in the space of a few minutes. Some of my men got into the house and I stationed them round the windows because I expected the Germans to counter-attack. The Germans didn't counter-attack and I was in the house, couldn't move forward because there was so much machine gun fire outside. So I reported to the CO, I had signallers with my company. I told him what the situation was and I had instructions to stay for awhile. Then later to pull back slightly from the main road area. It was getting round towards dusk. Tanks can't stay in a built up area during the darkness because they're so subject to attack, so they had to withdraw. We had had a fairly strenuous day one way and another and I think it was at about 10 o'clock I was called to the set and the CO said, "You will maintain contact!" Which was devastating really because it meant that we weren't going to be relieved. *Major Laurie Stringer, B Coy, 16th DLI*

The town was secured as the Germans fell back without counter-attacking. In their absence the Italian civilians made their feelings plain. It was the first large town to be captured by the Durhams with a population of around 20,000.

The welcome given to the Battalion by the joyous population was one of tremendous enthusiasm. Women and children clapped and shouted and even flung their arms around the necks of the troops. Partisans paraded the streets proudly displaying their armbands. The older folks were rather more subdued but showed their gratitude by placing bunches of flowers on the bodies of those who had given their lives in effecting the relief of the town. In the main square lay shattered busts of Mussolini which had been thrown from the windows of the Fascist Headquarters. This was a great day for the Durhams and for the people they had liberated. *Major Laurie Stringer, B Coy, 16th DLI*[13]

British tanks entering Cesena, 20 October 1944.
IWM NA 19640

In all 73 German POWs were taken. It is fair to say that not all of them were so welcoming.

There were some virulent troops. The MO moved up a forward RAP and a mortally wounded Corporal from the German 91st Light Regiment was brought into the RAP. It was quite clear he wasn't going to last the distance to the clearing station. He'd been blown up in one of the houses in Cesena. I lit a cigarette and bent down to put it between his lips and he spat at me! This man was within minutes of death and he wouldn't even take a cigarette from me. There were some like that. Most of them were perfectly normal people like ours, just happened to be Germans instead of British. *Major Viz Vizard, HQ Coy, 16th DLI*

On 21 October the battalion was pulled back for a rest at Montefiore where they remained until 6 November. Virr, who had been on leave, saw them arrive. He was shocked.

German prisoners of war captured in Cesena, 20 October 1944. IWM NA 19641

I was there when they came out of the line. That was the time when I realised what we actually looked like after we'd been in action. It was the only time I'd not been in with them myself. Their faces looked ashen and drawn. You don't realise when you're in yourself – it shocked me. *Sergeant William Virr, B Coy, 16th DLI*

By this time it was clear that the battalion was suffering from long term battle fatigue caused by repeated exposure to danger in harsh conditions.

We got across this range of hills – and that's the end of it. Then you cross the next range, then the next range, you went from one line to another. This was the last line, they took some budging at that time the Germans. You gradually got them out of their positions and they withdrew, only for you to find that they'd got another line with another name somewhere behind it. It was a very frustrating period. *Driver Tom Lister, MT Section, Headquarters Coy, 16th DLI*

Their officers had been telling them that it could not last much longer for over a month.

In efforts to encourage the troops that the infantry 'slogging match' would soon be over and the armour would then be able to break through onto the plains of Lombardy, stories were circulated, somewhat prematurely, that "the next ridge is the last." Troops heard this rumour so many times during this stage of the campaign that they, in turn, circulated the story that, "The enemy had a large team of bull-dozers specially trained for the purpose of creating fresh ridges as they fell back!" *Major Laurie Stringer, B Coy, 16th DLI*[14]

They hadn't finished yet.

They left Montifiori for the concentration area La Fratta, near Bertinoro, where they remained until 14 November, when they moved up into the line to take over from 128 Brigade at San Varano. At first things went smoothly despite the appalling wet weather which turned even roads into quagmires. They were now on the great Italian flood plain and faced a series of rivers and canals. Next day they crossed the River Lazarro with minimal cost and advanced in good order to establish a defensive line along the River Bolzanino. On 16 November A and C Companies moved forward towards the Cosina Canal but they met strong German opposition and fell back almost to their start lines. B Company relieved them and began a series of patrols designed to test and tease the Germans. Sergeant Virr was briefed by Major Stringer.

He showed me these houses on these aerial photographs and said, "I want you to go out there and make some noise – a nuisance patrol you could call it. If you can get a prisoner, take a prisoner!" It was about three o'clock in the morning. It was pitch dark. I don't think there was a moon or anything. I took about four men that's all. I and one of the other lads had Tommy guns. We went out, past a pile of rubble after we'd gone about 200 yards. We could see where it was because we could see flames burning, flickering in this house. We carried on and finished up going through a soggy, wet field. We got more or less up to the farmhouse. One of the lads was deaf, he shouldn't have been there but he used to play hell with you if you didn't pick him to go on patrol! I said to him, "Right, cover me, I'm going to go forward to try and see if I can hear or see anything." I was just going to set off and this lad says, "What did you say?" I had to stop – I went back and told him again! Just then the door opened and this German came out with his coat down to his ankles, his rifle and just finishing his ciggie off. He was waiting for his mate, who came out and they were coming towards us. We opened fire on them, threw a grenade – we were supposed to make a noise and we did do. Then we went! We set off back. The Germans opened up with this machine gun and this mortar although they didn't really know where we were. We got back to our old positions and Stringer didn't believe me really that I'd been right out there. As I got back to our house there was these two Germans – they'd followed us

Men of 16th Durham Light Infantry during a rest period. IWM NA 20226

wanting to surrender! They couldn't catch us we must have been going that fast! *Sergeant William Virr, B Coy, 16th DLI*

Next day B Company were ordered into the attack on the 'Sleep' farmhouses.

'H' Hour was at 13.30. My plan was to send one platoon to an intermediate objective to make that 'firm' and then to take the two other platoons slightly left flanking round on the left hand side supported by fire from the intermediate position and I had a troop of tanks under command. The intermediate objective was a group of very, very ramshackle buildings which were hardly standing, they were almost razed to the ground. Very, very little cover at all but it was slightly raised from the rest of the surrounding countryside. There were something like 800 yards of almost open country that I had to travel over to get to my objective. Artillery and mortar fire were to come down just after 'H' hour. Just prior to crossing the start line the Desert Air Force were to come over and dive bomb the enemy lines. *Major Laurie Stringer, B Coy, 16th DLI*

When the time came, the pilots made a terrible error.

Unfortunately they mistook our line for the enemy line and they came over a minute before 'H' hour and dive bombed and machine gunned my forward position. This was most unpleasant and it was there that Denis Worrall, who happened to be up forward, saw what was happening and he stood in the middle of the road, he hadn't got a steel helmet on, waving his stick at these aircraft to try and let them know they were machine gunning the wrong line. There he stood in the middle of that Italian road and he was unperturbed and really didn't bat an eyelid. Fortunately they didn't create many casualties as far as my company was concerned and we were able to move forward. None-the-less it was a distraction and an unpleasant incident at a time when everyone was keyed up to go forward. *Major Laurie Stringer, B Coy, 16th DLI*

This kind of incident was probably inevitable in the confusion of war, but insult was added to injury in a crassly phrased claim published in *Eighth Army News* that, "The Desert Air Force was giving even closer support to the forward infantry." Having passed on his orders, Stringer watched his men move forward across the open field.

I gave the subaltern my orders and he moved forward at 'H' hour. I watched with my binoculars to see what sort of progress he was making. After he'd gone about 300-400 yards he stopped and there was no further move forward. I couldn't understand why this was. So I said to my Sergeant Major, "Sergeant Major, I'm going forward to see why Mr X's platoon is not moving forward." I went forward to where his platoon were lying along a bank and I said to him, "Why aren't you moving forward?" He said, "I can't, Sir!" I said, "Why not?" He said, "We're heavily pinned down by fire!" I said, "You've got a troop of tanks on your right giving you fire support – you are to move forward!" He said, "I can't move forward! I can't do it." I took him by the arm, I didn't get excited, I said, "You must move forward!" With that he left me and ran in the opposite direction. It was a very, very tricky situation. I was worried because the men had seen this incident and I wondered what their reaction would be. *Major Laurie Stringer, B Coy, 16th DLI*

The officer had lost his nerve and was subsequently court martialled. Stringer led the men forward himself under a fair amount of machine gun fire and a small group got to the ruined outbuildings. Here the situation deteriorated radically.

> I couldn't raise my head because as soon as you moved the machine guns started opening up again. That is where I saw a small family of rabbits round their mother just nearby and I said to myself, "If I get out of this situation I will never complain again!" *Major Laurie Stringer, B Coy, 16th DLI*

Snipers were also increasing the casualty list.

> We had two brothers in our company in the same section together and it was while we were amongst this rubble that the younger one lifted his head up and the sniper hit him straight through the head. His brother was there at the side of him. *Sergeant William Virr, B Coy, 16th DLI*

The position was clearly untenable.

> Suddenly on my right I saw quite a heavy contingent of Germans moving forward and there was no doubt about the fact that they were going to counter-attack me on that position. It became untenable. There was a ditch running just away from this intermediate objective and I took the men into the ditch. We were able to crawl along the ditch and into a deep pond some way away. One of the tanks had been knocked out but the other two were quite superb. They didn't pull back, they fired everything they'd got and covered our retreat back to this pond. *Major Laurie Stringer, B Coy, 16th DLI*

The crew of the abandoned tank also retired down the drainage ditch. Here there was an illustration of the desperate humour that could co-exist with gut wrenching terror.

> The only way back was along this ditch which was half full of water. The Germans were firing, clipping the top of the ditch. When I got in, the driver from the tank was in front of me. You were stretched out full length. You couldn't get up because they were firing across the top. They used to wear like a boiler suit and it was gradually filling with water. I said, "Go on!" He said, "I can't move, I'm like a Michelin man!" I pulled his trousers out of his gaiters and said, "Right, unzip it and crawl out!" I held his trouser bottoms and he crawled out of his tank suit. He just had his underpants on underneath – and a revolver! That was how we finished up at the other end of the ditch. *Sergeant William Virr, B Coy, 16th DLI*

They finally got back to the start line and began to lick their wounds. As a postscript there was one more illustration of the power of humour.

> We were in these houses drying our clothes off. One of the lads came out and he just had his overcoat, long johns and boots. He went to parade for something and the Company Sergeant Major

said, "I'll put you on a charge – you're improperly dressed – you haven't got your hat on!" He was kidding him! *Sergeant William Virr, B Coy, 16th DLI*

That night the battalion moved back for three days rest at Villa Grappa. When they returned to the line early on 21 November they were able to move right up to the Cosina Canal in readiness for their part in a mass Corps attack to be launched on the night of 22 November. Lieutenant Collins, who had been posted to command the 'dismounted' Carrier Platoon, took up a position in a farmhouse on the near bank of the Cosina looking some 200 yards across the other side to a large group of farm buildings obviously occupied by the Germans. They were awaiting orders and generally keeping an eye on the Germans' activities.

We tried to sally forth to make an exploratory patrol across the river and they opened fire and drove us back. What we observed was that the enemy were dug in on the far side of the river. In other words they had outposts, they weren't just in the buildings. Then I went upstairs in the farmhouse to look through a window to try and locate their machine gun posts. With my binoculars I was searching the ground and suddenly there was a great clattering and a long burst of machine gun fire, which spouted all around this window – broke through the plaster on the walls on either side, through the window and none of them hit me. But they might have done and you get to the point where you think, "My Gosh! I'm leading a charmed life!" *Lieutenant Russell Collins, Carrier Platoon, Support Coy, 16th DLI*

Later they made a further attempt to get a patrol across the river.

We went down into the river and all of us got down into the river bed. It was clear that there was a German machine gun dug in only about perhaps 20 yards the other side of the river. Of course we were in the river bed so we were all right. We had some grenades and I gave orders that we would try and knock this thing out with grenades. There were two or three of us and we were trying to lob these grenades into this machine gun post. Every so often they would fire back, so we had to nip up very quickly, throw our grenades and get down again. We did that alternately and there was a soldier standing next to me, I can see him very clearly, he was closer to me than you are now – about three or four feet away. In turn – just turn and turn about – we stood up and threw a grenade and when we had done that four or five times, there was a searing burst of fire when it was his turn – it went right through his head. That was really shattering; he was obviously dead before he hit the ground. That again was the luck of the draw, you see, I mean I had a fifty-fifty chance there. *Lieutenant Russell Collins, Carrier Platoon, Support Coy, 16th DLI*

Shortly after this, back observing from the shattered window, Collins saw movement from the German positions.

> I saw the Germans get up out of this same trench, two of them, the machine gun team, put a flag on the end of a stick and walk, not towards us, but back towards the farm buildings. Now I was very puzzled by this and I thought this was a ruse to get us to come out again. I'm afraid I was very suspicious about the whole thing, and I really had very little sympathy for those chaps by then. I had a great anguished debate with myself, whether we should shoot them or not. I thought, "Is it a decoy? Are they trying to get us to come out?" Because there was no obvious sound of a battle. In retrospect they must have thought their base had been taken. But anyway I shot them. I felt I really had to give our own chaps the benefit of the doubt. There were very few people I've shot in cold blood, particularly in the back, when they're waving a white flag, but there was nothing else for it really – so that was the end of them. *Lieutenant Russell Collins, Carrier Platoon, Support Coy, 16th DLI*

That afternoon Sergeant Virr, who had served right through the Italian campaign, found that his allotted measure of luck had finally ran out. He had taken out a fairly large patrol accompanied by Lieutenant Grey to try and find a suitable crossing for the imminent attack across the Cosina.

> We had to cross a deep dyke, up to your chest in water. We followed the path at the other side of the dyke. It went along a gully with a steep embankment up to the right, then the ground dropped away into a valley. The Germans had cleared everything so they got a field of fire, cut all the trees and bushes down and

German soldier operating a Schmeisser sub-machine gun over a trench position. It was fire from one of these weapons that caught Sergeant Virr in the leg. TAYLOR LIBRARY

chucked them into this bit of a ditch. We were walking on and I was leading man – I didn't want to, but I had to because I was leading the patrol. We were going along this gully and it sort of bore round to the right. As I went round there was a dugout dug into this embankment. At the entrance was a German sat on a chair bored to death! We both saw each other at the same time, both for a second flabbergasted. He jumped up, ran inside and hid. I thought, "I'm not coming running in after you, you've probably gone in and picked your rifle up waiting for me!" I shouted at him to come out. He wouldn't, I could hear him inside, he was frightened to bloody death, whimpering, probably expecting me to throw a grenade in. I shouted at him to come out, said I wouldn't shoot – "Nicht schiessen!" But at the top of the banking they also had a bloke in a slit trench – he popped over with his Schmeisser and hit me. I immediately fired back at him, his head was just stuck over the top, then I jumped, leapt into all this brushwood, in case he fired again. He never fired again. I don't know whether I hit him or not. I knew I'd been hit and I said to the lads, "Give us a pull up, I've been hit!" The officer said, "You'd better get back!" So a couple of the lads walked me back. I said, "Have a look, just see if my balls are all right!" I'd been hit at the back of my leg and it had come out – grazed my scrotum – into the right leg and must have hit the bone. They got me at the side of road, ripped my pants and said, "You're all right!" Two lads came running down with a stretcher, I climbed on it and they carried me back to the farmhouse. *Sergeant William Virr, B Coy, 16th DLI*

The Durhams' section of the Corps attack was launched at 20.00 on a two company front with A Company on the left and B Company on the right.

It was an appalling night, it was raining cats and dogs. Just near to my start line, which was just south of the Cosina River, there were two enormous haystacks. The Germans set light to these haystacks and they blazed away, lighting up the area for hundreds of yards in all directions. The plan was for a barrage to come down just before I crossed the start line and then moved forward, a creeping barrage on to my objective, a group of buildings called Corla the other side of the river. The ground led down to the river slowly and then the river was about 20 yards wide – that's all – it was a very small river but it was quite deep, strangely enough. Then the ground rose slightly on the other side, 400-500 yards the other side of the river to Corla. *Major Laurie Stringer, B Coy, 16th DLI*

The barrage commenced on time.

A few of the shells dropped short and this didn't help matters.

One of my men started screaming at the top of his voice, absolutely hysterical. It only wants someone to do that and it has a very adverse effect upon the rest of the company who are already tensed up. I caught hold of him by the front of his battledress and said, "I am telling you to stop that noise!" It didn't make a scrap of difference at all to him, he just kept on screaming. Imagine it, rain, two haystacks alight, ground soggy, going into the attack and there was this man creating an unpleasant situation. I knew there was only one thing I could do – I hit him with my fist on the chin and it stopped him! I never regretted doing that, if I was faced with the same situation again I would do exactly the same. It was the only way that I saw that I was able to stop him. As far as he was concerned that was the end of his fighting, he went back as a battle exhaustion case and I didn't ever see him again. *Major Laurie Stringer, B Coy, 16th DLI*

The two companies moved across the swirling river.

At 'H' hour we moved forward, I was in the middle of the company, with two platoons up and one back. David Buchanan, a Scottish subaltern, was commanding one of the two platoons. We moved down to the river, there was machine gun fire, Spandaus, firing the whole time. We got across the river, it was not easy because the Germans had positions covering the river and the company on the left weren't able to cross at all because the Germans had Spandaus covering every 30-40 yards of the river. I was right up and I said, "David, take your platoon on to Corla, see what you can find out and let me know." David went forward and there then commenced some quite heavy fighting. *Major Laurie Stringer, B Coy, 16th DLI*

With A Company failing to get across, B Company, although initially successful, were extremely vulnerable to counter-attack. Corporal Kenneth Lovell was sent forward with Corporal Pettifer to establish contact with Lieutenant David Buchanan's platoon.

We set off, went over the river and I fell in a bomb hole going over. I'm not a very good swimmer and I came up spitting water. What I didn't realise at the time was that my Tommy gun had gone into the clay mud. We used them without butts, like squirt guns. Having got out of the river, we went forward and got to the edge of this ring of light, almost like daylight, from the haystacks on fire. When the Germans withdrew from farmhouses, they used to set fire to the haystacks to give their mortars and artillery an aiming point if they needed to counter-attack. The stacks really were blazing at this farmhouse we'd taken. There was about 150 yards of really open ground in front of the farmhouse all round but especially on our side. One of the other Platoon Sergeants was a little chap called Joe Thompson. He was a very short chap, I don't think he would have been much more than 5' 2." Very deep voice, Yorkshire accent. We jumped into a bomb hole and I said, "Right, hang about Pettifer, let's see what's happening, we don't know whether the platoon's still there." Pettifer said to me, "I can hear Sergeant Thompson over there!" I listened and sure enough it sounded like Sergeant Thompson. So I said to Pettifer, "Keep me covered, I'll go over and ask Joe where Lieutenant Buchanan and the rest of the platoon is." So he stayed in the bomb hole and kept me covered. I crept forward and there was this short chap and I couldn't make it out, but it sounded a deep voice, I thought, "Oh, Joe Thompson!" Then I got up, walked up and tapped him on the shoulder and I said, "Hey Joe, where's Mr Buchanan?" The German soldier turned round and said, "Ist ein Tommi! Hande hoch!!" Well I pulled the trigger of my Tommy gun and it virtually exploded – the breech block and the covering blew back just past my arms. It's lucky I wasn't holding it in my stomach otherwise it would have taken my inside out. The gases couldn't escape because it had been stuffed up with clay. So I was taken prisoner. There were about ten Germans setting up a couple of machine gun posts ready to counter-attack. *Corporal Kenneth Lovell, B Coy, 16th DLI*

Lovell spent the next seven months in a German POW camp. The situation was becoming increasingly chaotic and Major Stringer decided to see for himself what was going on.

I said, "I'm going forward to see what's happening!" I got up to Corla and I went round into the farmyard. I saw a section of men in a slit trench, or bomb hole. I got to within 20 yards and I shouted out to them, "Which section are you!" Imagine my surprise when seven German helmets popped their heads above this hole! There was some bitter fighting all of a sudden. I just managed to gain the cover of some buildings on my left hand side and the Germans counter-attacked pretty strongly and drove us back to the other side of the river. We had to retreat. There was some heavy and very confused fighting. Grenades and small arms fire – small arms fire mainly. It was in the middle of the night – I think it was a very disorganised retreat really. Sometimes you just don't know what is going on. When the men realised what the situation was and the enemy started advancing I gave the order for the platoons to retreat across the river. I got into the river again and the water was up to my chest. We got back across the river and the fighting died down. Things began to stabilise. *Major Laurie Stringer, B Coy, 16th DLI*

The attack had been a complete failure in the Durhams' sector, although the 2/5th Foresters had got across the Cosina and the integrity of yet another German river line was breached. Stringer was still trying to sort out his battered company.

> My men told me that David Buchanan had been hit and as soon as I heard that I decided I would try and find him. Circumstance were with me because I took two men and a stretcher and there, just my side of the river, he must have got back some how or other, I saw David lying in a furrow. He couldn't move. I went up to him and I heard the best words that I heard said to me during the whole of my military career, "Sir, I knew you would come!" You might say it's sentimental, you might say there wasn't much importance to that statement, but to me there was. He'd been shot through the legs and we were able to get him onto this stretcher and back to safety. Dear David – he was a splendid officer and that was the end of his fighting days. *Major Laurie Stringer, B Coy, 16th DLI*

On the 23 November, C Company advanced through the bridgehead established by the Foresters and Corla was finally captured and consolidated. A general battalion advance then followed towards Casa Bruciati. During this last phase of fighting Collins and his dismounted

View of Faenza from an OP just outside town. The Sherman tank is engaging German positions in Faenza, 24 November 1944. IWM NA 20222

Carrier Platoon were ordered to put in an attack on some farm buildings. He responded with a strange mixture of screaming nerves and cool professionalism.

> We were on the left flank as the attack came in. I had to make the plan to go and do it. I remember agonising with myself but I decided on that occasion I really couldn't, I couldn't be the first man forward there. I'd done it so many times and I'd really got to the end of my tether then. But then you see, I did have four sections, each commanded by a Sergeant. If there ever was a man who never showed any fear it was Sergeant Chilvers, who led that attack then and he got a Military Medal. We very quickly followed up, with my platoon headquarters and the other sections, surrounded the place and got right in. There was not much firing and the first thing you have to do is to secure the place, exploit through the objective, make sure they have not just gone back 20 yards and are waiting to jump in on you again. Then you immediately make an all round defence by saying "Right you, Sergeant, cover that sector, from there to there; Sergeant, you cover that sector over there. Go and find some fire positions and I'll come round in a minute to see you." Off they went and I started on my rounds. It was dusk and I came around one corner, and a voice said "Halt, who goes there?" "BANG!" All in one moment. It was a carrier driver, who was shaking like a leaf and had his rifle at the hip. He was called Yorkie Streeton and that was the last shot that was ever fired at me in anger in Italy! Once again it missed and that's why I'm here and able to tell the tale.
> *Lieutenant Russell Collins, Carrier Platoon, Support Coy, 16th DLI*

The Gothic Line campaign with its misery of ridges, rivers, mortars, rain and mud was finally over for Collins, his men and the all rest of the 'Faithful' Durhams as the 128th Brigade took up their place in the vanguard of the advance on to the River Lamone. In all, during that miserable campaign, they had suffered 429 casualties, of which 21 were officers.

The Battalion was moved back to the Forli area where they began what everyone hoped and prayed would be a long rest. Almost immediately though the battalions rumour mill began to move into over-drive. This time there really was something in it for advance parties from each company were assembled and despatched. Then the whole battalion moved back all the way to Rome where they were thrust upon a fleet of American Dakotas and found themselves aloft en route for Greece. What was going on?

CHAPTER THIRTEEN

Greece

On 3 December the Durhams flew in to Kalamachi airfield near Athens. The situation which greeted them was tense as two rival Greek partisan/political factions fought for dominance. The left wing Greek People's Army of Liberation (ELAS) and the nationalistic Greek Democratic Front (EDES) had seized the opportunity posed by the German withdrawal from Greece to try and take control. ELAS in particular, which had been trained and supplied with weapons by the British to fight the German occupation of Greece, was seen as a threat by Churchill due to its alleged links with Soviet Communism. At the moment the Durhams landed widespread hostilities had not yet erupted although there were isolated violent exchanges between the various bands of partisans and the Greek police. Lieutenant General Sir Richard Scobie was the British commander given the thankless task of resolving this awkward situation.

The rest of 139 Brigade had also moved to Greece: the 2/5th Leicester were also in Athens; whilst the 2/5th Foresters were sent to Salonika. Initially the Durhams took up positions in the centre of Athens itself.

> I got an instruction from Headquarters to go and occupy the hill on which the Philipapou Monument stood. I was told that we

View over Athens, 16 December 1944. IWM NA 20898

were unlikely to have any particular opposition. So I merely detailed a platoon to go down the road about half a mile, turn right, climb the hill, find the Philipapou Monument, sit down and let me know when they got there. I eventually got a runner back who said that they had occupied the Philipapou Monument. So I said, "Right-ho, I'll go and join them!" We got out a jeep and couple of chaps and we went down the road. I turned right and went up onto the Philipapou Monument and the runner said, "This isn't where we went!" We occupied it, because there was nobody there and we discovered in fact that the Platoon Commander obviously didn't know his right from his left – he'd turned left and he'd occupied the Acropolis! *Major Ronnie Sherlaw, 16th DLI*

Major Stringer (seated) *views ruins of the Parthenon – caused by time – unlike the war-torn ruins he has been used to over the previous months.*

The reactions of different men to the chance of seeing and touching the glories of ancient Greece varied greatly.

In my childhood I had always been reading the Classics and the thought of going to Athens was something quite remarkable to me. Something that I thought I should never have been able to take advantage of. One of the companies that night was placed on the Acropolis itself. Nothing much happened and next morning I said to Signaller Tony Sacco, "How was it, Tony," and he said, "Nothing else but bloody stones up there and it's freezing cold" I thought, "Well, that's the practical view of what the Acropolis was like!" *Signaller*

Athens December 1944 Edward Grey, from Sunderland, is on the right.

Ronald Elliott, HQ Coy, 16th DLI

During this early phase the troops were not usually fired on.

There had been some sort of shooting incident in the street and there was an angry mob around. One didn't know at all what to do, we really had no rules of engagement or anything like that. I determined the only way to deal with it was by a show of strength. So I fell in my platoon, very conspicuously in the street, went into open order and ordered them to fix bayonets. Then we marched briskly down the street to where this mob was and of course everybody just melted into the side lines. Then there were people there weeping and wailing over a man who'd been shot through the head – it was obviously an assassination of some sort. Then we were thanked by the people who offered us wine to drink, which turned out to be Retsina which we'd never had before. Retsina's got a very, very bitter taste of resin – I thought we were being poisoned and I declined to drink it, which was very embarrassing really. *Lieutenant Russell Collins, Carrier Platoon, Support Coy, 16th DLI*

Officers and NCOs of A Company, Athens February 1945.

At first the men had considerable sympathy for the ELAS partisans, who so recently had been fighting their mutual enemy the Germans and who seemed to be standing up for working class Greeks against a corrupt establishment.

All of the army by that time was pretty well socialist. Everyone was of the view that the Conservatives were to blame for all sorts of ills that we had in the war, the general level of the economy and the way that people felt about the future. So that, by and large, they were all pretty well Labour. Even though people admired Churchill for his ability to lead the country, his politics were completely suspect – he was a Conservative and was blackened with the rest of the Conservatives. We felt that what the Government was trying to do in Greece was to restore the monarchy, which we all surmised was really not what the people wanted, but was going to be imposed upon them. Therefore in the beginning there was a fair amount of favourable feeling towards this insurgency. *Signaller Ronald Elliott, Signal Section, HQ Coy, 16th DLI*

As the civil war erupted the battalion was withdrawn to the sea front area of Phaleron, whilst the Leicesters occupied the port of Piraeus. Demonstrations organised by ELAS seemed to show that they had a considerable amount of support amongst the ordinary Greek population. It became increasingly apparent that the British were not holding the ring between the two sides, but had their own agenda, which was distinctly anti-ELAS.

It was a Sunday morning and there were thousands of them coming along the coast road. They were chanting, a demonstration, like. We had a bloke called Lieutenant General Scobie that was in charge and they were coming along shouting. I was saying to myself, "What are they saying?" They were saying, "Scobie is a bastard! Scobie is a bastard!" Chanting like that. I think that the other half, the Royalists that wanted the King back – they were in a minority! Or they didn't dare say anything! *Private George Bland, Carrier Platoon, Support Coy, 16th DLI*

There was still an unwillingness on both sides to start a real 'shooting war' and local initiatives were pursued to try and avoid casualties.

I was lucky in recruiting a girl who had excellent English and she put me in touch with the chap who was the leader of the ELAS in that area. He said that if we would agree not to shoot at them he would agree not to shoot at us for a period of a week when we could perhaps come to some terms. I said I wasn't in position to do that sort of thing but that I would have a word with the Colonel. The Colonel agreed that we should have a local armistice. Every morning for about three days I would start at this bottom end of Phaleron, I would take out my pistol and put it on the ground. He would put his gun down and we'd walk up and shake hands. We had about three days of peace. Then on the third night the ELAS broke the peace and attacked one of my platoons and in fact killed somebody. So that ended the peace. We were very fed up about it and the Colonel felt that I'd been a bit optimistic about what we could do with these chaps and I think I probably was. But we felt that if we could do that then at least we'd give the local residents peace. It was just one of those things where you have one or two subversives and they'd decided they'd do something on their own. *Major Ronnie Sherlaw, D Coy, 16th DLI*

Support Company sergeants in Phaleron, Athens, February 1945.

The situation began to escalate on 12 December. As the sniping began, the troops had real difficulties in determining who exactly their enemies were. This led to a feeling of insecurity.

> The enemy were just the same as any other Greeks as far as we knew, they didn't have any uniform as such. So there was always this problem of knowing who they were. Although people were quite glad to be away from the main battlefront and it certainly wasn't as hard as fighting the Germans! It was a situation that was quite completely different to the way that we had been used to fighting. There were aspects of it that people felt uneasy about. As an average infantryman, one of the first questions that you ask when you're going into a new battle position is, "Which way is the

Members of the Signal Platoon.

front?" So that you know that if the worst comes to the worst which way you can go to get out of the bloody place. In this sort of situation, which is a typical urban 'battlefront' it's all around you and one feels somewhat unhappy about that. *Signaller Ronald Elliott, Signal Section, HQ Coy, 16th DLI*

They also began to dislike the tactics adopted by many of the ELAS insurgents.

The ELAS tended to use women, they'd have women coming along the street, just as though they were housewives having a demonstration, followed by armed men behind them using the women as a shield, or even children, having children around, so that you couldn't fire at them. So it got very dirty in that sense. This is about the time, as will always happen in these situations, that the soldiers' attitude changed from being politically favourable to being militarily against them. Because they weren't in our sense, playing particularly fair. Before very long, it was just they were them and we were us – it was just a combat situation. I think in the end we tended to feel that they were Communist and really probably weren't out to do any more for the population, they weren't particularly supported by the ordinary man in the street. Churchill was trying to re-impose the King, the Communists were trying to impose Communist rule so that really in effect one was almost as bad as the other – and we were somewhere in between I guess! *Signaller Ronald Elliott, Signal Section, Headquarters Coy, 16th DLI*

The troops would retaliate when fired on, but the risk of civilian casualties was high, for human nature could not entirely be over-ruled by troops with bullets flying around them.

We tried to avoid real civilians but people don't pay a lot of attention to that. I've got to be truthful! I mean you wouldn't deliberately shoot at civilians, but if there's any doubt in your mind and you might be wrong, then it's better to be safe than sorry – you'd let fly! *Sergeant Tommy Chadwick, C Coy, 16th DLI*

The situation was a strange amalgam of peace and war. During the day things were usually quiet and almost normal.

Things were fairly static and we were just in some houses, and the front line was over the other side of the street, technically, but there wasn't any obvious signs of anyone being there. Just on the opposite side of the road was this wine shop. So we used to make sorties over there for wine. We were very keen on banana wine and so when things were quiet and no one was looking we used to hop over there and buy ourselves some banana wine! We had Alan Hay, who was a bluff, hearty character and he came along and saw us quaffing this banana wine. He asked us what the devil we were doing and where we had got it from? We told him and he was aghast, "You're not to go over there again – you'll get killed, that's the front line over there!" We said, "Well, you know, you should try this – it's good stuff!" So he had a drink and he coughed around a bit and said, "Hmmmhhh! Well if you ever get any more – get some for me!" It was an odd sort of half war if you like. *Signaller Ronald Elliott, Signal Section, Headquarters Coy, 16th DLI*

However in the evening there was no doubt that the streets of Phaleron were mean indeed.

There were a few of us who were quite musical and we used to sing in the mess in the evening just for fun. We used to sing in little quartets; hymn tunes were about all we knew. Frank Johnson was one of four of us, Ronnie Sherlaw, was another, 'Giff' Footer and myself. Poor old Frank went out to try and sort out somebody, and one of the ELAS snipers got him. *Lieutenant Russell Collins, Carrier Platoon, Support Coy, 16th DLI*

Inevitably a certain amount of paranoia became apparent as was noted in an addendum to the battalion war diary.

Lessons learnt from recent fighting: Civilians: Used by enemy to try and gain information re our dispositions and strength etc. Every civilian, no matter how innocent he or she may look, is a potential enemy. No civilian can really be trusted. *Colonel Denis Worrall, 16th DLI*[15]

The battalion took up defensive positions in houses along the seafront. At night the whole scene was illuminated by the searchlights of the Royal Navy ships patrolling in the Bay of Phaleron. Intelligence had warned that ELAS were planning a major attack on the night of 13 December. Some of the Durhams still did not appreciate the seriousness of the threat and were caught unawares.

One night the Sergeant Major came to us. He says, "Right you are, we're going out to the Lieutenant's billet, I've heard word there's going to be an attack and I want to warn him!" By this time it was about half past ten at night, so it was dark. We went in front of our barrier, very careful, to go to his house. They were left of us about 50 yards in front of the barrier in a little side street. The first house on the right was a big house and they were all in there. We goes in and all we could hear was the piano playing and drunken singing – I'll never forget the song he was singing, 'If I had a Paper Doll to call My Own'! The Sergeant Major bustled his way in and there was the Lieutenant as drunk as a kitty cat, he was – he was paralytic. They had got some vino and they were all drunk! No guards on the door. The Sergeant Major tried to get some sense into them but he couldn't and at the finish the Lieutenant ordered him away. He came back and he said, "Well, I've done my best!" We manned the barriers all night and, sure enough, there was an attack and the house he was in was blown up. The Lieutenant got taken prisoner with a full platoon of 30 men in the house, all drunk. *Private James Corr, B Coy, 16th DLI*

ELAS attacked in large numbers right along the line using grenades and dynamite as well as small arms. Major Alan Hay had recovered from his hand wound and rejoined the battalion.

Battalion headquarters was in a small villa. Just next door there was a block of flats where the cooks and clerks were. It was a three storey building, built of concrete. At this time Colonel Worrall was away and Major Denny was in charge. I was kept at battalion headquarters as a second in command. On the night in question I had been along the front to visit the outer companies and I came back and put the jeep behind the block of flats where there was some open ground, about 100 yards by a 100 yards roughly. I went into the battalion headquarters and just lay down to rest. We didn't take our clothing off, when a bullet came through the window and we could hear other fighting outside. We tried to find out what it was and we gathered that a very strong party of ELAS had congregated in this open area but behind a stone wall. *Major Alan Hay, Headquarters Coy, 16th DLI*

Fires burning in Athens, January 1945.
IWM NA 21420

Major Denny asked Hay to take command of the cooks and clerks in the neighbouring three storey block.

I put what men I could find in open positions, but of course they were targets by the window, so we got up to the flat roof. I said, "What ammunition have we got?" Well being battalion headquarters they didn't have any ammunition and I said, "Well, look round for anything you can get!" We were then coming under very heavy attack and these people were shouting. The civilians who were still on the top floor, just a family with two kids, were trying to tell us that they were going to blow the building block up – they were interpreting because these ELAS were telling us to surrender because they would blow the block up. We could hear them hammering and knocking, there were so many and we really couldn't disperse them because the angles for rifle fire from the top were really too acute. I think I had four grenades so I had to wait until enough of these ELAS guerrillas came into view before I hurled a grenade. We would have a lull and let these people come over the wall, stream over the wall, let them get there and then release a grenade. They got to the bottom of the stairs of this subsidiary building and we drove them off. These grenades were very effective – you could see them going down. There was still knocking going on down below and firing at the windows. They didn't charge but they were creeping forward when

Devastation on the streets of Athens – civilians run for cover past a British barbed wire barricade. IWM NA 21028

they thought our firing had gone down – because we didn't have much to fire at them. They came from over the wall at the other end of the open ground facing us. There seemed to be crowds behind this. We didn't know how many at that time but there was an awful lot – hundreds. They were all raging and shouting and this that and the other – a real mob. They were going to drive us into the sea, they'd been saying that for long enough. I waited and waited and then threw another grenade. These people were screaming and shouting that they were going to blow us up. We were by that time all on the roof, there were concrete stairs coming up, so I thought, "I'll keep this one grenade as a last resort when they charge the stairs. There was a parapet you could keep behind, so unless they'd had mortars they couldn't catch us. Anyway there was this hammering going on down below. Then the explosion went off... The whole of the outside of the flats collapsed, just like a cardboard box and of course one of the casualties was my jeep. The outer floors collapsed – we were a bit further back. I was stunned by some masonry, I can't have had my tin hat on because I had a gash across my head. Then they charged – but they were just making a noise. White flags appeared shortly from the mob and they wanted to collect their wounded. By this time it was getting towards morning so we waited until they collected their wounded. In fact we didn't have anything to fire at them and then we started to count the cost. They came with barrows and bits of sheet with red crosses painted on them, they shouted, just to get their dead and wounded. I would think that there could have been a hundred. We didn't have any casualties except the Sergeant Cook and some others were buried in the rubble and we had to get them out. They were all right, they had cuts and bruises. *Major Alan Hay, Headquarters Coy, 16th DLI*

All along the waterfront the Durhams fought to avoid being over-run. However, with the exception of one platoon in B Company, all held out. This was the high tide of the ELAS revolt. More units flooded in as reinforcements and the coast road to Piraeus was opened. The Durhams began to advance, house by house, street by street, consolidating as they progressed by wiring off the controlled areas.

A lot of the houses had no windows, so that made life a lot easier. The success rate of the house clearing was about 10% because they weren't in uniform. They could ground their arms and walk out of the back door down the street, most likely with a pistol in their pocket! So it was treacherous more than vicious. *Sergeant Tommy Chadwick, C Coy, 16th DLI*

One experienced soldier, impatient with the rate of progress launched his own offensive.

One night I saw Les was a little 'tipsy', for want of another word. He decided to go and settle the war himself, so he ups and waltzes down this street firing at everything he saw. Some of these chaps were on rooftops, firing from behind chimney pots. How he wasn't shot that night I will never know. He was fated. He ultimately came back and Casey was waiting for him. He said, "I want you!" Les said, "I have been carrying out my duties, Sir! A one-man fighting patrol, I have nothing to report, Sir!" *Sergeant Tommy Chadwick, C Coy, 16th DLI*

Slowly the battalion edged forward. As each area was cleared, a charm offensive tried to woo the Greeks civilians by providing food and medical supplies. This proved effective and gradually it seemed that mass support for ELAS leached away. Colonel Worral noted.

Lessons learnt from recent fighting: The soup kitchen may be a better weapon than the rifle. A great

An ELAS fighter lays dead in the street. British soldiers move along the pavement with caution.
IWM NA 20929

The ELAS worn no uniform and, after an action, could simply walk away as a civilian and disappear among the populace. This was frustrating for the Durhams engaged in a policing action.
IWM NA 20930

Athens 1945.

'The soup kitchen may be a better weapon than the rifle. A great interest should be taken in the distribution of food.' Food kitchens in action in Athens January 1945. IWM NA 21290

interest should be taken in the distribution of food. *Colonel Denis Worrall, 16th DLI*[16]

In early January a group of some 60 insurgents were located in an industrial area on the outskirts of Athens.

We were ordered to go and sort them out. We had to attack before light, but unfortunately the lads had been doing a bit of drinking the night before and when I got up expecting to see the Sergeants and men ready to move, there was nobody there – they'd slept in. The Major was going off his head and he said, "We'll never get there now before light!" We got them ready in double quick time and off we set with our interpreter, a student type of a lad, he was frightened to death. We were dodging along paths and hedgerows and it started to get light. Now in front of the factory was a great big open space, there was no cover at all. That's the reason we were supposed to have got there before light. We carried on and got to the factory wall. The Major went in and fortunately they'd done the same as we had – they'd slept in! I was following the Major and suddenly I was fired on by a machine gun with my two lads and we had to dodge behind a column in the wall. We stayed there, we couldn't get out. The firing came from a very high tower in the factory. I said, "This is no good!" I took a running dive through the hole in the wall where we'd got through, dashed up the side of the road behind the wall, got a tank commander and said, "Just see him off will you!" He put a round in his gun and blasted that chap up there. That was the end, we got them all out. Some had been shot, a sorry lot of dirty people, bearded, one with his jaw shattered with a bullet. We loaded them up into trucks ready for interrogation. We carried on up this road to another factory. As we went we were fired on again from up the road. The bullets were coming straight down the road. We had to get to this factory across the road. So we had to jump across two at a time. As soon as there was a lull in the firing where we thought the chap was changing ammunition, then I would send two men across. Now this was a cognac factory with two great big doors. I was organising something and one of the young officers got hold of my PIAT man and said, "Fire your PIAT and burst those doors open!" He was inexperienced about PIATs, you were supposed to be under cover to fire a PIAT because it has a terrible blast, a blow back. He fired this PIAT at the doors, hit the doors and finished up in hospital because he got the backlash. I had to tell the young officer a couple of home truths about the use of a PIAT! The soldiers filled their water-bottles up with this cognac. It was pure, bloody poison really – one signaller went blue in the face and finished up in hospital. We had to get all their water bottles empty. But some of them managed to smuggle them away. *Company Sergeant Major Les Thornton, C Coy, 16th DLI*

The troops were ecstatic at the prospect of free booze.

We ran in and we were squirting the barrels with Sten gun fire. Of course the stuff was pouring out all over the place so we were filling water bottles with it. Within half an hour we had about six men unconscious – so that put the mockers on it – but we kept our water bottles. Word got back to Major Casey and he banned it all – all the drink we had in our water bottles was to be put in jerry cans and kept till the end of the war. *Sergeant Tommy Chadwick, C Coy, 16th DLI*

It was increasingly obvious that ELAS had shot its bolt in the Athens area and by 5 January the area had been cleared.

ELAS forces were still active in the area of the Patras in the Peloponnese Peninsula. The Durhams were embarked on 6 January and arrived off Patras on 9 January. The 11th Indian Brigade were occupying Patras in a state of uneasy truce with the ELAS forces. Neither side seemed to wish to start hostilities but the tension was excruciating. It was feared that a forced landing might be needed which would have cost many lives. Brigadier Block sent ELAS a blunt ultimatum which demanded that they evacuate the town. To everyone's surprise this was accepted and the Durhams landed unopposed – much to their relief.

Although patrols were sent into the surrounding countryside, the stay at Patras was almost a holiday for the tired troops. During this period Sam Cawdron arrived with a reinforcement draft and, although he had served in the Royal Artillery in Italy, they were all treated as 'new boys'.

An officer met us and gave us a lecture of what to do and what not to do all about the women. All the loose women had been put inside barbed wire and there was only one entrance through the actual gate. That was out of bounds for troops to control VD. While he was telling us there was two women on the roof of their particular house performing all sorts of things for our benefit – amazing! *Fitter Sam Cawdron, MT Section, HQ Coy, 16th DLI*

The billets were rather unfortunately placed for the maintenance of good order – they were within clear sight of an obvious brothel. This kind of display was deeply disturbing to many of the men.

The girls used to be at the windows, the main windows of the brothel which faced where the factory windows were, more or less face to face across an intervening distance of about 50 yards. The girls used to be there with nothing on just enticing the soldiery with ribald remarks. Of course you couldn't go in the front because there were people guarding it, but one or two of the lads reckoned that there was a route over the roof tops and that they could get into the backdoor of the brothel. This route lay beneath the window of the Officers' Mess and this fellow came back one night steaming and wet. When he'd was going past the Officers' Mess one of the officers had pissed all over him out of the window! Which rather cooled his ardour a bit. *Signaller Ronald Elliott, Signal Section, Headquarters Coy, 16th DLI*

On 14 January a general truce was signed and by agreement the ELAS forces withdrew to specially designated areas. The Durhams were ordered back to Athens on 11 February, this time by road. One driver had a close escape.

I was at the tail end of the convoy. The roads were atrocious in parts, a white chalk dust and of course the further behind you were, the worse it was, you could hardly see out of the windscreens, you had to keep stopping and wiping this damned stuff off. It affected your breathing. The MT Officer was conducting the convoy and riding a motorbike – going to the head of the column, going back to the rear. We got four fifths of the way and he decided to call it a day, so he took my place in the truck and bunged me the motorbike. But unthinkingly, I'm sure he didn't do it on purpose, he didn't give me his goggles. I never thought about it. I was riding this bike and within a couple of kilometres I was virtually blind. I rubbed it, made it worse and I just couldn't go any further – I couldn't see – and I stopped. There was a railway signal box on my left and a house that looked like a farm on my right. So I thought, "Well, I'll go in here and see if I can get some water and wash my eyes out. I rode the bike into this entrance into a yard – and was surrounded by armed Greeks. They made me get off the bike and rather roughly pushed me into the house. They started to ask me a load of questions which I couldn't understand. I couldn't see very well and I asked for some water to wash my eyes from somebody who spoke English. He told them to give me it and I sluiced my eyes out. They were very, very sore. I'd never met the man, but I got the immediate impression that it was General Grivas, because I had an idea of his size and shape. He was dressed like that. He said, "I'm afraid you have to be kept here, we're going away, you'll have to be kept here until we've gone. We'll leave your bike, you stay in this room, it will be under guard, give us your word that you won't try to escape and we'll let you off in about an hour or so." Which they did! Of course by then the battalion was long settled back in Phaleron. When I arrived there was a hue and cry, "Where had I been, what had I been doing?" I could barely see properly and it was dark and I went to the Medical Aid Post and they syringed my eyes out and put some drops in. Then it suddenly occurred to me that I ought to report this. I asked where the Intelligence Officer was and went and reported this – and I got another rousting because I hadn't reported immediately my suspicions that this man was there. Subsequently it turned out it was him, he had been there. Of course the contention was that if I had reported it straight away they might have been able to do something about it. I never agreed with that because I didn't know where he was going – he could have been anywhere. *Driver Tom Lister, MT Section, HQ Coy, 16th DLI*

Once safe in Athens the party started as the men enjoyed their new freedom from danger.

That's where everybody headed for every night. You'd do a little sight seeing and then finish up in one of the cafes. You were going to sleep at night – which was a luxury – you hadn't been used to getting that much sleep. I drank retsina, croisee the local drink or ouzo. Very strong! The local retsina we used to say, "A shilling a

The 16th Durhams' band in Greece, 1945. Major Viz Vizard is on drums.

fire-bucket full!" It was that cheap. And the drachma – I think there was about 9,000,000 to a pound! There was the odd bar brawl, but not a lot, nothing serious. I found that the morning after what I call a heavy session, compared to some of them, I had such a proverbial hangover that I invariably always said, "That's it – I'm leaving that alone!" But by mid-day, you were young and fit, you'd recovered quite well, so a little encouragement from your pals, they were all going – so off you went again! *Sergeant Tommy Chadwick, C Coy, 16th DLI*

The Greek population seemed content and the battalion received many plaudits from local dignitaries for the restraint with which they had handled themselves during the 'troubles'.

Looking back on all this, the one thing that sticks out in my mind is the adaptability of the British soldier. You can pick him up and put him down into a totally unfamiliar alien atmosphere where he doesn't understand what people are talking about, he's highly suspicious of all the people around about and they're hostile, or they're friendly, or they're inbetween. But within the space of at the most 48 hours, he will have completely adapted himself to new surroundings like a chameleon. Before you know where you are, chickens appear, eggs, tomatoes, melons and so forth. Washing is being done by Greek women, the men are talking to them – how they do it I don't know, but there is this tremendous ability to adapt. It happened over and over again, whatever the circumstances – hostile, difficult, cold, wet – yes, never mind – you'd still get this adaptability to the environment. It was one of our great assets, I suppose it always has been one of our great assets. The British soldier is basically friendly and gets on with people. *Major Viz Vizard, HQ Coy, 16th DLI*

Sport took on an increasing importance and several sports days were held. On 21 March the battalion held a cross country run with some 60 men engaged.

21 March: Each Company was represented by ten runners over a course of 6 miles. The whole of the event was broadcast and the spectators at Battalion Headquarters were able to follow the progress of the runners by the aid of the running commentary and also a map which represented the course. Spaced at intervals on the course, men of the Signal Platoon gave an eye witness account of the runners as they passed and this account was relayed over an amplifier situated outside Battalion HQ. Over a very hard course the competitors soon spread out and after the second mile the first man had a lead of 800 yards. From the spectators' point of view

Sam Cawdron

the weather was ideal; the sun shining gloriously; a blue sky; a gentle breeze coming off the sea and as an added attraction light music was played to fill in the time between the different commentaries of the race. The competitors, however, had a much harder time and as they neared the finishing post they all bore signs of fatigue. The first man home was Private Little of B Company, followed by Private Richardson of C Company. Private Manners and Lieutenant Sanders of B Company coming in together for a close third. *War Diary, 16th DLI*

Behind these front runners came Sam Cawdron.

We went down a straight road to a point and then came back cross country. Up and down tank traps, gullies, ploughed fields, everything. What we didn't know till we got back was the Signal Section had put wires up right from the start right the way round the circuit. They were sat on poles, each with a blinking microphone, all the way round with speakers in the finishing circle. They were broadcasting all what was going off to the others waiting for us finishing. Well it was fantastic. After I finished I listened to one or two... There were between 60-80 running and I'd done short races but I'd never done a long one. I thought, "Well I'll stick it out!" Anyway I finished up 26th! So that wasn't bad! A fantastic day that day! *Fitter Sam Cawdron, MT Section, HQ Coy, 16th DLI*

Drinking, dancing, sports days and light training filled the days but still a shadow remained at the back of everyone's mind.

All the talk and speculation was where were we going next. We were hoping against hope that we were going to be selected to go to North West Europe, to join the much more glamorous party that was going on there. We abhorred the thought of going back to Italy again, where we'd fought two previous campaigns and had left a lot of our dead. We envied the chaps that had all the glamour – in any case it would mean going home first. It seemed to be a very much more straight-forward show there altogether. So we were hoping we would go there. But of course in the event we were told we were going back to Italy. *Lieutenant Russell Collins, Carrier Platoon, Support Coy, 16th DLI*

Chapter Fourteen

Victory

Major General Weir

After a forced lull in the winter, the Allies had once more gathered their strength for one last spring offensive in Italy. The Eighth Army, now under General Richard McCreery, had launched its assault on 9 April. They burst across the Senio and Santerno Rivers and pushed on towards the River Po with the intention of capturing Verona. Although great progress had been made, it was still expected that they would meet stern resistance on the Germans' last line of defence along the Adige River. This was the frightening prospect facing the returning Durhams.

On 13 April they set sail back to Italy aboard the *Ville d'Oran* landing at Taranto two days later. They were welcomed by a stirring message from their divisional commander.

> The last round of this gigantic struggle is on. The German Army, battered and dazed, is desperately trying to ward off the knock-out blow. We must hasten to the side of our comrades now engaged in the hard fighting and with all our strength, assist in the delivery of the blow which will bring the German Army to utter and complete defeat at our feet. *Major General Weir, Headquarters, 46th Division*

Brave words, but they did not really strike a chord with the men charged with once more risking their lives when everyone could see that they were all so close to the metaphorical finishing line.

> A lot of them weren't keen, which is understandable. To coin their phrase, "It was a bit late to get a wooden top coat!" They'd gone so long. *Sergeant Tommy Chadwick, C Coy, 16th DLI*

The Durhams spent a few days on yet more training before they were shipped up the coast to Ancona.

> It was a quicker way because the trains – they stopped at every chip shop did the trains! By road there was a problem, but whipping us up to Ancona! once we had disembarked there we were ready. Horrific. It took about 48 hours. It was really, really rough. We couldn't stand up, we were lying on the floor. The

buckets where the troops had been sick were flying across the floor. Honest to God it was like a fairground ship. It was the roughest trip I've ever had in my life. Fortunately I wasn't sick but most were. Some just laid there and never even moved. It was that bad! *Sergeant Tommy Chadwick, C Coy, 16th DLI*

They were concentrated at La Fratta near Bertinori. News was coming in that the River Po had been crossed and that the Germans were having difficulty in forming a cohesive front line. It was good news, but it still seemed to be too late to save them from more fighting.

They had been taking large numbers of German prisoners, we heard all about this and we thought, "That's the end of them!" But they still hadn't officially declared that it was the end of the war. We always felt that we were being held back, that Hitler was going to make a last stand in the Alps. They knew all the passes and we heard he was going to make a last desperate stand there. We thought, "Now we are being saved for this!" We'd not been given any other jobs, we were just told to be in readiness. We thought, "Yes, this is our job – to invade the Alps!" *Major Alan Hay, A Coy, 16th DLI*

Thoughts of the end of the war had been with them for the last six years. A mixture of long term hope mingled with dread for their immediate future.

We all used to think, "Now one day we'll waken up and it will be over!" You used to think fantastic things. If you were in the line and you had to take wounded back to a safe place you were always happy because you used to think, "Well, while I'm here the war might be over – somebody might sign the peace!" Which eventually did happen – but it didn't happen when you thought it would. Fantastic! *Driver Jackie Milburn, MT Section, HQ Coy, 16th DLI*

Then suddenly the blessed moment was upon them, so long desired and now achieved almost out of the blue.

It was the 8th May. We were called all together to sit on the grass and we heard Churchill's speech, "The European War is ended!" You can't express it. *Company Sergeant Major Les Thornton, C Coy, 16th DLI*

Freed from the burden of fear and doubt, most of the battalion exploded in a shock wave of wild emotion. To ease their inhibitions the men desperately sought the 'Holy Grail' of alcohol from anywhere they could find it. Many bought it from accommodating Italians.

We all clubbed our money together. The 15 cwt driver said, "I'll go down to Forli and get a carboy of wine!" It was about eight or nine kilometres so he came back very, very slowly on the bumpy roads with two in the back holding the carboy down. It was a great big glass carboy – massive. He just came in this farm gate and he went down in a ditch... CRASH! And there was the wine pouring out of the side. He was out of that cab and he was away! We never seen him for two days. *Private James Corr, B Coy, 16th DLI*

Some remembered the cognac salted away after the capture of the distillery in Greece.

Come the end of the war all the lads said, "Where's this booze from Phaleron?" They went to 'Long' Tom Reynolds and found the booze had burnt a bloody hole in the jerry cans! It was brandy or something that had to be diluted – no wonder the lads were unconscious! *Sergeant Tommy Chadwick, C Coy, 16th DLI*

Others got rum.

The rum ration came out, half of us didn't know where we were. That night I issued out all the mortar green, white and red flares, all the red Verey lights – and we had a Guy Fawkes night. Got the 2″ mortars out, popping the parachute flares in, red flares, white flares, green flares, Verey light pistols were being fired. Nobody cared. Even shots were fired. But nobody worried. *Company Sergeant Major Les Thornton, C Coy, 16th DLI*

Most people went wild with excitement.

By the time the official news came through it was, "Get your hands on any vino!" We had a party, first of all firing off all the Verey Lights, flashes and signals. I suppose some live ammunition went off but not officially, but all the lights went up in the air and we had quite a party. We had a competition for the best decorated jeep. First of all camouflage netting but anything that would give

Victory celebrations in Italy, May 1945: B Company jeep wears a gondola and local ladies join in the fun.

a bit of colour, they got some balloons from somewhere, they went round the Italians and got some dresses from them. It was just a huge laugh, drinking and absolutely relaxing. Those static units up in that area that had nice camps with flagpoles and whitewashed stones – who were not even supporting troops – we sent out parties to pinch their flags. Anything that was stupid we were very good at – and I was in the thick of it! *Major Alan Hay, A Coy, 16th DLI*

Two gallant officers found that they had one last sacrifice to make for their comrades!

Harry Mynheer got hold of one of the locals and borrowed an oxcart and covered wagon. They put on the side "Off to Blaydon Races." He said, You two dress up!" – Russell Collins and I! We borrowed frocks and stuffed some socks in – mine kept sagging! He was quite the part! Harry Mynheer got some old hat and we were all going to Blaydon Races. Everybody was drinking everything they possible could! Later, I don't know what time it was, but I can remember Russell firing a Bren gun up in the air – I said, "Now come off it – it'll only come down on us! *Lieutenant Lionel Dodd, Mortar Platoon, Support Coy, 16th DL*I

Victory celebrations in Italy, May 1945: Russell Collins and Lionel Dodd in drag.

The Officers' and Sergeants' Messes organised parties and Jackie Milburn who had had some success as a concert party comic was asked to help supply the entertainment.

At night time the officers had a house as their mess and they sent for me to go over and entertain them. I could do a few dirty monologues, one was 'The Nudist Camp' – I gave them that and they liked that one. They were giving me a whisky or two now and again. I gave them 'Dan McGrew', got the belt on with the revolvers and when it comes to the end it's 'Two guns blast in the dark'. Well I got that out and flopped down, when I came round, I got straight up and carried on, 'Two guns blast in the dark' – as if I'd not been away. They enjoyed that. *Driver Jackie Milburn, MT Section, HQ Coy, 16th DLI*

At the height of the party in the Officers' Mess

there was an unfortunate accident.

> Two officers got very drunk and went off in a jeep and forgot that the bridge had been blown! They were both badly injured. *Major Alan Hay, A Coy, 16th DLI*

Driver Milburn at least was in the clear.

> It was my jeep. I wasn't driving it, I'd had too much, I couldn't drive! *Jacky Milburn, MT Section, HQ Coy, 16th DLI*

Ronnie Sherlaw owned up to at least partial responsibility.

> Myself and two of my officers went down in my jeep. It was on the other side of a very small stream where the bridge had been blown and a diversion had been made. During the course of the evening they ran out of drink which was a very serious matter and somebody said to me, "Is there anything you can do?" I said, "Oh, yes, I've got some, we'll go and get some!" One of my officers, Freddy Dries said, "I'll take you!" I said, "OK!" He got into the jeep driving seat, I was next to him and he shot away. Of course he'd be half tight. He shot away from the headquarters, down there, didn't notice the bridge had been blown and went straight across with that jeep. It is no exaggeration that as the jeep was in the air I stepped out of it onto the other side, the jeep went over and Dries was underneath it. The jeep wasn't in very good shape and Dries was in less of a good shape.... He had a broken leg. So it wasn't a good VE Day for us at all. *Major Ronnie Sherlaw, 16th DLI*

The more thoughtful were aware that although they were celebrating, the end of a long and bloody war is also a time for melancholy.

> We could hear people letting off rifles and machine guns in agony and ecstasy at the end of the war. When it came it was an anti-climax actually – something you'd been looking forward to all your wartime career and when it came it really didn't give you all of the kick that you thought it ought to have done. It was just as though it fizzled out rather towards the end. They did say that it was as dangerous in Forli that night as it was on any battlefront. So there it was... It was the end of the war and everybody was able to breathe a sigh of relief. For the first time you could feel the pressure was off you, you didn't have this feeling in your stomach that you could be going into dangerous situations. *Signaller Ronald Elliott, Signal Section, Headquarters Coy, 16th DLI*

And above all they had won. One battalion – the 16th Battalion Durham Light Infantry – had together done more to win the war than many so-called 'elite' units. They, alongside all the other ordinary line infantry units, had finally won the war on the ground against the best the Germans could throw at them.

Perhaps we should leave the last word to Lieutenant 'Winkler'

Collins. A young man who had proved himself beyond doubt in action, but who had also had enough of life threatening situations – at least for the time being.

> I was absolutely relieved, particularly as then we didn't have to go into action a third time in Italy. There was a great sense of euphoria, it was really marvellous. *Lieutenant Russell Collins, Carrier Platoon, Support Coy, 16th DLI*

Postcript

Almost before their hangovers had dissipated, the Durhams were moved straight up into Austria where they formed part of the Allied Army of Occupation. Over the next six months demobilisation was the watchword of the moment. Slowly the close knit team, so carefully forged in the fires of war, dissolved once more into its component elements. The wartime volunteers and conscripts returned to their disrupted civilian lives; the few regulars who were not time expired went back to their regular units. After just a few short months the battalion was no longer viable as a unit and in February 1946 it was disbanded, never to be reformed.

Since that time, with the exception of a slim volume produced by Major Laurie Stringer, the achievements of this remarkable group of men have been largely unsung. Hopefully this book will help to redress the balance.

1 Stringer, Laurence, *The History of the Sixteenth Battalion Durham Light Infantry*, Graz, 1946, p17
2 Private Thomas Anderson.
3 Private Joseph Tuck.
4 Captain Jones, loose manuscript held in Sound Archive
5 Ibid, Preston quoted in Stringer, p33
6 Sergeant D Kennedy
7 Lieutenant A Critchley. The war diary records his death from walking into a German mine field on 22 December.
8 Sergeant Joseph Makepiece
9 Captain Jones, loose manuscript held in Sound Archive
10 Ibid, Stringer, p46
11 Corporal H Vick
12 Captain Jones, loose manuscript held in Sound Archive
13 Ibid Stringer, p47
14 Ibid Stringer, p45
15 16th Bn DLI War Diary, Public Record Office
16 16th Bn DLI War Diary, Public Record Office

ROLL OF HONOUR

Fatal casualties of the 16th Battalion, Durham Light Infantry for the period September 1943 to May 1945.

Regarding the reference numbers which accompany each War Cemetery listing, the first refers to the Plot, the second to the Row and the third to the specific Grave. Thus 'VII B 20' means: Plot 7, Row B, Grave 20.

This is a work in progress, so any further information, particularly regarding incomplete Next of Kin records, is most welcome. Please write to me care of the Imperial War Museum Sound Archive. An expanded version of this listing, covering the entire period 1940–1946, has been deposited with the Sound Archive and with the DLI Museum in Durham City.

Researcher and Compiler Tom Tunney

Addinall, Pte Charles 4623092
Died: 8 December 1943 [age not recorded]
Cassino War Cemetery, Italy VII B 20
No CWGC Next of Kin details
Born York; enlisted York

Alcroft, Cpl Frederick 3131515
Died: 16 October 1944 [age not recorded]
Assisi War Cemetery, Italy II F 8
No CWGC Next of Kin details
Born Ayr; enlisted Ayr
Recorded. as 16th Btn DLI by CWGC on burial
Since amended to 10th Btn DLI.
Died 10 Oct 1943 according to War Office Roll.

Alexander, Pte John Robson 4469427
Died: 30 January 1944 aged 26
Cassino Memorial, Italy Panel 10
Son of Robert & Margaret Alexander, of South Shields, Co Durham

Alford, Pte Ronald 5445453
Died: 14th December 1944 aged 21
Phaleron War Cemetery, Greece 19 E 10
Son of Samuel & Rosina Alford, St Annes, Bristol

Allenby, Pte James Gordon 4469428
Died: 10 October 1943 [age not recorded]
Naples War Cemetery, Italy III K 7
Born Yorkshire; enlisted Yorkshire

Anderson, Pte Thomas 4468361
Died: 13 October 1943 aged 20
Minturno War Cemetery, Italy IV E 18
Son of John & Ann Anderson, Ryhope Colliery, Co Durham

Angus, Pte John Thomas 4461666
Died: 13 September 1944 aged 28
Coriano Ridge War Cemetery, Italy XVII K 10
Son of John Thomas & Barbara Angus
Born Co Durham; enlisted Yorkshire

Appleby, Pte Roger Stobbs 4463105
Died: IC) October 1944 aged 31
Assisi War Cemetery, Italy II D 11
Son of John & Dorothy A Appleby, Stamfordham, Northumberland

Apps, Pt:e Albert Pearson 4386185
Died: 23 September 1943 aged 29
Salerno War Cemetery, Italy II B
No CWGC Next of Kin details
Born E London; enlisted E London
Recorded as 8th Btn DLI by CWGC

Armitage, Pte William 4466054
Died: 19 October 1944 aged 31
Forli War Cemetery, Italy I B 1
Born Gateshead; enlisted Sunderland

Backhouse, Sgt George 1800352
Died: 1 September 1944 aged 22
Montecchio War Cemetery, Italy II F 8
Son of Samuel & Annie Backhouse, Earlsheaton, Yorkshire

Baglin, Pte Ronald James 4040817
Died: 15 December 1943 aged 35
Minturno War Cemetery, Italy II E 18
Son of Thomas Henry & Susannah Baglin; husband of Edith S Baglin
Born W London; enlisted W London

Bainbridge, Pte Charles Victor 4466665
Died: 12 September 1944 aged 33
Coriano Ridge War Cemetery, Italy IV G 8
Son of William & Dorothy Bainbridge; husband of Majorie Bainbridge, Stockton-on-Tees, Co Durham

Baldwin, Pte Alfred 4464889
Died: 23 September 1943 aged 29
Cassino Memorial, Italy Panel 10
Son of Rose Baldwin; husband of Janet Victoria Baldwin, Fairweather Green, Yorkshire

Ballance, Major Tristan George Lance MC 73434
Died: 4 December 1943 aged 27
Minturno War Cemetery, Italy II E 21
Son of Sir Hamilton Ashley Ballance KBE CB MS FRCS & of Lady Ballance, of Redgrave, Suffolk. BA (Oxon) Awarded the 16th DLI's first Military Cross, for his actions during Battle of Sedjenane, 2 March 1943.

Barnes, Pte Gordon 11415723
Died: 13 September 1944 aged 35
Coriano Ridge War Cemetery, Italy IV E 4
Son of Edward & Elizabeth Barnes, of Hinckley, Leicestershire; husband of Mary Ellen Barnes, of Hinckley

Barrett, Pte Percy 4464692
Died: 17 May 1945 aged 31 Klagenfurt War Cemetery, Austria 6 A 10 No CWGC Next of Kin details Born Yorkshire; enlisted Yorkshire

Bath, Cpl Alexander Campbell 4470023
Died: 10 October 1943 aged 21
Naples War Cemetery, Italy III D 11
Son of Frederick & Mary E Bath, of Sunderland

Beattie, Pte Richard 6297836
Died: 19 September 1943 aged 21
Salerno War Cemetery, Italy IV F 10
Son of Daniel & Jane Beattie, of Sunderland

Bedford, Pte Harry 14219167
Died: 10 October 1944
Assisi War Cemetery, Italy II F 9
No CWGC Next of Kin details
Born Yorkshire; enlisted Wakefield

Bell, Cpl John 14272525
Died: 8 December 1943 aged 24
Cassino War Cemetery, Italy VII B 22
Born Co Durham; enlisted Co Durham
Recorded as 9th Btn DLI by CWGC

Bell, Cpl Patrick 3595861
Died: 27 September 1944 aged 36
Coriano Ridge War Cemetery, Italy XVIII F 5
Son of James & Helen Bell; husband of Elizabeth Bell, Carlisle

Berridge, Pte Albert Kitchener 14521011
Died: 19 October 1944 aged 29
Forli War Cemetery, Italy I B 2
Son of William & Maud Berridge; husband of Irene Elizabeth Berridge, of Meir, Staffordshire

Best, Pte John 1720771
Died: 11 September 1944 aged 29
Coriano Ridge War Cemetery, Italy XVII K 9
Son of Charles & Alice Best; husband of Ada May Best, Middlesborough

Blair, Pte William 14557091
Died: 20 September 1944 aged 22
Coriano Ridge War Cemetery, Italy XVIII C 8
Son of John & Francis Anne Blair, Wrekenton, Co Durham

Bland, Cpl Joseph 4465725
Died: 19 September 1943 aged 33
Salerno War Cemetery, Italy VII A 45
Son of Edward & Frances Bland, of Darlington

Bottomley, Pte Jack 5962069
Died: 31 August 1944 aged 21
Montecchio War Cemetery, Italy IV B 13
Son of Horace & Minnie Bottomley, Bradford

Boyes, Pte Thomas Alec 4469448
Died: 13 October 1943 aged 27
Minturno War Cemetery, Italy IV E 17
Born Yorkshire; enlisted Yorkshire

Bradford, Pte Arthur 4624526
Died: 11 September 1943 aged 26
Salerno War Cemetery, Italy II B 47
Son of John & Sarah Bradford, Wolverhampton; husband of Alice Edna Bradford, Wolverhampton

Bradley, Cpl James 3973761
Died: 29 October 1943 aged 20
Minturno War Cemetery, Italy VIII B 2
Son of Wilfred &Lily Bradley, of Farnsworth

Brett, Pte John 4469131
Died: 17 May 1944 aged 23
Sidon War Cemetery, Lebanon I D 11
Son of Patrick & Margaret Brett, Blaydon, Co Durham

Broom, Pte Charles 4203718
Died: 15 September 1943 aged 27
Salerno War Cemetery, Italy V A 10
Son of William & Alice Broom, Liverpool

Brown, Pte James 4622092
Died: 19 September 1943 aged 23
Salerno War Cemetery, Italy IV C 14
Son of Albert & Eliza Brown, of Leeds,

Brown, Sgt Wilfred 4454524
Died: 16 October 1943 aged 29
Naples War Cemetery, Italy III M 5
Son of William & Annie Eliza Brown, Spennymoor, Co Durham; husband of Mary Brown

Buckley, Pte Albert 4468349
Died: 13 October 1943 aged 20
Minturno War Cemetery, Italy VIII C 18
Son of Henry & Lily Buckley, of Stockton-on-Tees

Burnett, Pte Robert 2383245
Died: 30 April 1945 aged 24
Salerno War Cemetery, Italy V F 36
Son of Robert & Jessie S Burnett, of Blantyre

Burton, Pte Samuel John 5439294
Died: 28 September 1944
Ancona War Cemetery, Italy IV C 16
Born Cornwall; enlisted Cornwall

Buttle, Pte George Edward 4469461
Died: 16 April 1945 aged 34
Durnbach War Cemetery, Germany 3 A 19
Born Co Durham; Stockton-on-Tees; Died POW

Casson, Cpl Walter Daniel 5950938
Died: 12 September 1943 aged 24
Salerno War Cemetery, Italy IV D 44
Son of Edward & Charlotte Casson; husband of Catherine Casson, of Bonnyrigg, Midlothian
Born N London; enlisted Essex

Caush, Pte Albert 4461915
Died: 14 December 1944 aged 29
Phaleron War Cemetery, Greece 17 D 7
Son of Joseph & Elizabeth Caush, of North Shields; husband of Helen Caush, of North Shields

Chandler, John Robert 4465579
Died: 15 July 1944
Caserta War Cemetery, Italy II B 7
Son of John Robert & Annie Chandler, of Hendon, Sunderland

Charlton, L/Sgt James 4462398
Died: 13 October 1943 aged 30
Minturno War Cemetery, Italy V A 12
No CWGC Next of Kin details
Born Sunderland; enlisted Sunderland

Christie, Sgt John 4466396
Died: 20 September 1944 aged 33
Coriano Ridge War Cemetery, Italy XVIII A 10
Son of John & Sarah Christie South Shields; husband of Mary Ellen Christie, South Shields

Clark, WOII (CSM) Arthur 4974963
Died: 19 October 1944 aged 27
Coriano Ridge War Cemetery, Italy IV G 11
Son of William & Alice Clark, of Ilkeston; husband of Dorothy Mary Clark, Ilkeston

Clark, 2/Lt Leslie William 301496
Died: 13 October 1943 aged 30
Minturno War Cemetery, Italy VIII D 16
Son of Albert & Lilly Alice Clark, Doncaster; husband of Doreen Mabel Clark

Clarkson, Pte George William 4469081
Died: 1 September 1944 aged 21
Gradara War Cemetery, Italy I A 42
Son of James Garfield Clarkson & Florence Mary Clarkson;husband of Dorothy Maud Clarkson
Born Co Durham; enlisted Co Durham

Clayton, Pte Charles Douglas 14403535
Died: 13 October 1943 aged 19
Minturno War Cemetery, Italy VIII C 20
Son of Eugene & Gladys Clayton, of Norton-on-Tees

Clifton, Pte Ronald Frederic 4470302
Died: 10 October 1943 aged 20
Cassino Memorial, Italy Panel 10
Son o:f Charles & Margaret Clifton, Bromley, Kent

Cockerill, Pte Frederick 4468870
Died: 16 November 1944 aged 22
Meldola War Cemetery, Italy I B 26
Husband of Gladys Cockerill, of Middlesborough

Collings, Pte Derek William 14236594
Died: 30 January 1944 aged 20
Cassino Memorial, Italy Panel 10
Son of Stanley & Olive Collings, of Nottingham

Cook, Pte George 4693806
Died: 13 September 1943 aged 27
Salerno War Cemetery, Italy I B 45
Son of Benjamin Cook & Mary Macella Cook, Thorne

Cooper, Pte Norman Leslie 4467138
Died: 6 February 1944 [age not recorded]
Minturno War Cemetery, Italy I E 6
Son of Albert & Ada Cooper, of West Bromwich

Cooper, Pte Walter 4464934
Died: 12 September 1944 aged 32
Coriano Ridge War Cemetery, Italy IV G 9
Son of Joe Edward & Emily Cooper, of Barkisland, Yorkshire; husband of Vera Cooper

Cope, Cpl Dennis 4698285
Died: 3 December 1943 aged 19
Minturno War Cemetery, Italy I J 9
Son of William & Sarah Jane Cope, Leeds

Court, Pte George Henry 4699055
Died: 10 October 1943 [age not recorded]
Naples War Cemetery, Italy III K 8
Son of George Henry & Isabella Court, of Robin Hood Bay, Yorkshire

Critchley, Lt Albert 269949
Died; 23 December 1943 aged 23
Cassino War Cemetery, Italy VII E 20
Son of Arthur & Florence Critchley, Altrincham; husband of Peggy Critchley,

Crosby, C/Sgt John 4457728
Died: 21 September 1944 aged 25
Coriano Ridge War Cemetery, Italy XVIII E 11
Son of John & Agnes Crosby; husband of Margaret Lilian Crosby, of Harrow, Middlesex

Croucher, L/Cpl Harry William James 14654621
Died: 23 November 1944 aged 28
Meldola War Cemetery, Italy I C 25
Son of Harry William & Rose May Croucher; husband of Dorothy Ivy Croucher, Dagenham

Crowther, L/Sgt George 4625177
Died: 3 December 1943 aged 32
Minturno War Cemetery, Italy I J 11
Son of Charles & Alice Crowther, of Leeds; husband of Doreen Crowther

Crummack, Pte William 4699622
Died: 13 October 1943 aged 20
Minturno War Cemetery, Italy V C 13
Son of William & Hannah Elisa Crummack, Leeds

Cundall, Pte William 4464929
Died: 23 December 1943 aged 30
Cassino War Cemetery, Italy VII E 19
Son of William & Alice Maude Cundall, of Leeds; husband of Elizabeth Cundall

Cusick, L/Cpl Robert 3451575
Died: 23 September 1943 aged 25
Salerno War Cemetery, Italy II B 30
Son of Margaret Cusick, of Hurst, Ashton-under-Lyne, Lancashire

Dabner, Sgt Thomas C Wallace MM 4457133
Died: 12 September 1944 aged 26
Coriano Ridge War Cemetery, Italy XIX J 4
Son of Thomas Wallace & Doris Dabner, of Sunderland. MM for actions with the 11th DLI, France 21/5/40.

Davenport, Pte Bernard 4035437
Died: 6 December 1943 aged 25

Minturno War Cemetery, Italy IV F 21
Son of Henry Richard & Charlotte Davenport Oswestry, Shropshire

Davidson, Pte William 14328718
Died: 28 September 1944 aged 20
Coriano Ridge War Cemetery, Italy XVIII F1
Son of George & Mary Ann Davidson, of Consett

Davies, Pte Eurfryn 3972836
Died: 24 September 1943 aged 32
Salerno War Cemetery, Italy IV D 43
Son of Evan & Susie Davies, Penclawdd, Glam

Davis, Pte Edward Charles 4038692
Died: 3 September 1944 aged 28
Montecchio War Cemetery, Italy IV B 7
Born SW London; enlisted SW London

Dawson, Pte George, 4470214
Died: 26 November 1943 aged 21
Minturno War Cemetery, Italy VII J 21
Son of Hugh & Elizabeth Ellen Dawson, of Clock Face, St Helens, Lancashire

Day, C/Sgt Charles 4691157
Died: 21 September 1944 aged 23
Coriano Ridge War Cemetery, Italy XVIII A 9
Son of James & Kate Ellen Day, Sheffield

Dickeson, Cpl James Allen 4466720
Died: 20 September 1944 aged 34
Coriano Ridge War Cemetery, Italy XVIII C 10
Son of James Allen Dickeson & Ada Dickeson; husband of Mary Dickeson, Seaham Harbour

Dixon, Pte Robert 4465584
Died: 10 October 1943 aged 33
Naples War Cemetery, Italy III D 9
Son of Robert & Constantia Dixon, Sunderland

Dolly, L/Cpl John 2764063
Died: 11 September 1943 aged 21
Salerno War Cemetery, Italy I B 44
Son of John & Margaret Dolly, Denaby Main

Douglass, Pte James 4468455
Died: 23 November 1944 aged 22
Meldola War Cemetery, Italy I B 25
Son of Jane Ann Douglass, of Sunderland

Duffy, 2/Lt Herbert 301497
Died: 11 September 1943 aged 26
Salerno War Cemetery, Italy III F 13
Son of James & Margaret Duffy, of Ashton-under-Lyne; husband of Hilda May Duffy,

Durose, Pte Francis Thomas 4467059
Died: 2 February 1945 [age not recorded]
Prague War Cemetery, Czechoslovakia IV D 3
Son of Francis Edwin & Alice Durose; husband & of Margaret Leitch Durose, of Dalkeith, Midlothian. Enlisted Birmingham. Died POW

East, L/Cpl Cecil Henry 5384578
Died: 10 October 1944 aged 22
Assisi War Cemetery, Italy II E 9
Son of John & Mary Alice East, of Slough, Buckinghamshire

Eden, Pte William 4458342
Died: 30 January 1944 aged 25
Minturno War Cemetery, Italy V C 21
Son of William & Elesibeth Eden; husband of Gladys Eden, Grimsby

Elvidge, Sgt Jack 4696058
Died: 14 January 1944 aged 27
Cassino War Cemetery 14 B 8
Son of John & Rose Elvidge, of South Kirkby

Esson, Pte William 4466432
Died: 26 February 1944 aged 32
Brookwood Memorial, Surrey Panel 21 Column 2 Son of James & Sarah Esson
Recorded as Army Catering Corps attached 16th DLI by the CWGC

Evans, Pte Frank 4470375
Died: 24 September 1943 aged 20
Salerno War Cemetery, Italy IV D 19
Born Lancashire; enlisted Lancashire

Faulkner, Pte, Kenneth 4131132
Died: 7 February 1944 aged 28
Naples War Cemetery, Italy II D 10
Son of Charles & Rose Faulkner, of Birkenhead; husband of Dorothy May Faulkner, of Tranmere

Fearnley, Pte Arthur Joseph 4470191
Died: 23 December 1943 [age not recorded]
Minturno War Cemetery, Italy V L 20
Born Salford; enlisted Salford

Ferrell, L/Sgt George 4466434
Died: 12 October 1943 aged 33
Naples War Cemetery, Italy III N 15
husband of Margaret Ferrell, of Ashington, Northumberland

Forbes, Sgt Albert 4609128
Died: 27 September 1944 aged 33
Coriano Ridge War Cemetery, Italy XVIII F 2
Son of David Frank & Ruth Annie Forbes, of Heckmondwike; husband of Marion Forbes

Foster, Pte Robert 14328731
Died: 1 September 1944 aged 20
Gradara War Cemetery, Italy I A 43
Son of Robert & Mary Ann Forster
Born Co Durham; enlisted Gateshead

Gardiner, Pte John George 4164549
Died: 28 December 1944 aged 31
Phaleron War Cemetery, Greece 19 A 5
Son of Joseph & Isabella Gardiner, of Bishop Auckland, Co Durham; husband of Esher Gardiner, of Bishop Auckland
Army Number 4464549 on War Office Roll

Geary, Pte Wilfred 3452467
Died: 17 November 1944 aged 26
Forli War Cemetery, Italy VI D 17
Son of Ralph Teasdale Geary & Margaret Geary, Seaham,Co Durham; husband of Irene Geary

Gee, Pte Arthur 4469893
Died: 31 August 1944 aged 28
Gradara War Cemetery, Italy II B 8
Son of Arthur & Harriet Gee, of Bridlington,Yorkshire; husband of Florence Gee, Bridlington

Gibson, Pte Allen 4465742
Died: 23 September 1943 aged 32
Salerno War Cemetery, Italy V F 18
Born Co Durham; enlisted Co Durham

Glen, Lt John Gibson 308673
Died: 11 September 1944 aged 26
Bari War Cemetery, Italy XI B 3
Son of William & Joan Glen, of Edinburgh
Recorded by CWGC as 96 Heavy AA Regt, RA
16th DLI War Diary confirms posting to 16th DLI

Godsmark, Pte Francis Alfred 4469516
Died: 13 October 1943 aged 27
Minturno War Cemetery, Italy V A 11
Son of George Henry & Lavina Godsmark, of Middlesborough; husband of Beatrice Godsmark

Goldstone, Cpl Maurice 1475530
Died 27 September 1944 [age not recorded]
Coriano Ridge War Cemetery, Italy XVIII F 4
Son of Max & Annie Goldstone, of Leeds,

Goodman, Pte Frederick Henry 4465624
Died: 30 January 1944 aged 30
Cassino Memorial, Italy Panel 10
Son of William & Gertrude Goodman; husband of Sarah Goodman, of Romford, Essex

Gray, Pte William Henry 4466455
Died: 29 November 1943 aged 32
Minturno War Cemetery IV A 8
Son of John & Alice E Gray, Newcastle-on-Tyne

Green, Sgt Jack Lorton 4033832
Died: 1 September 1944 aged 23
Montecchio War Cemetery, Italy IV B 11
Son of John & Caroline Jane Green; husband of Hannah Green, of Northwich, Cheshire

Gregory, Pte William Henry 4468458
Died: 3 October 1943 aged 19
Salerno War Cemetery, Italy IV D 24
Son of Harry & Ruth Gregory, of Middlesborough

Gullam, Sgt Henry George 4031651
Died: 14 January 1945 aged 31
Fayid War Cemetery, Egypt 5 B 13
Son of Elizabeth Gullam, of Cosheston,

Haley, Pte John Smith 14254205
Died: 11 September 1944 aged 20
Geel War Cemetery, Belgium III A 21
Son of John & Annie Haley, of Newton Hill, Yorkshire. Recorded as 16th DLI by CWGC, almost certainly with 6th, 8th, or 9th Battalion DLI at time of death.

Hall, Cpl Jack MM 4696086
Died: 19 October 1944 aged 28
Forli War Cemetery, Italy I A 12
Son of George & Ellen E Hall, of Leeds; husband of Doreen Hall. MM for actions 1/9/1944

Hancock, Cpl William Valentine 4466768
Died: 13 September 1944 aged 33
Coriano Ridge War Cemetery, Italy IV E 8
Son of William & Jane Hancock; husband of Margaret Jane Hancock, of Whitley Bay

Harrison, 2/Lt Douglas Richard Montgomery 301336
Died: 12 September 1943 aged 32
Salerno War Cemetery, Italy IV C 37
Son of Thomas & Mabel Maud Harrison; husband of Elizabeth Mildred Harrison, Gateshead,

Harrison, Pte George 14257505
Died: 30 January 1944 aged 31
Cassino Memorial, Italy Panel 10
Son of James Henry & Elizabeth Ann Harrison. Born Salford; enlisted Salford

Hart, L/Cpl Edward Anthony Peter 14205730
Died: 27 September 1944 [age not recorded]
Assisi War Cemetery, Italy II B 4
Born Hertfordshire; enlisted Hertfordshire

Harvey, Pte Charles William 869350
Died: 24 December 1944 aged 30
Phaleron War Cemetery, Greece 19 E 5
Nephew of Nellie Henry, of Middlesborough.

Hayes, Pte George 7951834
Died: 12 September 1944 aged 22
Coriano Ridge War Cemetery, Italy XIX A 3
Son of George & Alice Hayes, of Bolton

Heriot, Pte Robert Gordon 14205818
Died: 16 September 1943 aged 20
Cassino Memorial, Italy Panel 10. Son of Mrs L M Heriot, of Great Yarmouth, Norfolk

Heslington, Pte John 4469800
Died: 15 September 1943 aged 20
Cassino Memorial, Italy Panel 10
Son of John & Albertina Heslington, of Low Spennymoor, Co Durham

Higginson, Pte Norman 4620093
Died: 3 December 1943 aged 27
Minturno War Cemetery, Italy I J 10
Son of Harry & Mary Jane Higginson; husband of Winifred May Higginson, of Garlinge, Kent. Born & enlisted Newcastle

Hill, Pte Henry Charles 5346259
Died: 14 October 1943 aged 30
Naples War Cemetery, Italy I L 10
Son of Edward & Fanny Hill; husband of Kathleen Rose Hill, Thatcham, Berkshire

Hobson, Pte William 14555594
Died: 30 January 1944 aged 20
Cassino Memorial, Italy Panel 10
Son of Albany & Alice Hobson, of Oulton,Yorkshire

Holder, L/Cpl Albert Edward 4622978
Died: 3 December 1943 aged 30
Minturno War Cemetery, Italy I J 14
Son of William Henry & Fanny Emma Holder; husband of Margaret Holder of Kirkstall, Leeds

Hood, 2/Lt William Frederick 255419
Died: 31 August 1944 [age not recorded]
Montecchio War Cemetery, Italy IV B 8

Hopper, Pte Albert Edward 4469421
Died: 12 October 1944 aged 21
Coriano Ridge War Cemetery, Italy XV C 1
Son of Albert Edward & Ethel Hopper, Darlington

Hopper, Pte Stanley 4620097
Died: 19 September 1943 aged 27
Bone War Cemetery, Algeria VII D 3
Son of William & Annie Hopper, of Jarrow, Co Durham; husband of Margaret Hopper

Horn, Pte Lawrence Horace, Pte, 4464776
Died: 15 September 1943 aged 29
Salerno War Cemetery, Italy III D 8
Son of Herbert William & Emma Horn
Born Hudderfield; enlisted Yorkshire

Hoy, Sgt William Miller 4454567
Died: 1 October 1943 aged 24
El Alia Cemetery, Algeria 12 C 36
Son of William & Margaret Hamilton Hoy; husband of Edna May Hoy, of Gateshead

Hutton, Pte John Davidson 4469550
Died: 3 September 1944 aged 28
Montecchio War Cemetery, Italy IV B 6
Son of Robert & Mary Hutton; husband of Freda Hutton, of Blackhill, Co Durham
Recorded as 1st Btn DLI by CWGC

Isaac, L/Cpl Noah 4621021
Died: 19 September 1944 aged 29
Coriano Ridge War Cemetery, Italy XIX A 1
Son of Noah & Beatrice Isaac, of Romford

Jackson, Pte Alan 4470078
Died: 12 May 1944 aged 20
Prague War Cemetery, Czechoslovakia I B 12
Son of Henry & Esther Jackson, of Willington, Co Durham
Died while POW, most probably due to the heavy US daylight bombing raids on this day: see also Pte Charles Moore.

Jackson, Pte Fred 4758730
Died: 30 January 1944 aged 37
Cassino Memorial, Italy Panel 10
husband of M Jackson, of Silsden, Yorkshire

Jerrison, Sgt Joseph 4036366
Died: 12 September 1944 aged 27
Coriano Ridge War Cemetery, Italy IV E 1
Son of William & Mabel Jerrison, of West Bromwich, Staffordshire; husband of Hilda Rose Jerrison, of West Bromwich

Johns, Pte William, Rossiter 4456155
Died: 9 September 1943 aged 32
Salerno War Cemetery, Italy IV E 31
Son of Henry Pearce Johns & Catherine Jane Johns; husband of Mary Emma Johns, of Durham. Recorded as 16th Btn DLI by CWGC on burial; since amended to 18th Btn DLI

Johnson, Lt Frank 300166
Died: 9 December 1944 [age not recorded]
Phaleron War Cemetery, Greece 17 B 8
Son of John Harcourt Johnson & Emma Johnson, of Wakefield

Jones, Cpl Gwilym Thomas, Cpl, 4198235
Died: 22 September 1943 aged 24
Catania War Cemetery, Italy III D 22
Son of Mary J Jones, of Talysarn, Caernarvonshire
Recorded as 8th Btn DLI by CWGC

Jones, Pte Iorwerth 3969349
Died: 13 September 1944 aged 31
Coriano Ridge War Cemetery, Italy IV E 7
Born Glamorgan; enlisted Glamorgan

Keenan, L/Cpl Dennis 4542527
Died: 23 December 1944 aged 24
Athens Memorial, Greece Face 7
Son of Lilian Keenan; husband of Nora Keenan, of Bramley, Leeds; Born Co Durham;

Kemp, Pte Frederick Leonard 4469252
Died: 27 August 1944 aged 24
Ancona War Cemetery, Italy IV J 5
Son of Frederick & Mary Kemp, of Thornaby-on-Tees, Yorkshire

Kennedy, Sgt Douglas 4459612
Died: 6 December 1943 aged 26
Cassino War Cemetery, Italy VII B 18
Son of Thomas & Jane Ellen Kennedy, of South Shields, Co Durham; husband of Elsie Kennedy, of South Shields

Kirkup, Capt Frederick David Brookes 68316
Died: 9 September 1943 aged 27
Salerno War Cemetery, Italy IV B 27
Son of Col Ernest Hodgson Kirkup & Helen Chadwick Kirkup, of Low Fell, Co Durham

Lawther, Cpl Edward 4470087
Died: 15 November 1944 aged 23
Forli War Cemetery, Italy IV D 16
Husband of Emily Lawther, Philadelphia, Co Durham

Leadbitter, L/Cpl George MM 4469562
Died: 8 December 1943 aged 28
Cassino War Cemetery, Italy VII B 21
Son of William & Mary Leadbitter of Newcastle-on-Tyne Awarded the 16th DLI's first M M, for the Battle of Sedjenane, on 2 March 1943.

Learoyd, L/Cpl Robert Jones Darwin 4466806
Died: 3 September 1944 aged 33
Coriano Ridge War Cemetery, Italy IV B 1
Son of Samuel & Martha Jane Learoyd; husband of Florence Maud Learoyd, of Billingham

Leather, Pte Frederick Kenneth 3975599
Died: 13 October 1943 aged 21
Minturno War Cemetery, Italy IV E 20
Son of Albert & Sarah Alice Leather, Longsight, Manchester

Lefever, Pte Herbert Anthony 2391183
Died: 23 September 1943 aged 20
Cassino Memorial, Italy Panel 10
Born E London; enlisted London

Leonard, Pte William Henry 4037641
Died: 3 September 1944 aged 29
Montecchio War Cemetery, Italy IV B 12
Son of William Henry & Annie Leonard of Birmingham; husband of Beatrice Annie Leonard, of King's Heath, Birmingham

Logan, Captain Thomas Ralph 203926
Died: 14 September 1943 aged 23

Salerno War Cemetery, Italy IV B 12
Son of John Logan & Phyllis Logan, of Gosforth, Newcastle-on-Tyne

Loosemore, Herbert 4698891
Died: 7 March 1944 aged 21
Cassino Memorial, Italy, Panel 10
Born Sheffield; enlisted Sheffield

Lyle, Cpl Samuel 1460132
Died: 11 September 1944 aged 27
Coriano Ridge War Cemetery, Italy XVII K 8
Born Glasgow; enlisted Glasgow

Makepiece, Sergeant Joseph 4450018
Died: 30 January 1944 aged 33
Cassino Memorial, Italy Panel 10
Son of Mr & Mrs Robert Makepiece, of Crook, Co Durham; husband of E Makepiece, Byker, Newcastle-on-Tyne

Manning, Cpl Edward Charles 13016560
Died: 21 November 1944 aged 34
Cesena War Cemetery, Italy VI F 10
Son of Frederick John & Eliza Manning; husband of Irene Louisa Manning, Pound Hill, Wilts

Mantle, Pte Leonard George, 4470325
Died: 23 September 1943 aged 20
Salerno War Cemetery, Italy II B 33
Son of George Henry & Gertrude May Mantle, Kent

Marshall, 2/Lt Stanley Chuter 321146
Died: 31 August 1944 aged 25
Montecchio War Cemetery, Italy IV B 9
Son of Henry Chuter & Alice Marshall; husband of Murial Daisy Marshall, of Hern Hill, London

Martin, Pte William 4612008
Died: 29 August 1944 aged 31
Montecchio War Cemetery, Italy II J 10
Son of Albert William & Edith Emma Martin; husband of Winifred Annie Martin, of Halifax

Mattin, Arthur, WOII (CSM) MM, 5947792
Died: 4 September 1944 aged 29
Montecchio War Cemetery, Italy IV B 14
husband of Eileen D Mattin, of Kettering,

Mawson, Arnold, Pte 14409283
Died: 30 January 1944 aged 21
Cassino Memorial, Italy Panel '1O'
Son of Alfred & Sarah Ellen Mawson

McDonald, Pte John, 6215804
Died: 30 October 1943 [age not recorded]
Minturno War Cemetery, Italy VIII B 1
Son of William & Margaret McDonald; husband of Bridget McDonald, Stepney, London

McMillan, Pte Robert Brown 14588578
Died: 12 September 1944 aged 20
Coriano Ridge War Cemetery, Italy IV E 3
Son of Alexander & C McMillan, of Dykehead, Lanarkshire

McTaggart, L/Cpl James 14364988
Died: 29 March 1945 aged 31
Rome War Cemetery, Italy II D 13
Son of John & Agnes McTaggart; husband of Janet Gemmell McTaggart, of West Kilbride

McWaters, Alfred, Pte, 14364991
Died: 30 January 1944 aged 31
Minturno War Cemetery, Italy V G 23
Son of Alex&er & Emily McWaters of Glasgow; husband of Margaret Forbes McWaters

Meek, Pte Ernest Wilfred 4470472
Died: 29 October 1943 aged 19
Minturno War Cemetery, Italy V A 10
Son of Frederick & Susannah Meek, of Middlesborough, Yorkshire

Mills, Pte John Alexander 4470328
Died: 9 September 1943 aged 21
Salerno War Cemetery, Italy I E 21
Son of John & Emily Mills of Shepherd's Bush

Milner, Pte William 14375847
Died: 6 December 1943 aged 34
Cassino War Cemetery, Italy VII B 19
Son of William Dobson & Amelia Milner; husband of Margaret Jane Milner of Eastbourne, Darlington, Co Durham

Millett, Pte Clifford 7614876
Died: 6 December 1943 aged 25
Minturno War Cemetery IV F 22
Son of Thomas Henry & Mary Elizabeth Millett, of Pendleton, Salford, Lancashire

Mitchell, Lt Kenneth 258320
Died: 11 September 1944 aged 21
Montecchio War Cemetery, Italy IV B 10
Son of Thomas & Eleanor Annie Mitchell, of Blackhill, Co Durham

Moore, Pte Charles 4468724
Died: 12 May 1944 aged 36
Prague War Cemetery, Czechoslovakia.
Son of Charles & Elizabeth Moore; husband of Nellie Moore, of Browney, Co Durham
Died while POW, most probably due to the heavy US daylight bombing raids on this day: see also Pte Alan Jackson.

Morgan, Pte Wallace 14343219
Died: 29 August 1944 aged 28
Montecchio War Cemetery, Italy II J 8
Son of William & Mary Morgan; husband of Stella Morgan, of Clee Hill, Shropshire

Morris, Pte Cyril 14253438
Died: 16 September 1943 aged 19
Salerno War Cemetery, Italy III D 2
Son of George Henry & Selina Morris, of Moorends, Yorkshire

Morris, Pte Jack Joshua 4210076
Died: 18 September 1943 aged 19
Salerno War Cemetery, Italy I B 39
Son of Jack William & Catherine Morris, of Bony-Maen, Swansea

Moss, Pte Robert 14209714
Died: 18 September 1943 aged 27
Salerno War Cemetery, Italy I B 42
Son of John Henry & Mary Alice Moss, of Stockport, Cheshire ; husband of Beatrice Moss, of Edgeley, Stockport

Mutter, Pte Alex 1685962
Died: 23 November 1944 aged 28
Cesena War Cemetery, Italy VI B 11
Son of Andrew & A Mutter, Winchburgh, West Lothian

Nash, Cpl Sidney Lawrence 4618148
Died: 11 February 1944 aged 35
Beach Head War Cemetery, Anzio, Italy XXII F 11
Son of Arthur Edward Lawrence Nash & Edith Nash; husband of Gwendoline Nash, Amblerthorne, Yorkshire

Newland, Pte Alfred John 1517940
Died: 13 September 1944 aged 25
Coriano Ridge War Cemetery, Italy IV G 6
Son of James & Gertrude E Newland, of Starling' s Green, Essex

Nichols, Pte Eric 4210077
Died: 20 September 1944 [age not recorded]
Coriano Ridge War Cemetery, Italy XVIII A 12
Son of Albert Edward & Constance Nichols of Llandudno, Caernarvonshire

O'Brien, Cpl Anthony 1814335
Died: 24 December 1944 aged 34
Phaleron War Cemetery, Greece 19 E 6
Son of James & Rose Ellen O'Brien, Middlesborough, Yorkshire

O'Brien, Pte William, Patrick 6215869
Died: 18 November 1943 [age not recorded]
Cassino Memorial, Italy Panel 10
No CWGC Next of Kin details
Born EC London; enlisted E London
Recorded as 8th Battalion DLI by CWGC

Oliver, Cpl Fred 4462514
Died: 1 October 1943 aged 25
Catania War Cemetery, Italy III D 25
Son of George & Elizabeth Oliver, husband of Jean Oliver .Born & enlisted Durham City

Page, Pte Leslie Percy 14218701
Died: 10 October 1944 aged 21
Assisi War Cemetery, Italy II D 10
Son of Percy J & Elsie K Page of Walton-on-Thames, Surrey

Parkinson, Cpl Jack Stanley, 14400955
Died: 16 November 1944 aged Z3
Meldola War Cemetery, Italy I C 27
Son of Annie Parkinson
Born Halifax; enlisted Halifax

Paterson, Pte Robert 13055126
Died: 18th September 1943 aged 24
Salerno War Cemetery, Italy I B 38
Son of William & Elizabeth Paterson,Newhaven,

Pauly, Cpl George 4470334
Died: 12 September 1944 aged 21
Coriano Ridge War Cemetery, Italy IV E 5
Born SW London; enlisted SW London

Phipps, Pte Frederick Denniss 4467100
Died: 23 September 1943 aged 33
Salerno War Cemetery, Italy II C 18
Son of Fred & Nellie Phipps, of Stratford-on-Avon Recorded as 9th Battalion DLI by CWGC

Plows, Cpl Arthur 3195644
Died: 3 December 1943 aged 29
Minturno War Cemetery, Italy IV A 2
Son of Alfred Edward & Margaret Hilda Plows, of York; husband of Elsie Plows, of Fishergate

Poole, Pte Edgar 4623029
Died: 2 September 1944 aged 31
Montecchio War Cemetery, Italy II F 3
husband of Nellie Poole, of Harehills, Leeds

Preece, L/Cpl John 4694477
Died: 10 October 1943 aged 23
Naples War Cemetery, Italy III K 9
Son of John Thomas Preece & Lucy Ellen Preece, Maltby, Yorkshire

Preston, Pte Clifford 4466561
Died: 13 October 1943 aged 33
Cassino Memorial, Italy Panel 10
No CWGC Next of Kin details
Born Co Durham; enlisted Co Durham

Price, L/Sgt Albert 4688283
Died: 27 September 1944 aged 32
Coriano Ridge War Cemetery, Italy XVIII F 3
No CWGC Next of Kin details
Born York; enlisted York

Ramsden, Pte David 4692272
Died: 3 December 1943 aged 25
Minturno War Cemetery, Italy IV F 17
Son of David Wright Ramsden & Ethel Ramsden, of Leeds, Yorkshire; husband of Gladys Ramsden, of Armley, Leeds

Reading, Sgt Norman Joseph 4037694
Died: 10 October 1944 aged 29
Assisi War Cemetery, Italy II D 9
Son of Joseph & Sarah Elizabeth Reading; husband of Hilda Elsie Reading, Sheldon Warwickshire

Readshaw, Pte Cyril 4469611
Died: 7 February 1944 aged 27
Minturno War Cemetery, Italy V G 18
Son of James S & Elizabeth May Readshaw, Darlington, Co Durham

Richardson, Cpl Thomas 4466269
Died: 15 September 1943 aged 31
Salerno War Cemetery, Italy V A 11
Son of Thomas & Ann Richardson; husband of Emily Beatrice Richardson, of Framwellgate Moor, Co Durham

Richardson, Thomas, Pte, 4469616
Died: 10 October 1943 aged 27
Naples War Cemetery III, Italy D 10
Son of James Andrew & Edith Richardson; husband of Lily Richardson, Walker, Newcastle-on-Tyne

Robson, Cpl George Henry 14413939
Died: 22 November 1944 aged 22
Meldola War Cemetery, Italy I D 26
Son of George Henry & Annie Robson, West Hartlepool.Recorded as '1/6 Bn' DLI by CWGC

Savage, Pte William George, 902487
Died: 13 September 1944 aged 22
Coriano Ridge War Cemetery, Italy IV E 2
Son of Harry S & Florence A Savage, of Forest Gate, Essex

Senior, L/Cpl Harry 4464832
Died: 29 August 1944 aged 30
Montecchio War Cemetery, Italy II C 9
Son of Arthur & Annie Senior of Leeds, Yorkshire; husband of Amy Senior, of Leeds

Senior, Pte Joe Harrison 4624006
Died: 1 September 1944 aged 31
Montecchio War Cemetery, Italy II C 10
Son of Charles & Ann Senior, of Meltham, Yorkshire; husband & of Nellie Senior

Shackleton, Cpl Irwin 1683889
Died: 12 September 1944 aged 33
Coriano Ridge War Cemetery, Italy IV D 2
Son of Joseph & Margaret Shackleton, of Silsden, Yorkshire; husband of Myra Shackleton

Shadbolt, Pte Victor 5344371
Died: 13 September 1944 aged 24
Coriano Ridge War Cemetery, Italy IV E 6
Born E London; enlisted E London

Sharp, Pte Robert 14574709
Died: 1 September 1944 aged 22
Gradara War Cemetery, Italy I A 41
Son of George & Edith Sharp, Dunston, Gateshead

Shortt, Pte William 4203216
Died: 18 September 1943 aged 29
Salerno War Cemetery, Italy I B 41
Son of John & Ellen Beard, of Tooting, Surrey

Simpson, Lt Charles Stronach 261699
Died: 30 January 1944, aged 30
Minturno War Cemetery, Italy VI C 23
Son of Charles S & Elsie Ann Simpson, of Kirkton Ordiquhill, Banffshire
Recorded as Gordon Highlanders by CWGC 16th DLI War Diary confirms posting to 16th DLI

Skilton, Pte Harry, Levison, 5049882
Died: 10 October 1943 aged 26
Naples War Cemetery, Italy III K 6
Son of Thomas Henry & Mary Ann Skilton, of Fenton, Stoke-on-Trent

Smith, Pte Eric 4698141
Died: 29 October 1944 aged 22
Minturno War Cemetery, Italy VIII B 3
Son of Mr & Mrs J H Smith, of Easingwood, Yorkshire; husband of F Smith, of Grimsby

Smith, Capt Frank Stuart 253707
Died: 22 September 1943 [age not recorded]
Salerno War Cemetery, Italy VI E 42
No CWGC Next of Kin details
Born Birmingham; enlisted Birmingham

Smith, Pte Leslie William 4469343
Died: 3 November 1943 aged 23
Milan War Cemetery, Italy VI B 2
Son of Francis William & Annie Elizabeth Smith of Pickering, Yorkshire

Starr, Pte Harry, Pte 5444749
Died: 23 September 1943 aged 23
Salerno War Cemetery, Italy II B 34
Son of William Thomas Starr & Elizabeth Starr; husband of Matilda Starr, of Redfield, Bristol

Steele, Pte Ronald 4699867
Died: 20 October 1944 aged 21
Bari War Cemetery, Italy XI A 5
Son of Fred & Ada Steele, of Barnsley

Stevenson, Cpl Jack 1683908
Died: 13 September 1944 aged 24
Coriano Ridge War Cemetery, Italy IV G 7
Son of Harry & Elsie Stevenson, Leeds, Yorkshire; husband of Laura Stevenson

Strothard, Lt Fred Wray 253977
Died: 3 December 1943 aged 25
Minturno War Cemetery, Italy I J 8
Son of Joseph William Strothard (formerly Flt Sgt RAF), & Annie Strothard, of Tadcaster

Sturgeon, Pte Charles Raymond 4396422
Died: 27 December 1944 aged 33
Forli War Cemetery, Italy V C 12
Son of Charles Edward & Mary Elizabeth Sturgeon, of Darlington, Co Durham; husband of Winifred Sturgeon, of Darlington

Sultman, Pte Morris 3775539
Died: 3 December 1943 aged 24
Minturno War Cemetery, Italy I J 12
Son of Issy & Raymond Sultman, of Liverpool

Taylor, Pte George 14574724
Died: 3 September 1944 aged 22
Coriano Ridge War Cemetery, Italy IV B 2
Son of George Richard & Verona Taylor, of Bedlington, Northumberland

Thomas, Pte Joseph 4201092
Died: 30 January 1944 aged 20
Cassino Memorial, Italy Panel 10
Son of Richard & Margaret Thomas, of Bangor

Thompson, Pte Cyril 3967296
Died: 4 October 1943 aged 25
Catania War Cemetery, Italy III B 28
Son of George & Elizabeth Thompson
Born E London; enlisted E London

Thomson, Lt Archibald 303067
Died: 12 September 1944 aged 28
Coriano Ridge War Cemetery XIX A 12
Son of Archibald & Margaret Thomson, of Billingham, Co Durham Recorded as Royal Northumberland Fusiliers by CWGC.
16th DLI War Diary confirms his joining the 16th DLI on 9/9/44 & his death in action on 12/9/44

Threadgold, Sgt Donald, MM 4689911
Died: 12 September 1943 aged 34
Salerno War Cemetery, Italy I B 43
Son of Charles & Ada Threadgold; husband of Lucy Threadgold, Batley, Yorkshire
MM for actions on 22/4/43

Todd, Pte Isaac 14272620
Died: 13 October 1943 aged 19

Minturno War Cemetery, Italy VII F 8
Son of Edward Todd & of Alice Mary Todd, Barley Mow, Chester-le-Street, Co Durham

Tomlinson, Pte Joseph Leslie 3975361
Died: 23 September 1943 aged 20
Salerno War Cemetery, Italy II B 32
Son of Joseph & Margaret Tomlinson: nephew of Caroline Haughton, Manchester

Tuck, Pte Joseph 4617392
Died: 12 October 1943 aged 24
Minturno War Cemetery, Italy VIII C 19
No CWGC Next of Kin details
Born Lancashire; enlisted Halifax

Turle, Pte Joseph Henry George 5680620
Died: 10 October 1944 aged 33
Assisi War Cemetery, Italy II F 10
Son of Joseph Henry & Fanny Turle of Bristol; husband of Lavinia Elizabeth Turle, Horfield, Bristol

Urwin, Pte William 14566847
Died: 16 November 1944 aged 27
Meldola War Cemetery, Italy I B 27
Son of William & Phyllis Urwin, of Wardley Colliery, Gateshead, Co Durham

Ventham, L/Cpl Edward James 4398248
Died: 23 November 1944 aged 35
Meldola War Cemetery, Italy I C 26
No CWGC Next of Kin details
Born E London; enlisted W London

Vick, Cpl Harry 1470848
Died: 10 October 1944, aged 30
Assisi War Cemetery, Italy II E 8
Son of Henry Sidman & Mary Frances Vick, Leeds

Vile, Pte John Kenneth, 4699761
Died: 20 September 1944 aged 22
Coriano Ridge War Cemetery, Italy XVIII A 11
Son of George Stephen & Bridgid Vile, Huddersfield

Wadsworth, Pte Sam Wrigley 4619305
Died: 4 December 1943 aged 27
Minturno War Cemetery, Italy 1 B 20
Son of James & Florence Gertrude Wadsworth of East Ardsley, Wakefield

Wakelin, L/Cpl Thomas 3605435
Died: 28 August 1944 aged 24
Montecchio War Cemetery, Italy II D 11
Son of Isaac & Helen Wakelin
Born Bradford; enlisted Manchester

Walters, Pte James 4987361
Died: 17 November 1944 aged 37
Forli War Cemetery, Italy V1 1 15
No CWGC Next of Kin details
Born Derbyshire, enlisted Derbyshire

Watson, Pte Alec T 11256615
Died: 23 November 1944 aged 23
Meldola War Cemetery, Italy 1 D 27
Son of Alec Francis & Florence Watson, of Hanley. Staffordshire; husband of Majorie Watson, of Hanley

Waymark, Lt Stanley Charles John 276223
Died: 10 October 1944 [age not recorded]
Assisi War Cemetery, Italy II C 11
Son of Tom & Ann May Waymark; husband of Margaret L J Waymark, Hornchurch, Essex

Webb, Pte Reginald Nelson 2059903
Died: 10 October 1944 aged 22
Assisi War Cemetery, Italy II E 10
Son of Horatio Nelson Webb & Elizabeth May Webb of Birmingham

Weir, Pte Bernard 1592389
Died: 20th September 1944 aged 29
Coriano War Cemetery, Italy XVIII C 9
husband of Sarah Weir of Greenock, Renfrewshire

Welsh, Pte James 14243059
Died: 30 January 1944 aged 20
Cassino Memorial, Italy Panel 10
Born E London; enlisted Essex

Weston, Sergeant Douglas Arthur 4542382
Died: 23 November 1944 aged 28
Meldola War Cemetery, Italy I A 19
Son of Lucy Weston of Gleadless, Sheffield

Whitehead, Lt Wilson 130828
Died: 10 October 1943 [age not recorded]
Naples War Cemetery, Italy III D 13
No CWGC Next of Kin details

Whiteley, Pte Jack Lloyd 4626967
Died: 17th September 1943 aged 21
Cassino Memorial, Italy Panel 10
Son of Selwyn Whiteley & of Edith May Whiteley, of Halifax, Yorkshire

Whitemore, Pte William 4464877
Died: 8 December 1943 aged 29
Ancona War Cemetery, Italy III E 10
Son of Wilfred & S Anne Whitemore; husband of Dorothy Whitemore, of Thongsbridge, Yorkshire

Wiles, Pte Robert William 4465926
Died: 3 December 1943 aged 33
Minturno War Cemetery, Italy IV J 2
No CWGC Next of Kin details
Born Gateshead, enlisted Gateshead

Willis, Pte Albert Frank 1531356
Died: 13 September 1944 aged 27
Coriano Ridge War Cemetery, Italy IV G 12
Son of Thomas Henry & Alice Mary Willis, of Ely, Glamorgan

Wilson, Pte John Edward 4460740
Died: 30 January 1944 aged 27
Cassino Memorial, Italy Panel 10
Son of Albert Edward Wilson & of Margaret Wilson, of Jarrow, Co Durham

Wilson, Pte Vincent 4464681
Died: 15 February 1944
Anzio War Cemetery, Italy II D 7 [age not recorded] No CWGC Next of Kin details
Born Sunderland

Winter, Pte James 4466642
Died: 30 January 1944 aged 32
Cassino Memorial, Italy Panel 10
Son of James & Ethel Winter; husband of Gladys Winter, of Seaham, Co Durham

Wood, Pte Kenneth Hanson 4695710
Died: 14 October 1943 aged 29
Minturno War Cemetery, Italy VII D 24
Son of George & Ida Wood; husband of Mabel Wood, of Great Ayton, Yorkshire

Woodfinden, Pte John 101247
Died: 30 January 1944 aged 34
Cassino Memorial, Italy Panel 10
Son of Lydia Woodfinden, of Stockport

Yates, Lt Ernest 253708
Died: 14 October 1943 aged 26
Minturno War Cemetery, Italy VII D 25
Son of Edwin & Mary Yates, of Glossop,

Young, Pte Leslie 4469863
Died: 19 October 1944 aged 21
Coriano Ridge War Cemetery, Italy IV G 10
No CWGC Next of Kin details
Born Co Durham, enlisted Co Durham